Syntax

A minimalist introduction

ANDREW RADFORD

Department of Language and Linguistics
University of Essex

CAMBRIDGE
UNIVERSITY PRESS

CAMBRIDGE UNIVERSITY PRESS
Cambridge, New York, Melbourne, Madrid, Cape Town, Singapore, São Paulo

Cambridge University Press
The Edinburgh Building, Cambridge CB2 8RU, UK

Published in the United States of America by Cambridge University Press, New York

www.cambridge.org
Information on this title: www.cambridge.org/9780521581226

First published 1997
Sixth printing 2003

A catalogue record for this publication is available from the British Library

Library of Congress Cataloguing in Publication data
Radford, Andrew.
Syntax: a minimalist introduction/Andrew Radford.
        p.   cm.
Abridged version of author's *Syntactic theory and the structure of English*
Includes bibliographical references and index.
ISBN 0 521 58122 2 / ISBN 0 521 58914 2 (paperback)
1. Grammar, Comparative and general – Syntax. 2. Minimalist theory
(Linguistics). 3. English language – Syntax. I. Title.
P291.R36 1997
415-DC20   96-25137 CIP

ISBN 978-0-521-58122-6 hardback
ISBN 978-0-521-58914-7 paperback

Transferred to digital printing 2007

Syntax: a minimalist introduction

This textbook provides a concise, readable introduction to contemporary work in syntactic theory, particularly to key concepts of Chomsky's minimalist program. Andrew Radford gives a general overview of the main theoretical concepts and descriptive devices used in 1990s work. *Syntax: a Minimalist Introduction* presupposes no prior knowledge of syntax or any language other than English: the analysis is based on Standard, Belfast, Jamaican, Shakespearean and Child English. There are exercises (with helpful hints and model answers) and a substantial glossary.

   This is an abridged version of Radford's major new textbook *Syntactic Theory and the Structure of English: a Minimalist Approach* (also published by Cambridge University Press), and will be welcomed as a short introduction to current syntactic theory.

Contents

Preface

This book is essentially an abridged version of my *Syntactic Theory and the Structure of English: a Minimalist Approach*. Although much of the text of this shorter book is taken verbatim from various sections of the longer one, the shorter book is intended to be used as a self-contained introduction to syntax, and as such has been designed with a number of specific criteria in mind.

One is that lengthy tomes are simply impractical to use as course-books on short courses where only a limited number of hours/weeks are available: Joe Emonds once remarked to me that a student complained to him about my 625-page *Transformational Grammar* book that 'This is the third syntax course I've been on where we only got half way through the coursebook by the end of the course.' The main text of the present book is around a third the length of the main text of *Transformational Grammar* and is designed explicitly to be used on short syntax courses. So, there's no excuse for not getting through *all* of it!

A second consideration which I have borne in mind is that students taking short introductory syntax courses want a general overview of key theoretical concepts and descriptive devices used in contemporary work in the 1990s; they do not want (nor is it realistic to give them) a historical account of how earlier work in the 1960s, 1970s and 1980s led up to (or compares with) current work. This book aims to introduce students to key concepts which are presupposed in works written within the broad framework of the *minimalist program* (in the version outlined in chapter 4 of Chomsky 1995).

A third factor which has influenced me is that many students on syntax courses are primarily interested in English, and may have a relatively limited knowledge of (or interest in) the syntax of other languages. For such students, detailed discussion of (for example) the syntax of Sardinian clitics or Japanese topic markers is likely to induce severe brain-strain and a terminal desire to give up syntax. Accordingly, the discussion in this book is primarily based on different varieties of English (not just Modern Standard English, but also e.g. the English of Shakespeare's plays). The book is therefore ideal for linguaphobic Anglophiles.

A fourth concern which I have taken into account is that many students are terrified by the terminological trauma of taking syntax.

Most introductions to syntax presuppose a substantial background knowledge of traditional grammatical terms like *subject, case, agreement,* etc., and then go on to introduce new tongue-twisting terms and conceptually constipated constructs on every page: if you're like me, by the time you reach page 742, you've forgotten what exactly the new term introduced on page 729 means (let alone which of the various definitions of *c-command* it is based on). To overcome the understandable fears which beginners have, I have used simple metaphors and analogies to introduce technical terms (for example, the term *c-command* is defined in terms of networks of train stations). And to help those of you who suffer from terminological amnesia, I've included a substantial *glossary* at the end of the book which provides simple illustrations of how key terms (and abbreviations) are used – not just theory-specific technical terms like *c-command*, but also traditional terms such as *subject*. A good way of reminding yourself of key concepts and constructs after you have completed chapter 10 is to read through the glossary.

My final aim has been to heed plaintive pleas from generations of students that although they can generally follow the text discussion in my 1981 and 1988 coursebooks, they have little or no idea how to go about doing the exercises at the end of each chapter. To help overcome this problem, I've included *model answers* and/or *helpful hints* for each of the exercises in this book.

A word of warning to students taking syntax for the first time: syntax can damage your health, producing (in some cases) an allergic reaction leading to severe scepticemia, and (in rare cases) an addictive response leading to acute arboriphilia. There is no known cure. However, you can take some sensible precautions to minimize the risks.

This book is not a novel: you can't simply pick it up and expect to flick through it in a couple of hours while listening to *Bad English* on your Walkman. The argumentation is dense, and cumulative: new concepts and constructs are introduced on every page, and familiarity with them is presupposed in later chapters. You should therefore treat it like cod liver oil – to be taken in small doses. Tackle it one chapter at a time, and (for example) only go on to chapter 4 when you have digested chapter 3: this may mean that you have to read some chapters several times. It's important to tackle the exercises at the end of each chapter, since it's only by doing so that you find out whether you really do understand the text discussion. (This is particularly important at key points in the text – e.g. in chapter 3, where tree diagrams appear for the first time, and where the exercises give you the opportunity of perfecting your arboreal artwork skills.)

The book becomes gradually more abstract as it goes on; the last four chapters are markedly more abstract than the chapters preceding them, and the last two (which introduce recent research of a highly speculative nature) provide an intimidating intellectual challenge: you can be forgiven for wanting to throw in the towel – or throw up – at that point. If you manage to make it through to the end, reward yourself by buying the real thing – no, not a bottle of Coke, but a copy of Chomsky's (1995) book *The Minimalist Program*. As noted at the beginning, this book is an abridged version of my *Syntactic Theory and the Structure of English* (= *STSE*). The two books are thus to a large extent parallel in structure, and can be used in conjunction with each other: hence, those who want to follow up the text discussion in some particular chapter of this book, or to have more extensive exercise material to practise on, can look at the more detailed text discussion and considerably expanded exercise material in the corresponding chapter of *STSE*.

Both books have benefited considerably from helpful suggestions made by colleagues and graduate students. In this connection, I'd like to say a big *thank you* to Laura Rupp, Sam Featherston and Martin Atkinson (Essex), and Jon Erickson (Cologne); and above all to the series editor Neil Smith (University College London) for his patient and good-humoured comments on numerous ((re-)re-)revised drafts. I'd also like to express my gratitude to students from all over the world who took the trouble to write to me with comments on my earlier *Transformational Syntax* book; you'll see that I've tried to accommodate many of your suggestions (e.g. for model answers to exercises, for a glossary of terms, etc.).

This book is dedicated to my wife Khadija for the friendship, love, support and encouragement she has always shown me, and for putting up with a houseful of discarded papers and smelly socks for so long.

❶ Grammar

Grammar is traditionally subdivided into two different but inter-related areas of study – **morphology** and **syntax**. Morphology is the study of how words are formed out of smaller units (traditionally called *morphemes*), and so addresses questions such as 'What are the various component parts (= morphemes) of a word like *antidisestablishmentarianism*, and what kinds of principles determine the ways in which the parts are combined together to form the whole?' Syntax is concerned with the ways in which words can be combined together to form phrases and sentences, and so addresses questions like 'Why is it OK in English to say *Who did you see Mary with?*, but not OK to say **Who did you see Mary and?*' (a star in front of an expression means that it's ungrammatical). 'What kinds of principles determine the ways in which we can and cannot combine words together to form phrases and sentences?'

However, grammar is traditionally concerned not just with the principles which determine the *formation* of words, phrases and sentences, but also with the principles which govern their *interpretation* – i.e. with the principles which tell us how to *interpret* (= assign meaning to) words, phrases and sentences. For example, any comprehensive grammar of English will specify that compound words like *man-eater* and *man-made* have very different interpretations: in compounds like *man-eater*, the word *man* is traditionally said to have a *patient* interpretation, in the sense that *man* is the patient/hapless victim on whom the act of eating is going to be performed; by contrast, in compounds like *man-made*, the word *man* is said to have an *agent* interpretation, in the sense that *man* is the agent responsible for the act of making. Thus, structural aspects of meaning are traditionally said to be part of the domain of grammar. We might therefore characterize grammar as the study of *the principles which govern the formation and interpretation of words, phrases and sentences*. In terms of the traditional division of grammar into morphology and syntax, we can say that morphology studies the formation and interpretation of words, whereas syntax is concerned with the formation and interpretation of phrases and sentences.

In a fairly obvious sense, any native speaker of a language can be said to know the grammar of his or her native language. After all, native speakers clearly know how to form and interpret words, phrases and sentences in their native language. For example, any native speaker of

English can tell you that the negative counterpart of *I like syntax* is *I don't like syntax*, and not e.g. **I no like syntax*: thus, we might say that native speakers know how to negate sentences in their language. However, it is important to emphasize that this grammatical knowledge is *tacit* (i.e. subconscious) rather than *explicit* (i.e. conscious): so, it's no good asking a native speaker of English a question such as 'How do you form negative sentences in English?', since human beings have no conscious awareness of the psychological processes involved in speaking and understanding a language. To introduce a technical term, we might say that native speakers have grammatical **competence** in their native language: by this, we mean that they have tacit knowledge of the grammar of their language – i.e. of how to form and interpret words, phrases and sentences in the language.

In work dating back to the 1960s, Chomsky has drawn a distinction between *competence* (the fluent native speaker's tacit knowledge of his language) and **performance** (what people actually say or understand by what someone else says on a given occasion). Competence is 'the speaker–hearer's knowledge of his language', while performance is 'the actual use of language in concrete situations' (Chomsky 1965, p. 4). Very often, performance is an imperfect reflection of competence: we all make occasional slips of the tongue, or occasionally misinterpret what someone else says to us. However, this doesn't mean that we don't know our native language, or don't have competence (i.e. fluency) in it. Misproductions and misinterpretations are *performance errors*, attributable to a variety of performance factors like tiredness, boredom, drunkenness, drugs, external distractions and so forth. Grammars traditionally set out to tell you what you need to know about a language in order to have native speaker competence in the language (i.e. to be able to speak the language like a native speaker): hence, it is clear that grammar is concerned with *competence* rather than *performance*. This is not to deny the interest of *performance* as a field of study, but merely to assert that performance is more properly studied within the different – though related – discipline of psycholinguistics, which studies the psychological processes underlying speech production and comprehension. It seems reasonable to suppose that competence will play an important part in the study of performance, since you have to understand what native speakers tacitly know about their language before you can study the effects of tiredness, drunkenness, etc. on this knowledge.

If we say that grammar is the study of grammatical competence, then we are implicitly taking a *cognitive* view of the nature of grammar. After all, if the term *grammatical competence* is used to denote what native speakers tacitly know about the grammar of their language, then grammar is part of the more general study of cognition (i.e. human knowledge). In the terminology adopted by Chomsky (1986a, pp. 19–56), we're studying language as a cognitive system *internalized* within the human brain/mind; our ultimate goal is to characterize the nature of the internalized linguistic system (or *I-language*, as Chomsky terms it) which enables humans to speak and understand their native language. Such a cognitive approach has obvious implications for the descriptive linguist who is interested in trying to describe the grammar of a particular language like English. What it means is that in devising a grammar of English, we are attempting to describe the grammatical knowledge possessed by the fluent native speaker of English. However, clearly this competence is not directly accessible to us: as noted above, you can't ask native speakers to introspect about the nature of the processes by which they produce and understand sentences in their native language, since they have no conscious awareness of such processes. Hence, we have to seek to study competence *indirectly*. But how?

Perhaps the richest vein of readily available evidence which we have about the nature of grammatical competence lies in native speakers' intuitions about the *grammaticality* and *interpretation* of words, phrases and sentences in their native language. For example, preschool children often produce past-tense forms like *goed, comed, seed, buyed*, etc. and any adult native speaker of (Modern Standard) English will intuitively know that such forms are ungrammatical in English, and will know that their grammatical counterparts are *went, came, saw* and *bought*. Similarly, any native speaker of English would intuitively recognize that sentences like (1a) below are grammatical in English, but that sentences like (1b) are ungrammatical:

(1) (a) If you don't know the meaning of a word, look it up in a dictionary
     (b)*If you don't know the meaning of a word, look up it in a dictionary

(Recall that a star in front of an expression means that it is ungrammatical; by convention, any expression which does not have a star in front of it is grammatical; note that stars go *before* – not *after* – ungrammatical words, phrases or sentences.) Thus, we might say that *intuitions about grammaticality* form part of the native speaker's grammatical competence. Equivalently, we can say that native speakers have the ability to make *grammaticality judgments* about words, phrases and sentences in their native language – i.e. the ability to judge whether particular expressions are grammatical or ungrammatical within their native language. An interesting implication of this fact is that if grammars model competence, a grammar of a language must tell you not only what you *can* say in the language, but also what you *can't* say, since native speaker competence includes not only the ability to make the judgment that certain types of sentence (e.g. (1a) above) are grammatical, but also the ability to judge that others (e.g. (1b) above) are ungrammatical. Indeed, much of contemporary work in syntax is concerned with trying to explain why certain types of structure are ungrammatical: it would perhaps not be too much of an exaggeration to say that whereas traditional grammars concentrate on *grammaticality* (i.e. on telling you how to form grammatical phrases and sentences), work on grammar within the Chomskyan paradigm tends to focus much more on explaining *ungrammaticality* (i.e. on explaining why certain types of structures are ungrammatical).

A second source of introspective evidence about the nature of grammatical competence relates to native speaker intuitions about the *interpretation* of words, phrases and sentences in their native language. For example, any native speaker of English can tell you that a sentence such as:

(2) Sam loves you more than Jim

is ambiguous, and has two different interpretations which can be paraphrased as in (3a–b) below:

(3) (a) Sam loves you more than Jim loves you
     (b) Sam loves you more than Sam loves Jim

So, it seems that the native speaker's grammatical competence is reflected not only in intuitions about *grammaticality*, but also in intuitions about *interpretation*.

Given that a grammar of a language is a model of the competence of a fluent speaker of the language, and given that competence is reflected in intuitions about grammaticality and interpretation, an important criterion of adequacy for a grammar of any natural language is that of *descriptive adequacy*. We can say that a grammar of a given language is *descriptively adequate* if it correctly describes whether any given string (i.e. sequence) of words in a language is or isn't grammatical, and also correctly describes what interpretation(s) the relevant string has. So, for example, a grammar of English would be descriptively adequate in the relevant respects if it told us that sentences like (1a) above are grammatical in English but those like (1b) are ungrammatical, and if it told us that sentences like (2) are ambiguous as between the two interpretations paraphrased in (3a) and (3b): conversely, our grammar would be descriptively inadequate if it wrongly told us that both the sentences in (1a–b) are grammatical in English, or that (2) can be paraphrased as in (3a), but not as in (3b).

While the concern of the descriptive linguist is to devise grammars of particular languages, the concern of the theoretical linguist is to devise a *theory of grammar*. A theory of grammar is a set of hypotheses about the nature of possible and impossible grammars of *natural* (i.e. human) languages: hence, a theory of grammar answers questions like: 'What are the inherent properties which natural language grammars do and don't possess?' Just as there are *criteria of adequacy* for grammars, so too there are a number of criteria which any adequate theory of grammar must satisfy. One obvious criterion is *universality*, in the sense that a theory of grammar should provide us with the tools needed to describe the grammar of *any* natural language adequately; after all, a theory of grammar would be of little interest if it enabled us to describe the grammar of English and French, but not that of Swahili or Chinese. So, what we mean by saying that *universality* is a criterion of adequacy for a theory of grammar is that a theory of grammar must enable us to devise a descriptively adequate grammar for every natural language: in other words, our ultimate goal is to develop a *theory of Universal Grammar*. In the linguistic literature, it is a standard convention to abbreviate the term *Universal Grammar* to *UG*, and hence to talk of devising a *theory of UG*.

However, since the ultimate goal of any theory is *explanation*, it is not enough for a theory of Universal Grammar simply to list sets of universal properties of natural language grammars; on the contrary, a theory of UG must seek to *explain* the relevant properties. So, a key question for any adequate theory of UG to answer is: '*Why* do natural language grammars have the properties they do?' The requirement that a theory should *explain* why grammars have the properties they do is conventionally referred to as the criterion of *explanatory adequacy*.

Since the theory of Universal Grammar is concerned with characterizing the properties of *natural* (i.e. human) language grammars, an important question which we want our theory of UG to answer is: 'What are the essential defining characteristics of natural languages which differentiate them from, for example, artificial languages like those used in mathematics and computing (e.g. Basic, Prolog, etc.), or from animal communication systems (e.g. the tail-wagging dance performed by bees to communicate the location of a food source to other bees)?' It therefore follows that the descriptive apparatus which our theory of Universal Grammar allows us to make use of in devising natural language grammars must not be so powerful that it can be used to describe not only natural languages, but also computer languages or animal communication systems (since any such excessively powerful theory wouldn't be able to pinpoint the criterial properties of natural languages which differentiate them from other types of communication system). In other words, a third condition which we have to impose on our theory of language is that it be maximally *restrictive*: that is, we want our theory to provide us with technical devices which are so *constrained* in their expressive power that they can only be used to describe natural languages, and are not appropriate for the description of other communication systems. Any such restrictive theory would then enable us to characterize the very essence of natural language.

The neurophysiological mechanisms which underlie linguistic competence make it possible for young children to *acquire* language in a remarkably short period of time: children generally start to form elementary two-word structures at around 18 months of age, and by the age of 30 months have acquired a wide range of different grammatical constructions and are able to produce sentences of considerable grammatical complexity. Accordingly, a fourth condition which any adequate linguistic theory must meet is that of *learnability*: it must provide grammars which are learnable by young children in a relatively short period of time.

A related requirement is that linguistic theory should provide grammars which make use of the *minimal* theoretical apparatus required to provide a descriptively adequate characterization of linguistic phenomena: in other words, grammars should be as simple as possible. Much of the work in syntax in the 1980s involved the postulation of ever more complex structures and principles: as a reaction to the excessive complexity of this kind of work, Chomsky in the 1990s has made **minimalism** (i.e. the requirement to minimize the theoretical and descriptive apparatus used to describe language) the cornerstone of linguistic theory. The *minimalist program for linguistic theory* which he has been developing (cf. Chomsky 1995) is motivated to a large extent by the desire to minimize the acquisition burden placed on the child, and thereby maximize the learnability of natural language grammars.

Our brief discussion of learnability leads us naturally to consider the goal of developing a *theory of the acquisition of grammar*. An acquisition theory is concerned with the question of how children acquire grammars of their native languages. One of the most fundamental questions which an acquisition theory seeks to answer is: 'How and when do children develop an initial grammar of the language they are acquiring, and what are the subsequent stages they go through in their grammatical development?'

Children generally produce their first recognizable word (e.g. *Mama* or *Dada*) by the age of 12 months. For the next six months or so, there is little apparent evidence of grammatical development, although the child's productive vocabulary typically increases by about three words a month until it reaches around a couple of dozen words at age 18 months. Throughout this *single-word stage*, children's utterances comprise single words spoken in isolation: e.g. a child may say *Apple* when reaching for an apple, or *Up* when wanting to get on her mother's knee. During the single-word stage, there is no evidence of the acquisition of grammar, in that children do not make productive use of *inflections* (e.g. they don't add the plural +*s* ending to nouns, or the past tense +*d* ending to verbs), and don't productively combine words together to form two- and three-word utterances. At around the age of 18 months, we find the first signs of the acquisition of grammar: children start to make productive use of inflections (e.g. using plural nouns like *doggies* alongside the singular form *doggy*, and participles like *going* alongside the uninflected verb form *go*), and similarly start to produce elementary two- and three-word utterances such as *Want Teddy, Eating cookie, Dolly go bed*, etc. From this point on, there is a rapid expansion in their grammatical development, so that by the age of around 30 months, children have typically acquired most of the inflections and core grammatical constructions used in English, and are able to produce adultlike sentences such as *Where's Mummy gone? What's Daddy doing? Can we go to the zoo, Daddy?* etc. (though of course occasional morphological or syntactic errors occur – cf. e.g. *We goed there with Daddy, What we can do?* etc.).

Thus, the central phenomenon which any theory of language acquisition must seek to explain is this: how is it that after a long drawn-out period of many months in which there is no obvious sign of grammatical development, at around the age of 18 months there is a sudden *spurt* as multiword speech starts to emerge, and a phenomenal growth in grammatical development then takes place over the next twelve months? This *uniformity* and (once the spurt has started) *rapidity* in the pattern of children's linguistic development are the central facts which a theory of language acquisition must seek to explain. But how?

Chomsky maintains that the most plausible explanation for the uniformity and rapidity of first language acquisition is to posit that the course of acquisition is determined by a biologically endowed innate *language faculty* (or *language acquisition program*, to borrow a computer software metaphor) within the brain, which provides children with a (genetically transmitted) algorithm (i.e. set of procedures) for developing a grammar, on the basis of their linguistic *experience* (i.e. on the basis of the speech input they receive). The way in which Chomsky visualizes the acquisition process can be represented schematically as in (4) below (where *L* is the language being acquired):

(4)

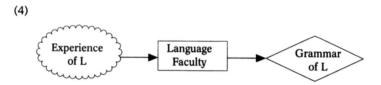

Children acquiring a language will observe people around them using the language, and the set of expressions in the language which the child hears – and the contexts in which they are used – in the course of acquiring the language constitute the child's linguistic *experience* of the language. This experience serves as input to the child's *language faculty*, which provides the child with a procedure for (subconsciously) analysing the experience in such a way as to devise a *grammar* of the language being acquired. Thus, the input to the language faculty is the child's experience, and the output of the language faculty is a grammar of the language being acquired.

The hypothesis that the course of language acquisition is determined by an innate language faculty is known popularly as the *innateness hypothesis*. Chomsky maintains that language acquisition is an activity unique to human beings, and different in kind from any other type of learning which human beings experience, so that learning a language involves mental processes entirely distinct from those involved in e.g. learning to play chess, or learning to ride a bicycle.

One piece of evidence which Chomsky adduces in support of positing an innate language faculty unique to humans is that language acquisition is a *species-specific* ability, possessed only by human beings: cf.

Whatever evidence we do have seems to me to support the view that the ability to acquire and use language is a species-specific human capacity, that there are very deep and restrictive principles that determine the nature of human language and are rooted in the specific character of the human mind.
(Chomsky 1972, p. 102)

Moreover, he notes, language acquisition is an ability which all humans possess, entirely independently of their general intelligence: cf.

Even at low levels of intelligence, at pathological levels, we find a command of language that is totally unattainable by an ape that may, in other respects, surpass a human imbecile in problem-solving activity and other adaptive behavior.
(Chomsky 1972, p. 10)

In addition, the apparent *uniformity* in the pattern of acquisition suggests that children have genetic guidance in the task of constructing a grammar of their native language: cf.

We know that the grammars that are in fact constructed vary only slightly among speakers of the same language, despite wide variations not only in intelligence but also in the conditions under which language is acquired.
(Chomsky 1972, p. 79)

Moreover, there is similar uniformity in the types of grammars developed by different speakers of a given language: cf.

Different speakers of the same language, with somewhat different experience and training, nonetheless acquire grammars that are remarkably similar.
(Chomsky 1972, p. 13)

Furthermore, the *rapidity* of acquisition (once the *grammar spurt* has started) also points to genetic guidance in grammar construction:

Otherwise it is impossible to explain how children come to construct grammars . . . under the given conditions of time and access to data.
(Chomsky 1972, p. 113)

(The sequence 'under . . . data' means simply 'in so short a time, and on the basis of such limited linguistic experience'.) What makes the uniformity and rapidity of acquisition even more remarkable is the fact that the child's linguistic experience is often *degenerate* (i.e. imperfect), since it is based on the linguistic *performance* of adult speakers, and this may be a poor reflection of their *competence*: cf.

A good deal of normal speech consists of false starts, disconnected phrases, and other deviations from idealized competence.   (Chomsky 1972, p. 158)

If much of the speech input which children receive is ungrammatical (because of performance errors), how is it that they can use this degenerate experience to develop a (competence) grammar which specifies how to form grammatical sentences? Chomsky's answer is to draw the following analogy:

Descartes asks: how is it when we see a sort of irregular figure drawn in front of us we see it as a triangle? He observes, quite correctly, that there's a disparity between the data presented to us and the percept that we construct. And he argues, I think quite plausibly, that we see the figure as a triangle because there's something about the nature of our minds which makes the image of a triangle easily constructible by the mind.   (Chomsky 1968, p. 687)

The obvious implication is that in much the same way as we are genetically predisposed to analyse shapes (however irregular) as having specific geometrical properties, so too we are genetically predisposed to analyse sentences (however ungrammatical) as having specific grammatical properties. A further argument Chomsky uses in support of the innateness hypothesis relates to the fact that language acquisition is an entirely subconscious and involuntary activity (in the sense that you can't consciously choose whether or not to acquire your native language – though you can choose whether or not you wish to learn chess); it is also an activity which is largely unguided (in the sense that parents don't teach children to talk): cf.

Children acquire . . . languages quite successfully even though no special care is taken to teach them and no special attention is given to their progress.
                    (Chomsky 1965, pp. 200–1)

The implication is that we don't learn to have a native language, any more than we learn to have arms or legs; the ability to acquire a native language is part of our genetic endowment – just like the ability to learn to walk.

  If (as Chomsky claims) human beings are biologically endowed with an innate language faculty, an obvious question to ask is what are the defining characteristics of the language faculty. An important point to note in this regard is that children can in principle acquire *any* natural language as their native language (e.g. Bosnian orphans brought up by English-speaking foster parents in an English-speaking community acquire English as their first language). It therefore follows that the language faculty must incorporate a set of *principles of Universal Grammar* – in the sense that the language faculty must be such as to allow the child to develop a grammar of *any* natural language on the basis of suitable linguistic experience of the language (i.e. sufficient speech input). Experience of a particular language L (examples of words, phrases and sentences in L which the child hears produced by native speakers of L) serves as input to principles of UG which are an inherent part of the child's language faculty, and UG then provides the child with an algorithm for developing a grammar of L.

If the acquisition of grammatical competence is indeed controlled by a genetically endowed language faculty incorporating principles of Universal Grammar, then it follows that certain aspects of child (or adult) competence are known without experience, and hence must be part of the genetic blueprint for language with which we are biologically endowed at birth. Such aspects of language would not have to be learned, precisely because they form part of the child's genetic inheritance. If we make the (not unnatural) assumption that the language faculty does not vary significantly from one (normal) human being to another, those aspects of language which are innately determined will also be *universal*. Thus, in seeking to determine the nature of the language faculty, we are in effect looking for universal principles which determine the very structure of language – principles which govern the kinds of grammatical operations which are (and are not) permitted in natural languages, principles of such an abstract nature that they could not plausibly have been learned on the basis of experience.

But how can we discover what these abstract universal principles are which constrain the range of grammatical operations permitted in natural language grammars? The answer is that since the relevant principles are posited to be universal, it follows that they will constrain the application of *every* grammatical operation in *every* language. Thus, detailed observation of even *one* grammatical operation in *one* language should reveal evidence of the operation of principles of Universal Grammar. By way of illustration, let's consider how *yes–no questions* are formed in English (i.e. questions to which *Yes* and *No* are appropriate as one-word answers). If we compare a simple declarative sentence (= statement) like (5a) below with its interrogative (= question) counterpart (5b):

(5) (a) Memories **will** fade away
    (b) **Will** memories fade away?

we see that the yes–no question in (5b) appears to be formed by preposing the bold-printed word *will* in front of the word *memories* (this particular grammatical operation is often referred to as *interrogative inversion*, the word *inversion* here serving to indicate a change of word order). We might therefore imagine that inversion involves some operation such as the following:

(6) Move the second word in a sentence in front of the first word.

However, it's easy enough to show that (6) is descriptively inadequate. For example, it would wrongly predict that the interrogative counterpart of (7a) below would be (7b):

(7) (a) Memories of happiness will fade away
    (b) *Of memories happiness will fade away?

Why is (6) wrong? The most principled answer which we can hope to give is that grammars of natural languages simply don't work like that. More specifically, we might suppose that what's wrong with an operation like (6) is that it is *structure-independent*, in the sense that it operates independently of (i.e. makes no reference to) the grammatical structure of the sentence, so that you don't need to know what the grammatical structure of the sentence is (i.e. which words belong to which grammatical categories, or which words modify which other words, etc.) in order to know how inversion works.

In fact, no linguist has ever claimed to have found any grammatical operation like (6) which operates in a completely structure-independent fashion in any natural language. It therefore seems reasonable to suppose that we would want to exclude structure-independent operations like (6) from our theory of grammar. One way of doing this would be to incorporate into our theory of Universal Grammar a principle such as (8) below:

(8) STRUCTURE DEPENDENCE PRINCIPLE
    All grammatical operations are structure-dependent.

What this means is that grammatical operations only apply to certain types of grammatical structure, not others. Let's look briefly at what is meant by *grammatical structure* in this context.

It is traditionally said that sentences are structured out of words, and phrases, each of which belongs to a specific *grammatical category* and serves a specific *grammatical function* within the sentence containing it. (We shall turn to consider categories in detail in the next chapter, so for the time being don't worry if you're not familiar with the terminology used here.) To see what we mean by this, consider the grammatical structure of our (pessimistic) sentence (7a) *Memories of happiness will fade away*. In traditional grammatical analysis, each of the words in the sentence would be assigned to a specific grammatical category: e.g. *memories* and *happiness* belong to the category of **noun**, *fade* is a **verb**, *will* is an **auxiliary** (so called because it provides additional – hence auxiliary – information about the action or process described by the verb, in this case indicating that the process of fading away will take place in the future), *of* is a **preposition** and *away* is traditionally classed as an **adverb** (though might be analysed as a prepositional particle). Certain of the words in the sentence combine together to form phrases, and each of these phrases in turn belongs to a specific category: for example, the string *memories of happiness* is a **noun phrase**, and the string *fade away* is a **verb phrase**. These two phrases are joined together by the auxiliary *will*, thereby forming the overall **sentence** *Memories of happiness will fade away*. Each of the various **constituents** (i.e. component parts) of the sentence also serves a specific grammatical function. For example, the noun phrase *memories of happiness* serves the grammatical function of being the **subject** of the auxiliary *will*, whereas the verb phrase *fade away* serves the function of being the **complement** of *will* (see the *glossary* if you are unfamiliar with these terms).

Having looked briefly at some traditional assumptions about grammatical structure, let's now return to our earlier discussion and see how we might develop a *structure-dependent* approach to the phenomenon of interrogative inversion. In keeping with suggestions made in traditional grammars, we might suppose that inversion involves an operation such as the following:

(9)   Move an auxiliary in front of a preceding noun expression which functions as its subject.

(A *noun expression* can be glossed as 'an expression comprising a noun together with any expressions modifying the noun'.) Such a characterization is overtly *structure-dependent* in the sense that it presupposes knowledge of the grammatical structure of a given sentence – i.e. knowledge of what grammatical categories the various expressions in the sentence belong to (e.g. *noun expression* and *auxiliary*), and what grammatical function they serve (e.g. *subject*). Consequently, in order to know whether inversion can apply in a given sentence, we need to know whether the sentence contains a subject noun expression followed by an auxiliary verb. In (5a), *memories* is a noun expression (comprising the single noun *memories*), and serves the grammatical function of being the subject of the auxiliary *will*. Thus, our structure-dependent characterization of inversion in (9) correctly predicts that (5b) *Will memories fade away?* is the interrogative counterpart of (5a) *Memories will fade away*. Likewise, it correctly predicts that the interrogative counterpart of (7a) is *Will memories of happiness fade away?*, in which we have an auxiliary (*will*) inverted with a noun expression (the noun phrase *memories of happiness*) which functions as its subject. Hence, the structure-dependent account makes correct predictions about both sets of sentences.

But no less importantly, our structure-dependent description of inversion also correctly predicts that inversion is not possible in cases such as:

(10) (a) Down **will** come taxes
       (b) ***Will** down come taxes?

(11) (a) John **received** a prize
       (b) ***Received** John a prize?

In (10b) we have the prepositional particle *down* inverted with the auxiliary *will*; and in (11b) we have the noun expression *John* inverted with the verb *received*. Since in neither case do we have inversion of a subject noun expression with an auxiliary, our structure-dependent characterization of English inversion correctly predicts that inversion cannot take place here. By contrast, our structure-independent characterization of inversion in (6) wrongly predicts that inversion should be possible in both cases.

So, the phenomenon of inversion in questions provides us with clear evidence in support of incorporating into our theory of grammar the **structure dependence principle** (8), which specifies that all grammatical operations are sensitive to the grammatical structure of the sentences they apply to. It seems reasonable to suppose that (8) is a fundamental principle of Universal Grammar, so that (8) holds for all grammars of all natural languages. If so, and if we assume that abstract grammatical principles which are universal are part of our biological endowment, then the natural conclusion to reach is that (8) is a principle which is wired into the language faculty, and which thus forms part of the child's genetic blueprint for a grammar. This in turn means that the innate language faculty incorporates a set of universal grammatical principles (i.e. UG principles) such as the structure dependence principle. Accordingly, we can revise our earlier model of acquisition in (4) above as in (12) below:

(12)

In this (revised) model, the child's experience is processed by the UG module which is an integral part of the language faculty.

A theory of grammar which posits that the internal grammatical structure of words, phrases and sentences in natural language is determined by innate principles of UG offers the important advantage that it minimizes the burden of *grammatical learning* imposed on the child. This is a vital consideration, since we saw earlier that *learnability* is a criterion of adequacy for any theory of grammar – i.e. any adequate theory of grammar must be able to explain how children come to learn the grammar of their native language(s) in such a rapid and uniform fashion. The UG theory developed by Chomsky provides a straightforward account of the rapidity of the child's grammatical development, since it posits that there is a universal set of innately endowed grammatical principles which determine the nature of grammatical structure and the range of grammatical operations found in natural language grammars. Since UG principles which are innately endowed do not have to be learned by the child, the theory of UG minimizes the learning load placed on the child, and thereby maximizes the learnability of natural language grammars.

Thus far, we have argued that the language faculty incorporates a set of universal grammatical principles (= UG principles) which are invariant across languages, and which determine the nature and acquisition of grammatical structure. However, it clearly cannot be that *all* aspects of the grammatical structure of languages are determined by innate grammatical principles; if this were so, all languages would have precisely the same grammatical structure, and there would then be no *structural learning* involved in language acquisition (i.e. no need for children to learn anything about the grammatical structure of sentences in the language they are acquiring), only *lexical learning* (viz. learning about the *lexis* (= vocabulary) of the language – i.e. learning the words in the language and their idiosyncratic linguistic properties, e.g. whether a given item has an irregular plural form, etc.). However, it is quite clear that although there are universal principles which determine the broad outlines of the grammatical structure of words, phrases and sentences in every natural language, there are also language-particular aspects of grammatical structure which children have to learn as part of the task of acquiring their native language. Thus, language acquisition involves not only *lexical learning* but also some *structural learning*. Our main concern here is to examine structural learning, and what it tells us about the language acquisition process.

Clearly, structural learning is not going to involve learning those aspects of structure which are determined by *universal* (hence innate) grammatical principles. Rather, structural learning will be limited to those *parameters* (i.e. dimensions, or aspects) of grammatical structure which are subject to language-particular variation (i.e. which vary from one language to another). In other words, structural learning will be limited to *parametrized* aspects of structure (i.e. those aspects of structure which are subject to parametric variation from one language to another). Thus, the obvious way to determine just what aspects of the grammatical structure of their native language children have to learn is to examine the range of parametric variation in grammatical structure between different (adult) natural languages.

We can illustrate one type of parametric variation across languages in terms of the following contrast between the Italian examples in (13a–b) below, and their English counterparts in (13c–d):

(13) (a) Maria parla francese   (b) Parla francese
      (c) Maria speaks French   (d) *Speaks French

As we see from (13a/c), in both Italian and English, finite verbs (i.e. verbs which carry present/past etc. tense) like *parla/speaks* license (i.e. can have) an overt subject like *Maria*; the two languages differ, however,

in that finite verbs also license a null (i.e. missing but understood)
subject in Italian (as we see from the fact that (13b) is grammatical in
Italian, and corresponds to English '*He/she* speaks French'), but not in
English (so that (13d) is ungrammatical in English). Thus, finite verbs in
a null subject language like Italian license either overt or covert (= null)
subjects, but in a non-null subject language like English, finite verbs
license only overt subjects, not null subjects. We might describe the
differences between the two languages by saying that Italian is a *null
subject language*, whereas English is a *non-null subject language*. More
generally, there appears to be parametric variation between languages as
to whether or not they allow finite verbs to have null subjects. The relevant parameter (termed the **null subject parameter**) would appear to
be a binary one, with only two possible settings, viz. *does/doesn't allow
finite verbs to have null subjects*. There appears to be no language
which allows the subjects of some finite verbs to be null, but not others –
e.g. no language in which it is OK to say *Drinks wine* (meaning 'He/
she drinks wine') but not OK to say *Eats pasta* (meaning 'He/she eats
pasta'). The range of grammatical variation found across languages
appears to be strictly limited: there seem to be just two possibilities –
languages either do or don't systematically allow finite verbs to have
null subjects (i.e. to have an *understood subject* which is not overtly
expressed).

A more familiar aspect of grammatical structure which is obviously
parametrized relates to *word order*, in that different types of language
have different word orders in specific types of construction. One type
of word-order variation can be illustrated in relation to the following
contrast between English and Chinese:

(14) (a) *What* do you think he will say?
      (b) Ni   xiangxin ta   hui shuo *shenme*
           you think   he   will say   *what?*

In English wh-questions (questions which contain a wh-word, i.e. a
word like *what/where/when/why* beginning with *wh-*), the wh-expression is moved to the beginning of the sentence. By contrast, in Chinese,
the wh-word does not move to the front of the sentence, but rather
remains *in situ* (i.e. in the same place as would be occupied by a corresponding noninterrogative expression), so that *shenme* 'what' is positioned after the verb *shuo* 'say' because it is the complement of the verb,
and complements are normally positioned after their verbs in Chinese.

Thus, another parameter of variation between languages is the *wh-parameter* – i.e. the parameter which determines whether wh-expressions can be fronted (i.e. moved to the front of the overall interrogative structure containing them) or not. Interestingly, this parameter again appears to be one which is *binary* in nature, in that it allows for only two possibilities – viz. a language either does or doesn't allow *wh-movement* (i.e. movement of wh-expressions to the front of the sentence). Many other possibilities for wh-movement just don't seem to occur in natural language: for example, there is no language in which the counterpart of *who?* undergoes wh-movement but not the counterpart of *what?* (e.g. no language in which it is OK to say *Who did you see?* but not *What did you see?*). Likewise, there is no language in which wh-complements of some verbs can undergo fronting, but not wh-complements of other verbs (e.g. no language in which it is OK to say *What did he see?* but not *What did he hear?*). It would seem that the range of parametric variation found with respect to wh-fronting is strictly limited to just two possibilities: viz. a language either does or doesn't allow wh-expressions to be systematically fronted.

A second type of word-order variation which we find concerns the relative position of **heads** and **complements** within phrases. It is a general (indeed, universal) property of phrases that every phrase has a head word which determines the nature of the overall phrase. For example, an expression such as *students of linguistics* is a plural noun phrase, because its head word (i.e. the key word in the phrase whose nature determines the properties of the overall phrase) is the plural noun *students*. The following expression *of linguistics* which combines with the head noun *students* to expand it into the noun phrase *students of linguistics* is said to be the *complement* of the noun *students*. In much the same way, an expression such as *in the kitchen* is a prepositional phrase which comprises the head preposition *in* and its complement *the kitchen*. Likewise, an expression such as *stay with me* is a verb phrase which comprises the head verb *stay* and its complement *with me*. And similarly, an expression such as *fond of fast food* is an adjectival phrase formed by combining the head adjective *fond* with the complement *of fast food*.

In English (and many other languages) head nouns, verbs, prepositions, adjectives, etc. precede their complements; however, there are also languages like Korean in which heads follow their complements. Thus, in informal terms, we might say that English is a **head-first** language, whereas Korean is a **head-last language**. The differences between the two languages can be illustrated by comparing the English examples in (15) below with their Korean counterparts in (16):

(15) (a) Close the door   (b) desire for change

(16) (a) Moonul dadala   (b) byunhwa-edaehan kalmang
           door   close   change-for   desire

In the English verb phrase *close the door* in (15a), the head verb *close* precedes its complement *the door*; if we suppose that *the door* is a determiner phrase, then the head of the phrase (= the determiner *the*) precedes its complement (= the noun *door*). Likewise, in the English noun phrase *desire for change* in (15b), the head noun *desire* precedes its complement *for change*; the complement *for change* is in turn a prepositional phrase in which the head preposition *for* likewise precedes its complement *change*. Since English consistently positions heads before complements, it is a *head-first* language. By contrast, we find precisely the opposite ordering in Korean. In the verb phrase *moonul dadala* (literally 'door close') in (16a), the head verb *dadala* 'close' follows its complement *moonul* 'door'; likewise, in the noun phrase *byunhwa-edaehan kalmang* (literally 'change-for desire') in (16b), the head noun *kalmang* 'desire' follows its complement *byunhwa-edaehan* 'change-for'; the expression *byunhwa-edaehan* 'change-for' is in turn a prepositional phrase whose head preposition *edaehan* 'for' follows its complement *byunhwa* 'change' (so that *edaehan* 'for' might more appropriately be called a *postposition*). Since Korean consistently positions heads *after* their complements, it is a *head-last* language. Given that English is *head-first* and Korean *head-last*, it is clear that the relative positioning of heads with respect to their complements is one word-order parameter along which languages will differ; the relevant parameter might be referred to as the **head (position) parameter**.

It should be noted, however, that word-order variation in respect of the relative positioning of heads and complements falls within narrowly circumscribed limits. There are many different logically possible types of word-order variation which just don't seem to occur in natural languages. For example, we might imagine that in a given language some verbs would precede and others follow their complements, so that (for example) if two new hypothetical verbs like *scrunge* and *plurg* were coined in English, then *scrunge* might take a following complement, and *plurg* a preceding complement. And yet, this doesn't ever seem to happen (rather *all* verbs typically occupy the same position in a given language with respect to a given type of complement).

What all of this suggests is that there are universal constraints on the range of parametric variation found across languages in respect of the relative ordering of heads and complements. It would seem as if there are only two different possibilities which the theory of grammar allows for, so that a given language must either be *head-first* (and so consistently position all heads before all their complements), or *head-last* (and so consistently position all heads after all their complements). Many other logically possible orderings of heads with respect to complements simply appear not to be found in natural language grammars. The obvious question to ask is why this should be.

The answer given by Chomsky is that the theory of Universal Grammar which is wired into the language faculty imposes genetic constraints on the range of parametric variation permitted in natural language grammars. In the case of the **head parameter** (i.e. the parameter which determines the relative positioning of heads with respect to their complements), UG allows only a binary set of possibilities – namely that a language may either be consistently *head-first* or consistently *head-last*. If this is so, then the only structural learning which children have to undertake when learning the word-order properties of the relevant class of constructions is to choose (on the basis of their linguistic experience) which of the two alternative settings of the parameter allowed by UG (viz. *head-first* or *head-last*) is the appropriate one for the language being acquired.

We might generalize our discussion at this point in the following terms. If the **head parameter** reduces to a simple binary choice, and if the **wh-parameter** and the **null subject parameter** also involve binary choices, it seems implausible that binarity could be an accidental property of these particular parameters. Rather, it seems much more likely that it is an inherent property of parameters that they constrain the range of structural variation between languages, and limit it to a simple binary choice. Generalizing still further, let us suppose that *all* grammatical variation between languages can be characterized in terms of a set of parameters, and that for each parameter, UG specifies a binary choice of possible values for the parameter. If this is so, then the only structural learning which children face in acquiring their native language is the task of determining the appropriate value for each of the relevant structural parameters along which languages vary. (Of course, children also face the formidable task of *lexical learning* – i.e. building up their vocabulary in the relevant language.)

If our reasoning here is along the right lines, then it leads us to the following view of the language acquisition process. The central task which the child faces in acquiring a language is to construct a grammar of the language. The child's language faculty incorporates a theory of Universal Grammar which includes (i) a set of universal *principles* of grammatical structure, and (ii) a set of structural *parameters* which impose severe constraints on the range of structural variation permitted in natural languages (perhaps limiting the range of variation to a series of binary choices). Since universal principles of grammatical structure don't have to be learned, the child's structural learning task is limited to that of *parameter-setting* (i.e. determining an appropriate *setting* for each of the relevant structural parameters). For obvious reasons, the model outlined here has become known as the **principles-and-parameters theory** (= **PPT**) of language.

The **principles-and-parameters theory** clearly has important implications for the nature of the language acquisition process: more precisely, such a model would vastly reduce the complexity of the acquisition task which children face. The **PPT** model would lead us to expect that those structural principles of language which are invariant across languages will not have to be learned by the child, since they will be part of the child's genetic endowment: on the contrary, all that the child has to learn are those grammatical properties which are subject to parametric variation across languages. Moreover, the child's learning task will be further simplified if it turns out (as we have suggested here) that the values which a parameter can have fall within a narrowly specified range, perhaps characterizable in terms of a series of binary choices. This simplified parameter-setting conception of the child's acquisition task has given rise to a metaphorical acquisition model in which the child is visualized as having to set a series of switches in one of two positions (*up/down*) – each such switch representing a different structural parameter. In the case of the **head parameter**, we might hypothesize that if the switch is set in the *up* position, the language will be head-first, whereas if it is set in the *down* position, the language will be head-last. Of course, an obvious implication of the *switch* metaphor is that the switch must be set in *either* one position *or* the other, and so cannot be set in both positions. (This would preclude the possibility of a language having both head-first and head-last structures.)

The assumption that acquiring the syntax of a language involves the relatively simple task of setting a number of structural parameters provides a natural way of accounting for the fact that the acquisition of specific parameters appears to be a remarkably *rapid* and *error-free* process in young children. For example, young children acquiring English as their native language seem to set the **head parameter** at its appropriate *head-first* setting from the very earliest multiword utterances they produce (at around age 18 months), and seem to know (tacitly, not explicitly, of course) that English is a *head-first* language. For example, the earliest verb phrases and prepositional phrases produced by young children consistently show verbs and prepositions positioned before their complements, as structures such as the following indicate (produced by a young boy called Jem at age 20 months; head verbs or prepositions are italicized, and their complements are in non-italic print):

(17) (a) *Touch* heads. *Cuddle* book. *Want* crayons. *Want* malteser.
           Open door. *Want* biscuit. *Bang* bottom. *See* cats. *Sit* down
      (b) *On* mummy. *To* lady. *Without* shoe. *With* potty. *In* keyhole.
           In school. *On* carpet. *On* box. *With* crayons. *To* mummy

The obvious conclusion to be drawn is that children consistently position heads before their complements from the very earliest multiword utterances which they produce. They do not use different orders for different words of the same type (e.g. they don't position the verb *see* after its complement but the verb *want* before its complement), or for different types of words (e.g. they don't position verbs before and prepositions after their complements).

A natural question to ask at this point is how we can provide a principled explanation for the fact that from the very onset of multiword speech we find heads correctly positioned before their complements. The **principles-and-parameters** model of acquisition enables us to provide an explanation for why children manage to learn the relative ordering of heads and complements in such a *rapid* and *error-free* fashion. The answer provided by the model is that learning this aspect of word order involves the comparatively simple task of setting a binary parameter at its appropriate value. This task will be a relatively straightforward one if UG tells the child that the only possible choices are for a language to be uniformly *head-first* or uniformly *head-last*. Given such an assumption, the child could set the parameter correctly on the basis of minimal linguistic experience. For example, once the child is able to parse (i.e. grammatically analyse) an adult utterance such as *Help Daddy* and knows that it contains a verb phrase comprising the head verb *help* and its complement *Daddy*, then (on the assumption that UG specifies that *all* heads behave uniformly with regard to whether they are positioned before or after their complements), the child will automatically know that *all* heads in English are normally positioned before their complements.

To summarize: in this chapter, we have been concerned with the nature and acquisition of *grammar*. We began by arguing that a grammar of a language is a model of the grammatical competence of the fluent native speaker of the language, and that grammatical competence is reflected in native speakers' intuitions about grammaticality and interpretation. We suggested that correspondingly, the main criterion of adequacy for grammars is that of *descriptive adequacy* (i.e. correctly accounting for grammaticality and interpretation). We noted that a theory of grammar is concerned with characterizing the general properties and organization of grammars of natural languages; we suggested that any adequate theory of language should be *universal*, *explanatory* and *restrictive*, and should provide grammars which are *minimally complex*, and hence *learnable*. We went on to look at the early stages of language acquisition, and argued that the most fundamental question for any acquisition theory to answer is why it should be that after a period of a year and a half during which there is no evidence of any grammatical development, most of the grammar of the language is acquired during the course of the following year. We outlined the *innateness hypothesis* put forward by Chomsky, under which the course of language acquisition is genetically predetermined by an innate language faculty. We noted Chomsky's claim that the language faculty incorporates a set of *UG principles* (i.e. universal grammatical principles). We argued that if principles of UG determine the nature of every grammatical operation and structure in every natural language, close examination of any one type of grammatical structure or operation in any one language will reveal evidence for the operation of UG principles – and we saw that the phenomenon of *inversion* in English provides evidence for postulating the **structure dependence principle**. We went on to suggest that languages differ in their structure along a range of different **grammatical parameters**. We looked at three such parameters – the **wh-parameter**, the **null subject parameter** and the **head parameter**.

We argued that each of these parameters is inherently binary in nature, and that consequently the structural learning which the child faces involves *parameter-setting* – i.e. determining which of the two alternative settings provided by UG is the appropriate one for each parameter in the language being acquired. We further argued that if the only structural learning involved in language acquisition is parameter-setting, we should expect to find evidence that children correctly set parameters from the very onset of multiword speech; and we presented evidence to suggest that from their very earliest multi-word utterances, children acquiring English as their mother tongue correctly set the **head parameter** at the *head-first* value appropriate for English.

Exercises

Exercise I

Below are examples of utterances produced by a girl called Lucy at age 24 months. Comment on whether Lucy has correctly set the three para-meters discussed in the text (the **head parameter**, the **wh-parameter** and the **null subject parameter**). Discuss the significance of the relevant examples for the parameter-setting model of acquisition.

	CHILD SENTENCE	ADULT COUNTERPART
1	What Daddy making?	'What's Daddy making?'
2	Want bye-byes	'I want to go to sleep'
3	Mummy go shops	'Mummy went to the shops'; this was in reply to 'Where did mummy go?'
4	Me have yoghurt?	'Can I have a yoghurt?'
5	Daddy doing?	'What's Daddy doing?'
6	Think Teddy sleeping	'I think Teddy's sleeping'; this was in reply to 'What d'you think Teddy's doing?'
7	What me having?	'What am I having?'; this followed her mother saying 'Mummy's having fish for dinner'
8	No me have fish	'I'm not going to have fish'
9	Where Daddy gone?	'Where's Daddy gone?'
10	Gone office	'He's gone to his office'

11	Want bickies	'She wants some biscuits'; this was her reply to 'What does Dolly want?'
12	What Teddy have?	'What can Teddy have?'
13	Where Mummy going?	'Where's Mummy going?'
14	Me go shops	'I want to go to the shops'
15	Daddy drinking coffee	'Daddy's drinking coffee'
16	What Nana eating?	'What's Grandma eating?'
17	Want choc'ate	'He wants some chocolate'; this was her reply to 'Teddy wants some more meat, does he?'
18	Dolly gone?	'Where's Dolly gone?'
19	Watch te'vision	'I'm going to watch television'
20	Me have more	'I want to have some more'
21	In kitchen	'In the kitchen' (reply to 'Where's Mummy?')
22	Me play with Daddy	'I want to play with Daddy'

Helpful hints

If Lucy has correctly set the **wh-parameter**, we should expect to find that she systematically preposes wh-expressions and positions them sentence-initially. If she has correctly set the **head parameter**, we should expect to find (for example) that she correctly positions the complement of a verb after the verb, and the complement of a preposition after the preposition; however, where the complement is a wh-expression, we expect to find that the complement is moved into sentence-initial position in order to satisfy the requirements of the **wh-parameter** (so that in effect the **wh-parameter** over-rides the **head parameter**). If Lucy has correctly set the **null subject parameter** we should expect to find that she does not use null subjects. However, the picture here is complicated by the fact that young children often produce truncated sentence structures in which the first word of the sentence is omitted (just as in diary styles, adults truncate sentences by omitting the subject when it is the first word in a sentence: cf. *Went to a party. Had a great time. Got totally sozzled*). Hence, when a child sentence has a missing subject, it is important to determine whether we are dealing with a *null subject* (i.e. whether the child has mis-set the null subject parameter), or a *truncated subject*. Since truncation occurs only sentence-initially (as the first word in a sentence), but null subjects can occur in any subject position in a sentence, one way of telling the difference between the two is to see whether children omit subjects only when they are the first word in the sentence (which would be the result of truncation), or whether they also omit subjects in noninitial positions in the sentence (as is the case in a genuine null subject language like Italian). Another way of differentiating the two is that in null subject languages we find that overt pronoun subjects are only used for emphasis, so that in an Italian sentence like *L'ho fatto io* (literally 'It have done **I**') the subject pronoun *io* 'I' has a contrastive interpretation, and the relevant sentence is paraphraseable in English as 'It was *I* who did it'; by contrast, in a non-null subject language like English, subject pronouns are not intrinsically emphatic – e.g. *he* doesn't have a contrastive interpretation in an English diary-style sentence such as *Went to see Jim. Thought he might help*. A third way of differentiating between sentences with null and truncated subjects is that in truncation structures we sometimes find that expressions other than subjects can be truncated (e.g. preposed complements).

In relation to the sentences in 1–22, make the following assumptions (where I use the informal term *covert subject* to mean 'understood null or truncated subject'). In 1 *making* is a verb which has the subject *Daddy* and the complement *what*; in 2 *want* is a verb which has a covert subject and the complement *bye-byes*; in 3 *go* is a verb which has the subject *Mummy* and the complement *shops*; in 4 *have* is a verb which has the subject *me* and the complement *yoghurt*; in 5 *doing* is a verb which has the subject *Daddy*, and its complement is a covert counterpart of *what*; in 6 *think* is a verb with a covert subject and its complement is *Teddy sleeping* (with *Teddy* serving as the subject of the verb *sleeping*); in 7 *having* is a verb which has the subject *me* and the complement *what*; in 8 *no* is a negative particle which has the complement *me have fish* (assume that *no* is the kind of word which doesn't have a subject), and *have* is a verb which has the subject *me* and the complement *fish*; in 9 *gone* is a verb which has the subject *Daddy* and the complement *where*; in 10 *gone* is a verb which has a covert subject and the complement *office*; in 11 *want* is a verb which has a covert subject and the complement *bickies*; in 12 *have* is a verb which has the subject *Teddy* and the complement *what*; in 13 *going* is a verb which has the subject *Mummy* and the complement *where*; in 14 *go* is a verb which has the subject *me* and the complement *shops*; in 15 *drinking* is a verb which has the subject *Daddy* and the complement *coffee*; in 16 *eating* is a verb which has the subject *Nana* and the complement *what*; in 17 *want* is a verb which has a covert subject and the complement *choc'ate*; in 18 *gone* is a verb which has the subject *Dolly* and its complement is a covert counterpart of *where*; in 19 *watch* is a verb which has a covert subject and the complement *te'vision*; in 20 *have* is a verb which has the subject *me* and the complement *more*; 21 is a phrase in which the preposition *in* has the complement *kitchen* (assume that phrases don't have subjects); and in 22 *play* is a verb which has the subject *me* and the complement *with Daddy* (and in turn *Daddy* is the complement of the preposition *with*).

Exercise II

In the text, we claimed that the **head parameter** always has a uniform setting in a given language: a language is either *head-first* (so that all heads precede their complements), or it is *head-last* (so that all heads follow their complements). However, although this would seem to be true of many languages (English included), there are other languages which don't show the same uniform setting for the **head parameter**. In this respect, consider the German phrases and sentences given below:

1. Hans muss stolz auf seine Mutter sein
   Hans must proud of his mother be
   'Hans must be proud of his mother'
2. Hans muss auf seine Mutter stolz sein
   Hans must of his mother proud be
   'Hans must be proud of his mother'
3. Hans geht den Fluss entlang
   Hans goes the river along
   'Hans goes along the river'
4. Hans muss die Aufgaben lösen
   Hans must the exercises do
   'Hans must do the exercises'
5. Ich glaube dass Hans die Aufgaben lösen muss
   I think that Hans the exercises do must
   'I think that Hans must do the exercises'

In relation to these sentences, make the following assumptions about their structure. In 1 and 2 *muss* is a verb, *Hans* is its subject and *stolz auf seine Mutter sein* is its complement; *sein* is a verb and *stolz auf seine Mutter* is its complement; *stolz* is an adjective, and *auf seine Mutter* is its complement; *auf* is a preposition and *seine Mutter* is its complement; *seine* is a determiner, and *Mutter* is its complement. In 3 *geht* is a verb, *Hans* is its subject and *den Fluss entlang* is its complement; *entlang* is a preposition (or, more precisely, a *postposition*) and *den Fluss* is its complement; *den* is a determiner and *Fluss* is its complement. In 4 *muss* is a verb, *Hans* is its subject and *die Aufgaben lösen* is its complement; *lösen* is a verb and *die Aufgaben* is its complement; *die* is a determiner and *Aufgaben* is its complement. In 5 *glaube* is a verb, *ich* is its subject and *dass Hans die Aufgaben lösen muss* is its complement; *dass* is a complementizer (i.e. a complement-clause introducing particle) and *Hans die Aufgaben lösen muss* is its complement; *muss* is a verb, *Hans* is its subject, and *die Aufgaben lösen* is its complement; *lösen* is a verb and *die Aufgaben* is its complement; *die* is a determiner and *Aufgaben* is its complement.

Helpful hints

Look at which categories are positioned before their complements and which after. Which words always seem to occupy a fixed position in relation to their complements, and which occupy a variable position? In the case of categories which sometimes go before (and sometimes after) their complements, try and establish whether the position of the head word is determined by *structural factors* (i.e. the type of structure involved) or *lexical factors* (i.e. the choice of head word).

❷ Categories

In the previous chapter, we concluded that the **structure dependence principle** determines that all grammatical operations in natural language are category-based (i.e. apply to whole categories of words or phrases rather than to individual expressions). In this chapter, we provide further evidence in support of this conclusion, and argue that a principled description of the grammar of any language (the language chosen for illustrative purposes being Standard English) requires us to recognize that all words in the language belong to a restricted set of **grammatical categories**.

A natural question to ask at this point is: 'What does it mean to say that words belong to grammatical categories?' We can define a *grammatical category* in the following way:

(1) A *grammatical category* is a class of expressions which share a common set of grammatical properties.

For example, by saying that words like *boy, cow, hand, idea, place, team*, etc. belong to the grammatical category *noun*, what we are saying is that they all share certain grammatical properties in common: e.g. the morphological property of having a plural form (ending in the suffix +*s*), and the syntactic property of being able to be premodified by *the*. As is implicit here, the bulk of the evidence in support of postulating that words belong to categories is *morphosyntactic* (i.e. morphological and/or syntactic) in nature.

The relevant morphological evidence comes from the *inflectional* and *derivational* properties of words: inflectional properties relate to different forms of the same word (e.g. the plural form of a noun like *cat* is formed by adding the plural inflection +*s* to give the form *cats*), while derivational properties relate to the processes by which a word can be used to form a different kind of word by the addition of another morpheme (e.g. by adding the suffix +*ness* to the adjective *sad* we can form the noun *sadness*). Although English has a highly impoverished system of inflectional morphology, there are none the less two major categories of word which have distinctive inflectional properties – namely *nouns* and *verbs*. We can identify the class of nouns in terms of the fact that they typically inflect for *number*, and thus have (potentially) distinct *singular* and *plural* forms – cf. pairs such as *dog/dogs, man/men, ox/oxen*, etc. Accordingly, we can differentiate a noun like *fool* from an adjective like *foolish* by virtue of the fact that only (regular) nouns like *fool* – not adjectives like *foolish* – can carry the noun plural inflection +*s*: cf. e.g.

(2)   They are *fools* (noun)/**foolishes* (adjective)

There are three complications which should be pointed out, however. One is the existence of irregular nouns like *sheep* which are invariable and hence have a common singular/plural form (cf. *one sheep, two sheep*). A second is that some nouns have no plural by virtue of their meaning: only those nouns (generally called **count nouns**) which denote entities which can be counted have a plural form (e.g. *chair* – cf. *one chair, two chairs*); some nouns denote an uncountable mass and for this reason are called **mass nouns** or **noncount nouns**, and so cannot be pluralized (e.g. *furniture* – hence the ungrammaticality of *one furniture, *two furnitures). A third complication is posed by noun expressions which contain more than one noun; only the head noun in such expressions can be pluralized, not any preceding noun used as a dependent or modifier of the head noun: thus, in expressions such as *car doors, wheel trims, policy decisions, skate boards, horse boxes, trouser presses, coat hangers*, etc. the second noun is the head noun and can be pluralized, whereas the first noun is a nonhead (i.e. is a modifier/dependent of some kind) and cannot be pluralized.

 In much the same way, we can identify verbs by their inflectional morphology in English. In addition to their uninflected *base* form (= the form under which they are listed in dictionaries) verbs typically have up to four different inflected forms, formed by adding one of four inflections to the appropriate stem form: the relevant inflections are the past/perfective participle suffix +*n*, the past-tense suffix +*d*, the third person singular present tense suffix +*s*, and the present/imperfective/progressive participle suffix +*ing* (see the *glossary* if these terms are unfamiliar), giving the range of forms illustrated in the table in (3) below:

(3) TABLE OF VERB FORMS

BASE	+N	+D	+S	+ING
hew	hewn	hewed	hews	hewing
mow	mown	mowed	mows	mowing
sew	sewn	sewed	sews	sewing
show	shown	showed	shows	showing
strew	strewn	strewed	strews	strewing

Like most morphological criteria, however, this one is complicated by
the irregularity of English inflectional morphology; for example, many
verbs have irregular *past* or *perfective* forms, and in some cases either
or both of these forms may not in fact be distinct from the (uninflected)
base form, so that a single form may serve two or three functions
(thereby *neutralizing* the relevant distinctions), as the table in (4)
below illustrates:

(4) TABLE OF TYPICAL IRREGULAR VERBS

BASE	PERFECTIVE	PAST	PRESENT	IMPERFECTIVE
go	gone	went	goes	going
speak	spoken	spoke	speaks	speaking
see	seen	saw	sees	seeing
_____come_____		came	comes	coming
wait	_____waited_____		waits	waiting
meet	_____met_____		meets	meeting
_____cut_____			cuts	cutting

(In fact, the largest class of verbs in English are those which have the
morphological characteristics of *wait*, and thus form both their past and
perfective forms by suffixing +(e)d.) The picture becomes even more
complicated if we take into account the verb *be*, which has eight distinct
forms (viz. the base form *be*, the perfective form *been*, the imperfective
form *being*, the past forms *was/were* and the present forms *am/are/is*).
The most regular verb suffix in English is +*ing*, which can be attached to
the base form of almost any verb (though a handful of defective verbs
like *beware* are exceptions).

   The obvious implication of our discussion of nouns and verbs here is
that it would not be possible to provide a systematic account of English
inflectional morphology unless we were to posit that words belong to
grammatical categories, and that a specific type of inflection attaches
only to a specific category of word. The same is also true if we wish to

provide an adequate account of *derivational morphology* in English (i.e. the processes by which words are derived from other words), for it turns out that particular derivational affixes can only be attached to words belonging to a particular category. For example, the negative prefixes *un+* and *in+* can be attached to adjectives to form a corresponding negative adjective (cf. pairs such as *happy/unhappy* and *flexible/inflexible*) but not to nouns (so that a noun like *fear* has no negative counterpart **unfear*), nor to prepositions (so that a preposition like *inside* has no negative antonym **uninside*). Similarly, the adverbializing (i.e. adverb-forming) suffix *+ly* in English can be attached only to adjectives (giving rise to adjective/adverb pairs such as *sad/sadly*) and cannot be attached to a noun like *computer*, or to a verb like *accept*, or to a preposition like *off*. Likewise, the nominalizing (i.e. noun-forming) suffix *+ness* can be attached only to adjective stems (so giving rise to adjective/noun pairs such as *coarse/coarseness*), not to nouns, verbs or prepositions. (Hence we don't find *+ness* derivatives for a noun like *boy*, or a verb like *resemble*, or a preposition like *down*.) There is clearly no point in multiplying examples here: it is clear that derivational affixes have categorial properties, and any principled account of derivational morphology will clearly have to recognize this fact (see Aronoff 1976 and Fabb 1988).

The *syntactic* evidence for assigning words to categories essentially relates to the fact that different categories of words have different *distributions* (i.e. occupy a different range of positions within phrases or sentences). For example, if we want to complete the four-word sentence in (5) below by inserting a single word at the end of the sentence in the position marked ___ :

(5) They have no ___

we can use an (appropriate kind of) noun, but not a verb, preposition, adjective or adverb, as we see from (6) below:

(6) (a) They have no *car/conscience/friends/ideas* (nouns)
     (b) *They have no *went* (verb)/*for* (preposition)/*older* (adjective)/
          conscientiously (adverb)

Thus, using the relevant syntactic criterion, we might define the class of nouns as the set of words which can terminate a sentence in the position marked ___ in (5).

Using the same type of syntactic evidence, we could argue that only a verb (in its uninflected *infinitive/base* form) can occur in the position marked ___ in (7) below to form a complete (nonelliptical) sentence:

(7) They/it can ___

And support for this claim comes from the contrasts in (8) below:

(8) (a) They can *stay/leave/hide/die/starve/cry* (verb)
     (b)*They can *gorgeous* (adjective)/*happily* (adverb)/*down*
          (preposition)/*door* (noun)

And the only category of word which can occur after *very* (in the sense of *extremely*) is an adjective or adverb, as we see from (9) below:

(9) (a) He is *very* **slow**   (*very* + **adjective**)
     (b) He walks *very* **slowly**   (*very* + **adverb**)
     (c) * *Very* **fools** waste time   (*very* + **noun**)
     (d)*He *very* **adores** her   (*very* + **verb**)
     (e)*It happened *very* **after** the party   (*very* + **preposition**)

(But note that *very* can only be used to modify adjectives/adverbs which by virtue of their meaning are *gradable* and so can be qualified by words like *very/rather/somewhat* etc.; adjectives/adverbs which denote an absolute state are *ungradable* by virtue of their meaning, and so cannot be qualified in the same way – hence the oddity of !*Fifteen students were very* **present**, *and five were very* **absent**, where ! marks semantic anomaly.) Moreover, we can differentiate adjectives from adverbs in syntactic terms. For example, only adverbs can be used to end sentences such as *He treats her* ___ , *She behaved* ___ , *He worded the statement* ___ : cf.

(10) (a) He treats her *badly* (adverb)/*kind* (adjective)/*shame* (noun)
      (b) She behaved *abominably* (adverb)/*appalling* (adjective)/
            disgrace/(noun)/*down* (preposition)
      (c) He worded the statement *carefully* (adverb)/*good* (adjective)/
            tact (noun)

And since adjectives (but not adverbs) can serve as the complement of the verb *be* (i.e. can be used after *be*), we can delimit the class of (*gradable*) adjectives uniquely by saying that only adjectives can be used to complete a four-word sentence of the form *They are very* ___ : cf.

(11) (a) They are very *tall/pretty/kind/nice* (adjective)
      (b)*They are very *slowly* (adverb)/*gentlemen* (noun)/*working*
            (verb)/*outside* (preposition)

Another way of differentiating between an adjective like *real* and an adverb like *really* in syntactic terms is that adjectives are used to modify nouns, whereas adverbs are used to modify other types of expression: cf.

(12) (a) There is a *real* **crisis**   (*real* + **noun**)
      (b) He is *really* **nice**   (*really* + **adjective**)
      (c) He walks *really* **slowly**   (*really* + **adverb**)
      (d) He is *really* **down**   (*really* + **preposition**)
      (e) He must *really* **squirm**   (*really* + **verb**)

Adjectives used to modify a following noun (like *real* in *There is a real crisis*) are traditionally said to be *attributive* in function, whereas those which do not modify an immediately following noun (like *real* in *The crisis is real*) are said to be *predicative* in function.

    As for the syntactic properties of prepositions, they alone can be intensified by *right* in the sense of 'completely', or by *straight* in the sense of 'directly':

(13) (a) Go *right* **up** the ladder
      (b) He went *right* **inside**
      (c) He walked *straight* **into** a wall
      (d) He fell *straight* **down**

By contrast, other categories cannot be intensified by *right/straight* (in Standard English): cf.

(14) (a) *He *right/straight* **despaired**   (*right/straight*+ **verb**)
      (b) *She is *right/straight* **pretty**   (*right/straight* + **adjective**)
      (c) *She looked at him *right/straight* **strangely** (*right/straight* + **adverb**)
      (d) *They are *right/straight* **fools**   (*right/straight*+ **noun**)

It should be noted, however, that since *right/straight* serve to intensify the meaning of a preposition, they can only be combined with those (uses of) prepositions which express the kind of meaning which can be intensified in the appropriate way (contrast the grammaticality of *He made right/straight **for** the exit* with the ungrammaticality of **He bought a present right/straight **for** Mary*).

    A further syntactic property of some prepositions (namely those which take a following (pro)nominal complement (traditionally called *transitive prepositions*)) which they share in common with (transitive) verbs is the fact that they permit an immediately following *objective pronoun* as their complement (i.e. a pronoun in its object form, like *me/us/him/them*): cf.

(15) (a) She was *against* him   (*transitive preposition* + **pronoun**)
     (b) She was *watching* him   (*transitive verb* + **pronoun**)
     (c) *She is *fond* him   (*adjective* + **pronoun**)
     (d) *She works *independently* him   (*adverb* + **pronoun**)
     (e) *She showed me a *photo* him   (*noun* + **pronoun**)

Even though a preposition like *with* does not express the kind of meaning which allows it to be intensified by *right* or *straight*, we know it is a (transitive) preposition by virtue of the fact that it is invariable (so not a *verb*) and permits an objective pronoun as its complement, e.g. in sentences such as *He argued with **me/us/him/them***.

Given that different categories have different *morphological* and *syntactic* properties, it follows that we can use the morphological and syntactic properties of a word to determine its categorization (i.e. what category it belongs to). The morphological properties of a given word provide an initial rough guide to its categorial status: in order to determine the categorial status of an individual word, we can ask whether it has the inflectional and derivational properties of a particular category of word. For example, we can tell that *happy* is an adjective by virtue of the fact that it has the derivational properties of typical adjectives: it can take the negative prefix *un*+ (giving rise to the negative adjective *unhappy*), the adverbializing suffix +*ly* (giving rise to the adverb *happily*), the comparative/superlative suffixes +*er*/+*est* (giving rise to the forms *happier/happiest*) and the nominalizing suffix +*ness* (giving rise to the noun *happiness*).

However, we cannot always rely entirely on morphological clues, owing to the fact that inflectional morphology is sometimes irregular, and derivational morphology often has limited productivity: this means that a word belonging to a given class may have only *some* of the relevant morphological properties, or even (in the case of a completely irregular item) *none* of them. For example, although the adjective *fat* has comparative/superlative forms in +*er*/+*est* (cf. *fat/fatter/fattest*), it has no negative *un*+ counterpart (cf. **unfat*), no adverb counterpart in +*ly* (cf. **fatly*) and (for many speakers) no noun counterpart in +*ness* (cf. **fatness*); even more exceptional is the adjective *little*, which has no negative *un*+ derivative (cf. **unlittle*), no adverb +*ly* derivative (cf. **littlely/*littly*), no productive noun derivative in +*ness* (cf. the awkwardness of ?*littleness*), and no productive *+er/+est* derivatives (the forms *littler/littlest* are not usual – at least, for me).

What makes morphological evidence even more problematic is the fact that many morphemes may have more than one use. For example, we noted earlier that *+n* and *+ing* are inflections which attach to verbs to give perfective or imperfective verb forms (traditionally referred to as *participles*). However, certain *+n/+ing* forms seem to function as *adjectives*, suggesting that *+ing* and *+n* can also serve as adjectivalizing morphemes. Thus, although a word like *interesting* can function as a verb (in sentences like *Her charismatic teacher was gradually interesting her in syntax*), it can also function as an adjective (used attributively in structures like *This is an interesting book*, and predicatively in structures like *This book is very interesting*). In its use as an adjective, the word *interesting* has the negative derivative *uninteresting* (cf. *It was a rather uninteresting play*), and the *+ly* adverb derivative *interestingly* (though, like many other adjectives, it has no noun derivative in *+ness*, and no comparative/superlative derivatives in *+er/+est*). Similarly, although we earlier identified *+n* as a verbal inflection (in forms like *grown/shown/blown/thrown* etc.), it should be noted that many words ending in *+n* can also function as adjectives. For example, the word *known* in an expression such as *a known criminal* seems to function as an (attributive) adjective, and in this adjectival use it has a negative *un+* counterpart (cf. expressions like *the tomb of the unknown warrior*). Similarly, the form *expected* can function as a perfective verb form in structures like *We hadn't expected him to complain*, but seems to function as an (attributive) adjective in structures such as *He gave the expected reply*; in its adjectival (though not in its verbal) use, it has a negative *un+* derivative, and the resultant negative adjective *unexpected* in turn has the noun derivative *unexpectedness*.

So, given the potential problems which arise with morphological criteria, it is unwise to rely solely on morphological evidence in determining categorial status: rather, we should use morphological criteria in conjunction with *syntactic* criteria (i.e. criteria relating to the range of positions that words can occupy within phrases and sentences). One syntactic test which can be used to determine the category that a particular word belongs to is that of **substitution** – i.e. seeing whether (in a given sentence), the word in question can be substituted by a regular noun, verb, preposition, adjective or adverb. We can use the *substitution* technique to differentiate between comparative adjectives and adverbs ending in +er, since they have identical forms. For example, in the case of sentences like:

(16) (a) He is *better* at French than you
      (b) He speaks French *better* than you

we find that *better* can be replaced by a *more + adjective* sequence like *more fluent* in (16a) but not (16b), and conversely that *better* can be replaced by a *more + adverb* sequence like *more fluently* in (16b) but not in (16a): cf.

(17) (a) He is *more fluent/*more fluently* at French than you
      (b) He speaks French *more fluently/*more fluent* than you

Thus, our *substitution* test provides us with syntactic evidence that *better* is an adjective in (16a), but an adverb in (16b).

The overall conclusion to be drawn from our discussion is that morphological evidence is suggestive rather than conclusive, and has to be checked against syntactic evidence. A useful syntactic test wnich can be employed is that if a morphologically irregular word can be substituted by e.g. a regular noun (i.e. can be replaced by a regular noun wherever it occurs), then the irregular word has the same categorial status as the regular word which can replace it, and so is a noun.

Thus far, we have looked at five traditional grammatical categories of English, viz. *noun, verb, preposition, adjective* and *adverb*. For typographical convenience, it is standard practice to use capital-letter abbreviations for categories, and so to use **N** for *noun*, **V** for *verb*, **P** for *preposition*, **A** for *adjective* and **ADV** for *adverb*. The words which belong to these five categories are traditionally said to be **contentives** (or **content words**), in that they have idiosyncratic *descriptive content*. However, in addition to *content words* languages also contain **function words** (or **functors**) – i.e. words which serve primarily to carry information about the *grammatical function* of particular types of expression within the sentence (e.g. information about grammatical properties such as number, gender, person, case, etc.). The differences between contentives and functors can be illustrated by comparing a (contentive) noun like *car* with a (functional) pronoun like *they*. A noun like *car* has obvious descriptive content in that it denotes an object which typically has four wheels, an engine, etc.; by contrast, a pronoun such as *they* has no descriptive content (e.g. you can't draw a picture of *they*), but rather is a functor which (as we shall see shortly) simply encodes a set of

grammatical (more specifically, person, number and case) properties
in that it is a third person plural nominative pronoun.

One test of whether words have descriptive content is to see
whether they have *antonyms* (i.e. opposites): if a word has an antonym,
it is a contentive (though if it has no antonym, you can't be sure whether
it is a functor or a contentive). For example, a noun/N such as *loss* has
the antonym *gain*; a verb/V such as *rise* has the antonym *fall*; an adjec-
tive/A such as *tall* has the antonym *short*; an adverb/ADV such as *early*
(as in *He arrived early*) has the antonym *late*; and a preposition/P such
as *inside* has the antonym *outside*. This reflects the fact that nouns,
verbs, adjectives, adverbs and prepositions typically have descriptive
content, and so are contentives. By contrast, a particle like infinitival
to, or an auxiliary like *do* (cf. '*Do* you want *to* smoke?'), or a determiner
like *the*, or a pronoun like *they*, or a complementizer (i.e. complement-
clause introducing particle) like *that* (cf. 'I said *that* I was tired') have
no obvious antonyms, and thus can be said to lack *descriptive content*,
and so to be *functors*. Using rather different (but equivalent) terminology, we might say that contentives have *lexical content* (i.e. idiosyncratic
descriptive content which varies from one lexical item/word to another), whereas functors have *functional content*. We might then say that
nouns, verbs, adjectives, adverbs and prepositions are **lexical categories**
(because the words belonging to these categories have lexical/descrip-
tive content) whereas particles, auxiliaries, determiners, pronouns and
complementizers are **functional categories** (because words belonging
to these categories have an essentially grammatical function). Having
briefly outlined the characteristics of functional categories, let's take a
closer look at the main functional categories found in English.

The first type of functional category which we shall deal with is the
category of **determiner** (abbreviated to **D**, or sometimes **DET**). Items
such as those bold-printed in (18) below (as used here) are traditionally
said to be determiners (because they determine the referential or quantificational properties of the italicized noun expression which follows
them):

(18) (a) I bought **a** *new battery* from **the** *local garage*
      (b) I prefer **this** *painting* to **that** *photo*
      (c) **My** *studio apartment* is no bigger than **your** *garage*
      (d) **All** *good comedians* tell **some** *bad jokes*

(Quantifying determiners are determiners like *all/some* which denote quantity, and are sometimes said to belong to the subcategory *quantifier*; referential determiners are determiners like *the/this/that/my* which are used to introduce referring expressions – e.g. an expression like *the car* in a sentence like *Shall we take the car?* is a referring expression in the sense that it refers to a specific car whose identity is assumed to be known to the hearer.) Since determiners are positioned in front of nouns (cf. **the** boys), and adjectives can similarly be positioned prenominally (cf. **tall** boys), an obvious question to ask at this point is why we couldn't just say that the determiners in (18) have the categorial status of adjectives. The answer we shall give is that any attempt to analyse determiners as adjectives in English runs up against a number of serious descriptive problems. Let's see why.

One reason for not subsuming determiners within the category of adjectives is that adjectives and determiners are syntactically distinct in a variety of ways, in respect of their *distribution*. For example, adjectives can be recursively (i.e. repeatedly) stacked in front of the noun they modify (in that you can go on putting more and more adjectives in front of a given noun), whereas determiners cannot be stacked in this way, and hence you can generally only have one determiner (of a given type – e.g. one referential determiner and one quantificational determiner) premodifying a noun:

(19) (a) ADJECTIVES: men; *handsome* men; *dark handsome* men; *tall dark*
                            handsome men; *sensitive tall dark handsome* men;
                            intelligent sensitive tall dark handsome men, etc.
      (b) DETERMINERS: the car; *a my* car; *that the* car; *that his the* car;
                            a that car, etc.

Moreover, both determiners and adjectives can be used together to modify a noun, but when they do so, any determiner modifying the noun has to precede any adjective(s) modifying the noun: cf. e.g.

(20) (a) **my** *nice new* clothes   (**determiner** + *adjective* + *adjective* + noun)
      (b) **nice* **my** *new* clothes   (*adjective* + **determiner** + *adjective* + noun)
      (c) **nice new* **my** clothes   (*adjective* + *adjective* + **determiner** + noun)

Thus, determiners seem to form a distinct distributional class (hence belong to a different category) from adjectives.

A further difference between determiners and adjectives can be illustrated in relation to what speaker B can – and cannot – reply in the following dialogue:

(21) SPEAKER A: What are you looking for?

SPEAKER B: *Chair/*Comfortable chair/**A** chair/**The** chair/**Another** chair/**This** chair/**My** chair

As already noted, nouns like *chair* have the property that they are *countable* (in the sense that we can say *one chair, two chairs*, etc.), and in this respect differ from nouns like *furniture* which are *uncountable* (hence we can't say *one furniture, *two furnitures, etc.). As we see from (21), a singular count noun like *chair* cannot stand on its own as a complete noun expression, nor indeed can it function as such even if premodified by an adjective like *comfortable*; rather, a singular count noun requires a premodifying determiner like *a/the/another/this/my* etc. This provides us with clear evidence that determiners in English belong to a different category from adjectives.

Indeed, a more general property which differentiates determiners from adjectives is that determiners tend to be restricted to modifying nouns which have specific *number/countability* properties. For example, the determiner *a* modifies a singular count noun, *much* modifies a (singular) mass noun, *several* modifies a plural count noun, *more* modifies either a plural count noun or a (singular) mass noun: cf.

(22) (a) Can you pass me **a** *chair/*chairs/*furniture*?

(b) He doesn't have **much** *furniture/*chair/*chairs* of his own

(c) He bought **several** *chairs/*chair/*furniture* in the sale

(d) Do we need **more** *furniture/chairs/*chair*?

By contrast, typical adjectives like *nice, simple, comfortable, modern*, etc. can generally be used to modify all three types of noun: cf.

(23) (a) We need a **nice, simple, comfortable, modern** *chair*

(b) We need some **nice, simple, comfortable, modern** *chairs*

(c) We need some **nice, simple, comfortable, modern** *furniture*

(It should be noted, however, that a handful of determiners like *the* can also be used to modify singular/plural count and noncount nouns alike.)

It seems reasonable to suppose that determiners constitute a *functional* category (whereas adjectives are a *lexical* category). After all, there is an obvious sense in which adjectives (e.g. *thoughtful*) have descriptive content but determiners do not – as we can illustrate in terms of the following contrast (? and ! are used to denote increasing degrees of semantic/pragmatic anomaly):

(24) (a) a *thoughtful* friend/?cat/??fish/???pan/!problem
      (b) **a/the/another/this/my** friend/cat/fish/pan/problem

As (24a) illustrates, an adjective like *thoughtful* can only be used to modify certain types of noun; this is because its descriptive content is such that it is only compatible with (for example) an expression denoting a rational entity. By contrast, determiners like those bold-printed in (24b) lack specific descriptive content, and hence can be used to premodify any kind of noun (the only restrictions being *grammatical* in nature – cf. e.g. the fact that *a(n)/another* can only be used to premodify a singular count noun). Thus, it seems appropriate to conclude that determiners constitute a functional category, and adjectives a lexical category.

It is a striking fact about determiners that many of them can not only be used to modify a following noun expression, but can also be used on their own (without any following noun): in this second type of use, they are traditionally categorized as *pronouns*. This dual use of the relevant words can be illustrated by examples such as (25) below, where the bold-printed items serve as *prenominal* determiners (premodifying an italicized noun expression) in the first example in each pair, but as *pronominal* determiners (standing on their own) in the second example:

(25) (a) **All** *guests* are welcome/**All** are welcome
      (b) **Many** *miners* died in the accident/**Many** died in the accident
      (c) **Several** *protesters* were arrested/**Several** were arrested
      (d) **Each** *son* was envious of the other/**Each** was envious of the other
      (e) I don't have **any** *cigarettes*/I don't have **any**
      (f) I prefer **this** *book*/I prefer **this**
      (g) Are you going to buy **those** *items*/Are you going to buy **those**?

There are so many words of this type that it seems implausible to suppose that their dual (prenominal/pronominal) use is mere coincidence. Rather, it seems more plausible to say that in both uses, the relevant items have the categorial status of *determiners* (or *quantifiers* in the case of the items italicized in (25a–e)), and that they can be used either *prenominally* (i.e. in front of a noun, as in *Look at **that** car!*) or *pronominally* (i.e. standing on their own, not modifying a following noun expression, as in *Look at **that**!*).

Although most determiners can be used both prenominally and pronominally, there are a few which can only be used prenominally: cf.

(26) (a) Don't touch *the* glass   (= prenominal determiner)
      (b)*Don't touch *the*   (= pronominal determiner)

(27) (a) *Every* student failed   (= prenominal quantifier)
      (b)*Every* failed   (= pronominal quantifier)

But are there conversely determiners which can be used only pronominally, not prenominally?

   In this connection, consider the categorial status of so-called *personal pronouns* like *I/me/we/us/you/he/him/she/her/it/they/them*.
These are called personal pronouns not because they denote people (the
pronoun *it* is not normally used to denote a person), but rather because
they encode the grammatical property of *person*. In the relevant technical sense, *I/me/we/us* are said to be *first person* pronouns, in that they
are expressions whose reference includes the person/s speaking; *you* is
a second person pronoun, in that its reference includes the addressee/s
(viz. the person/s being spoken to), but excludes the speaker/s;
he/him/she/her/it/they/them are third person pronouns in the sense
that they refer to entities other than the speaker/s or addressee/s.
Personal pronouns differ morphologically from nouns and other pronouns in Modern English in that they inflect for nominative/objective
case, as we can see from contrasts such as the following:

(28) (a) *John* admires *Mary*, and *Mary* admires *John*
      (b) **He/*Him** admires **her/*she**, and **she/*her** admires **him/*he**

Pronouns like *he/him* and *she/her* change their morphological form
according to the position which they occupy within the sentence, so that
the *nominative* forms *he/she* are required as the subject of a present-
tense verb like *admires* (or a past-tense verb), whereas the *objective*
(= *accusative*) forms *him/her* are required e.g. when used as the complement of a verb or preposition: these variations are said to reflect different **case forms** of the pronoun. By contrast, nouns such as *John* and
Mary don't inflect for nominative/objective case in Modern English,
and hence don't change their form according to whether they are used
as subjects or complements.

   Personal pronouns are clearly functors by virtue of the fact that they
lack descriptive content: thus, whereas a noun like *dogs* denotes a specific type of animal, a personal pronoun like *they* denotes no specific
type of entity, but has to have its reference determined from the linguistic or nonlinguistic context. We might argue that personal pronouns

simply encode sets of grammatical properties – viz. *person, number, gender* and *case* properties – as represented in the table in (29) below:

(29)

PERSON	NUMBER	GENDER	CASE	
			NOMINATIVE	OBJECTIVE
1	SG	–	I	me
1	PL	–	we	us
2	–	–	you	you
3	SG	M	he	him
3	SG	F	she	her
3	SG	N	it	it
3	PL	–	they	them

(SG = singular; PL = plural; M = masculine; F = feminine; N = neuter; – indicates that the item in question carries no specific gender/number restriction on its use.)

But what grammatical category do personal pronouns belong to? Studies by Postal (1966), Abney (1987) and Longobardi (1994) suggest that pronouns have the categorial status of determiners. This assumption would provide us with a unitary analysis of the syntax of the italicized items in the bracketed expressions in sentences such as (30a–b) below:

(30) (a) [*We* psychologists] don't trust [*you* linguists]
      (b) [*We*] don't trust [*you*]

Since *we* and *you* in (30a) modify the nouns *psychologists/linguists* and since determiners like *the* are typically used to modify nouns, it seems reasonable to suppose that *we/you* function as prenominal determiners in (30a). But if this is so, it is plausible to suppose that *we* and *you* also have the categorial status of determiners in sentences like (30b). It would then follow that *we/you* have the categorial status of determiners in both (30a) and (30b), but differ in that they are used prenominally in (30a), but pronominally in (30b). However, third person pronouns like *he/she/it/they* are typically used only pronominally – hence the ungrammaticality of expressions such as **they boys* in standard varieties of English (though this is grammatical in some nonstandard varieties of English – e.g. that spoken in Bristol in south-west England).

Having looked at prenominal and pronominal determiners, let's now turn to look at a very different kind of functional category.

Traditional grammarians posit that there is a special class of items which once functioned simply as verbs, but in the course of the evolution of the English language have become sufficiently distinct from other verbs that they are now regarded as belonging to a different category of **auxiliary** (conventionally abbreviated to **AUX**). Auxiliaries differ from other verbs in a number of ways. Whereas a typical verb like *want* may take a range of different types of complement (e.g. a subjectless infinitival *to*-complement as in *I want* [*to go home*], an infinitive with a (bold-printed) subject as in *I want* [**you** *to keep quiet*], or a noun expression as in *I want* [*lots of money*]), by contrast auxiliaries typically take a verb expression as their complement, and have the semantic function of marking grammatical properties associated with the relevant verb, such as *tense, aspect, voice, mood* or *modality*. The items italicized in (31) below (in the use illustrated there) are traditionally categorized as auxiliaries taking a [bracketed] verbal complement:

(31) (a) He *has/had* [gone]
      (b) She *is/was* [staying at home]
      (c) He *is/was* [seen regularly by the doctor]
      (d) He really *does/did* [say a lot]
      (e) You *can/could* [help]
      (f) They *may/might* [come back]
      (g) He *will/would* [get upset]
      (h) I *shall/should* [return]
      (i) You *must* [finish your assignment]

In the relevant uses, *have* is traditionally said to be a perfective auxiliary, *be* an imperfective/progressive auxiliary, *do* a dummy (i.e. meaningless) auxiliary, and *can/could/may/might/will/would/shall/should/ must* are said to be modal auxiliaries (see the *glossary* for glosses of these terms). A minor complication is posed by the fact that the items *have* and *do* have other uses in which they function as *verbs* rather than auxiliaries.

There are clear syntactic differences between auxiliaries and verbs. For example (as we saw in the previous chapter), auxiliaries can undergo *inversion* (i.e. can be moved into presubject position) in questions – as is illustrated by the following examples, where the inverted auxiliary is italicized, and the subject is bold-printed:

(32) (a) *Can* **you** speak Japanese?

(b) *Do* **you** smoke?

(c) *Is* **it** raining?

By contrast, typical verbs do not themselves permit inversion, but rather require what is traditionally called *do*-support (i.e. have inverted forms which require the use of the dummy auxiliary *do*): cf.

(33) (a) **Intends* **he** to come? (b) *Does* **he** intend to come?

(c) **Saw* **you** the mayor? (d) *Did* **you** see the mayor?

(e) **Plays* **he** the piano? (f) *Does* **he** play the piano?

A second difference between auxiliaries and verbs is that auxiliaries can generally be directly negated by a following *not* (which can usually contract down onto the auxiliary in the form of *n't*): cf.

(34) (a) John *could not/couldn't* come to the party

(b) I *do not/don't* like her much

(c) He *is not/isn't* working very hard

(d) They *have not/haven't* finished

By contrast, verbs cannot themselves be directly negated by *not/n't*, but require indirect negation through the use of *do*-support: cf.

(35) (a)* They *like not/liken't* me (b) They *do not/don't* like me

(c)* I *see not/seen't* the point (d) I *do not/don't* see the point

(e)* You *came not/camen't* (f) You *did not/didn't* come

(Note that in structures such as *John decided not to stay* the negative particle *not* negates the infinitive complement *to stay* rather than the verb *decided*.) And thirdly, auxiliaries can appear in sentence-final tags, as illustrated by the examples below (where the part of the sentence following the comma is traditionally referred to as a *tag*): cf.

(36) (a) You don't like her, *do* you?

(b) He won't win, *will* he?

(c) She isn't working, *is* she?

(d) He can't spell, *can* he?

In contrast, verbs can't themselves be used in tags, but rather require the use of *do*-tags: cf.

(37) (a) You like her, *do/*like* you?

(b) They want one, *do/*want* they?

So, on the basis of these (and other) syntactic properties, it seems that we are justified in positing that auxiliaries constitute a different category from verbs.

A fourth type of functor found in English is the **infinitive particle** *to* – so called because the only kind of complement it will allow is one containing a verb in the *infinitive* form. (The infinitive form of the verb is its uninflected base form, i.e. the citation form in dictionary entries.) Typical uses of infinitival *to* are illustrated in (38) below:

(38) (a) I wonder whether *to* [go home]
      (b) Many people want the government *to* [change course]
      (c) We don't intend *to* [surrender]

In each example in (38), the [bracketed] complement of *to* is an expression containing a verb in the infinitive form (viz. the infinitives *go*, *change* and *surrender*). But what is the categorial status of infinitival *to*?

We are already familiar with an alternative use of *to* as a preposition, e.g. in sentences such as the following:

(39) (a) He stayed *to* [the end of the film]
      (b) Why don't you come *to* [the point]?
      (c) He went *to* [the police]

In (39), *to* behaves like a typical (transitive) preposition in taking a [bracketed] determiner phrase (i.e. *the*-phrase) as its complement (viz. *the end of the film*, *the point* and *the police*). A natural suggestion to make, therefore, would be that *to* is a preposition in both uses – one which takes a following determiner phrase complement (i.e. has a determiner expression as its complement) in (39) and a following verbal complement in (38).

However, infinitival *to* is very different in its behaviour from prepositional *to* in English: whereas prepositional *to* is a contentive with intrinsic semantic content (e.g. it means something like 'as far as') infinitival *to* seems to be a dummy (i.e. meaningless) functor with no intrinsic semantic content. Because of its intrinsic semantic content, the preposition *to* can often be modified by intensifiers like *right/straight* (a characteristic property of prepositions) – cf.

(40) (a) He stayed *right* to the end of the film
      (b) Why don't you come *straight* to the point?
      (c) He went *straight* to the police

By contrast, the dummy functor infinitival *to* (because of its lack of descriptive content) cannot be intensified by *right/straight*: cf.

(41) (a) *I wonder whether *right/straight* **to** go home
      (b) *Many people want the government *right/straight* **to** change course
      (c) *We don't intend *right/straight* **to** surrender

Moreover, what makes the prepositional analysis of infinitival *to* even more problematic is that infinitival *to* takes an entirely different range of complements from prepositional *to* (and indeed different from the range of complements found with other prepositions in general). For example, prepositional *to* (like many other prepositions) takes a noun expression as its complement, whereas infinitival *to* requires a verbal complement – as we see from examples such as those below:

(42) (a) I intend to *resign* (= verb)/*to *resignation* (= noun)
      (b) She waited for John to *arrive* (= verb)/*to *arrival* (= noun)
      (c) Try to *decide* (= verb)/*to *decision* (= noun)

Significantly, genuine prepositions in English (such as those bold-printed in the examples below) only permit following verbal complements when the verb is in the *+ing* form (known as the *gerund* form in this particular use), not where the verb is in the uninflected base/infinitive form: cf.

(43) (a) I am **against** *capitulating*/*capitulate*
      (b) Try and do it **without** *complaining*/*complain*
      (c) Think carefully **before** *deciding*/*decide*

By contrast, infinitival *to* can only take a verbal complement when the verb is in the uninflected base/infinitive form, never when it is in the gerund form: cf.

(44) (a) I want to *go*/*going* there
      (b) You must try to *work*/*working* harder
      (c) You managed to *upset*/*upsetting* them

A further difference between infinitival and prepositional *to* (illustrated in (45) below) is that infinitival *to* permits *ellipsis* (i.e. omission) of its complement, whereas prepositional *to* does not: cf.

(45) SPEAKER A: Do you want *to* go **to** the cinema?
      SPEAKER B: No, I don't really want *to*   (infinitival)
                 *No, I don't really want *to* go **to**   (prepositional)

Thus, there are compelling reasons for assuming that infinitival *to* belongs to a different category from prepositional *to*. But what category does infinitival *to* belong to?

In the late 1970s, Chomsky suggested that there are significant similarities between infinitival *to* and a typical auxiliary like *should*. For example, they occupy the same position within the clause: cf.

(46) (a) It's vital [that John *should* show an interest]
    (b) It's vital [for John *to*   show an interest]

We see from (46) that *to* and *should* are both positioned between the subject *John* and the verb *show*. Moreover, just as *should* requires after it a verb in the infinitive form (cf. *You should show/*should showing/*should shown more interest in syntax*), so too does infinitival *to* (cf. *Try to show/*to showing/*to shown more interest in syntax*). Furthermore, infinitival *to*, like typical auxiliaries (e.g. *should*) but unlike typical nonauxiliary verbs (e.g. *want*), allows ellipsis of its complement: cf.

(47) (a) I don't really want to go to the dentist's, but I know I *should*
    (b) I know I should go to the dentist's, but I just don't want *to*
    (c) *I know I should go to the dentist's, but I just don't *want*

The fact that *to* patterns like the auxiliary *should* in several respects strengthens the case for regarding infinitival *to* and auxiliaries as belonging to the same category. But what category?

Chomsky (1981, p. 18) suggested that the resulting category (comprising finite auxiliaries and infinitival *to*) be labelled **INFL** or **Inflection**, though (in accordance with the standard practice of using single-letter symbols to designate categories) in later work (1986b, p. 3) he replaced **INFL** by the single-letter symbol **I**. The general idea behind this label is that finite auxiliaries inflect for tense/agreement, and infinitival *to* serves much the same function in English as infinitive inflections in languages like Italian which have overtly inflected infinitives (so that Italian *canta+re* = English *to sing*). We can then say (for example) that an auxiliary like *should* is a finite I/INFL, whereas the particle *to* is an infinitival I/INFL.

The last type of functional category which we shall look at is that of **complementizer** (abbreviated to **COMP** in earlier work and to **C** in more recent work): this is a term used to describe a special kind of (*italicized*) word which is used to introduce complement clauses such as those bracketed below:

(48) (a) I think [*that* you may be right]
      (b) I doubt [*if* you can help me]
      (c) I'm anxious [*for* you to receive the best treatment possible]

Each of the bracketed clauses in (48) is a *complement clause*, in that it functions as the complement of the word immediately preceding it (*think/doubt/anxious*); the italicized word which introduces each clause is known in recent work (since 1970) as a *complementizer* (but would be known in more traditional work as a particular type of subordinating *conjunction*). Complementizers are *functors* in the sense that they encode particular sets of grammatical properties. For example, complementizers encode (non)finiteness by virtue of the fact that they are intrinsically *finite* or *nonfinite* (see the *glossary* if these terms are unfamiliar). Thus, the complementizers *that* and *if* are inherently finite in the sense that they can only be used to introduce a finite clause (i.e. a clause containing a present- or past-tense auxiliary or verb), and not e.g. an infinitival *to*-clause; by contrast, *for* is an inherently infinitival complementizer, and so can be used to introduce a clause containing infinitival *to*, but not a finite clause containing a tensed (i.e. present/past-tense) auxiliary like *should*; compare the examples in (48) above with those in (49) below:

(49) (a) *I think [*that* you **to** be right]
      (b) *I doubt [*if* you **to** help me]
      (c) *I'm anxious [*for* you **should** receive the best treatment possible]

Complementizers in structures like (48) serve three grammatical functions: firstly, they mark the fact that the clause they introduce is the complement of some other word (*think/doubt/anxious*); secondly, they serve to indicate whether the clause they introduce is finite (i.e. contains a present/past tense verb/auxiliary) or infinitival (i.e. contains infinitival *to*); and thirdly, they mark the *illocutionary force* (i.e. semantic/pragmatic function) of the clause they introduce (thus, *if* introduces an interrogative clause, whereas *that/for* introduce other types of clause: e.g. *that* typically introduces a declarative/statement-making clause).

However, an important question to ask is whether we really need to assign words such as *for/that/if* (in the relevant function) to a new category of complementizer, or whether we couldn't simply treat (for example) *for* as a preposition, *that* as a determiner and *if* as an adverb. The answer is 'No', because there are significant differences between complementizers and other apparently similar words. For example, one difference between the complementizer *for* and the preposition *for* is that the preposition *for* has intrinsic semantic content and so (in some but not all of its uses) can be intensified by *straight/right*, whereas the complementizer *for* is a dummy functor and can never be so intensified: cf.

(50) (a) He headed *straight/right* **for** the pub   (= preposition)
      (b) The dog went *straight/right* **for** her throat   (= preposition)
      (c) * He was anxious *straight/right* **for** nobody to leave

                                                              (= complementizer)
      (d)* It is vital *straight/right* **for** there to be peace   (= complementizer)

Moreover, the preposition *for* and the complementizer *for* also differ in their syntactic behaviour. For example, a clause introduced by the complementizer *for* can be the subject of an expression like *would be unthinkable*, whereas a phrase introduced by the preposition *for* cannot: cf.

(51) (a) *For you to go there on your own* would be unthinkable (= *for*-clause)
      (b)* *For you* would be unthinkable   (= *for*-phrase)

What makes it even more implausible to analyse infinitival *for* as a preposition is the fact that prepositions in English aren't generally followed a [bracketed] infinitive complement, as we see from the ungrammaticality of:

(52) (a) * She was surprised *at* [there to be nobody to meet her]
      (b)* I'm not sure *about* [you to be there]
      (c) * I have decided *against* [us to go there]

On the contrary, as examples such as (43) above illustrate, the only verbal complements which can be used after prepositions are gerund structures containing a verb in the *+ing* form.

   A further difference between the two types of *for* is that if we replace a noun expression following the preposition *for* by an appropriate interrogative expression like *who?/what?/which one?*, the interrogative expression can be preposed to the front of the sentence (with or without *for*) if *for* is a preposition, but not if *for* is a complementizer. For example, in (53) below, *for* functions as a preposition and the (distinguished) nominal *Senator Megabucks* functions as its complement, so that if we replace *Senator Megbabucks* by *which senator?*, the wh-expression can be preposed with or without *for*: cf.

(53) (a) I will vote *for* **Senator Megabucks** in the primaries
   (b) **Which senator** will you vote *for* in the primaries?
   (c) *For* **which senator** will you vote in the primaries?

However, in (54a) below, the bold-printed expression is not the complement of the complementizer *for* (the complement of *for* here is the infinitival clause *Senator Megabucks to keep his cool*), but rather is the subject of the expression *to keep his cool*; hence, even if we replace *Senator Megabucks* by the interrogative wh-phrase *which senator*, the wh-phrase can't be preposed:

(54) (a) They were anxious *for* **Senator Megabucks** to keep his cool
   (b)***Which senator** were they anxious *for* to keep his cool?
   (c) *For **which senator** were they anxious to keep his cool?

Furthermore, when *for* functions as a complementizer, the whole *for*-clause which it introduces can often be substituted by a clause introduced by another complementizer; for example, the italicized *for*-clause in (55a) below can be replaced by the bold-printed *that*-clause in (55b):

(55) (a) Is it really necessary *for there to be a showdown*?
   (b) Is it really necessary **that there should be a showdown**?

By contrast, the italicized *for*-phrase in (56a) below cannot be replaced by a *that*-clause, as we see from the ungrammaticality of (56b):

(56) (a) We are heading *for a general strike*
   (b)*We are heading **that there (will/should) be a general strike**

Thus, there seems to be considerable evidence in favour of drawing a categorial distinction between the preposition *for*, and the complementizer *for*.

Consider now the question of whether the complementizer *that* can be analysed as a determiner. At first sight, it might seem as if such an analysis would provide a natural way of capturing the apparent parallelism between the two uses of *that* in sentences such as the following:

(57) (a) I refuse to believe **that** [*rumour*]
   (b) I refuse to believe **that** [*Randy Rabbit runs Benny's Bunny Bar*]

Given that the word *that* has the status of a prenominal determiner in
sentences such as (57a), we might suppose that it has the function of a
preclausal determiner (i.e. a determiner introducing the italicized clause
Randy Rabbit runs Benny's Bunny Bar) in sentences such as (57b).

However, there is strong empirical evidence against a determiner
analysis of the complementizer *that*. Part of the evidence is phonological in nature. In its use as a complementizer (in sentences such as (57b)
above), *that* typically has the vowel-reduced form /ðət/, whereas in its
use as a determiner (e.g. in sentences such as (57a) above), *that* invari-
ably has the unreduced form /ðæt/: the phonological differences
between the two suggest that we are dealing with two different items
here, one of which functions as a complementizer and typically has a
reduced vowel, and the other of which functions as a determiner and
always has an unreduced vowel.

Moreover, *that* in its use as a determiner (though not in its use as
a complementizer) can be substituted by another determiner (such as
this/the):

(58) (a) Nobody else knows about **that/this/the** *accident* (= determiner)
     (b) I'm sure **that/*this/*the** *you are right*   (= complementizer)

Similarly, the determiner *that* can be used pronominally (without any
complement), whereas the complementizer *that* cannot: cf.

(59) (a) Nobody can blame you for **that** *mistake* (prenominal determiner)
     (b) Nobody can blame you for **that**   (pronominal determiner)

(60) (a) I'm sure **that** *you are right*   (preclausal complementizer)
     (b)*I'm sure **that**   (pronominal complementizer)

The clear phonological and syntactic differences between the two uses
of *that* argue strongly that the particle *that* which serves to introduce
complement clauses should not be analysed as a determiner, but rather
should be assigned to the different category **C** of complementizer.

The third item which we earlier suggested might function as a complementizer in English is interrogative *if*. However, at first sight, it might
seem that there is a potential parallelism between the use of *if* and interrogative wh-adverbs like *when/where/whether*: cf.

(61) I don't know [*where/when/whether/***if** he will go]

Thus, we might be tempted to analyse *if* as an interrogative adverb.

However, there are a number of reasons for rejecting this possibility. For one thing, *if* differs from interrogative adverbs like *where/when/ whether* not only in its form (it isn't a *wh*-word, i.e. it doesn't begin with *wh*), but also in its distribution: for example, whereas typical wh-adverbs can occur in finite and infinitive clauses alike, the complementizer *if* is restricted to introducing finite clauses – cf.

(62) (a) I wonder [*when/where/whether/***if** I should go] [finite clause]
        (b) I wonder [*when/where/whether/*****if** to go]   [infinitive clause]

Moreover, *if* is different from interrogative wh-adverbs (but similar to other complementizers) in respect of the fact that it cannot be used to introduce a clause which serves as the complement of a preposition (like *about/over/at/on* in the examples below): cf.

(63) (a) I'm not certain **about** [*whether/when/where* he'll go]
        (b) *I'm concerned **over** [*if* taxes are going to be increased]
        (c) *I'm puzzled **at** [*that* he should have resigned]
        (d) *I'm not very keen **on** [*for* you to go there]

Finally, whereas a wh-adverb can typically be coordinated with (e.g. joined by *and/or* to) another similar adverb, this is not true of *if*: cf.

(64) (a) I don't know [*where* or **when** to meet him]
        (b) I don't know [*whether* or **not** he'll turn up]
        (c) *I don't know [*if* or **not** he'll turn up]

For reasons such as these, then, it seems more appropriate to categorize *if* as an interrogative complementizer, and *whether/where/when* as interrogative adverbs. More generally, our discussion highlights the need to posit an additional category C of complementizer, to designate clause-introducing items such as *if/that/for* which serve the function of introducing specific types of finite or infinitival clause.

Having looked at the characteristics of the major lexical and functional categories found in English, we are now in a position where we can start to *parse* (i.e. analyse the grammatical structure of) phrases and sentences. The first step in parsing any expression is to *categorize* each of the words in the expression. A conventional way of doing this is to use the traditional system of **labelled bracketing**: each word is enclosed in a pair of square brackets, and the lefthand member of each pair of brackets is given an appropriate subscript category label to indicate what category the word belongs to. To save space, it is conventional to use the following capital-letter abbreviations to represent categories:

(65) N = noun   V = verb
      A = adjective   ADV = adverb
      P = preposition   D/DET = determiner
      C/COMP = complementizer   I/INFL = auxiliary/infinitival *to*

Adopting this notation, we can represent the categorial status of each of the words in a sentence such as *Any experienced journalist knows that he can sometimes manage to lure the unsuspecting politician into a cunning trap* as in (66) below:

(66) [$_D$ Any] [$_A$ experienced] [$_N$ journalist] [$_V$ knows] [$_C$ that] [$_D$ he] [$_I$ can]
      [$_{ADV}$ sometimes] [$_V$ manage] [$_I$ to] [$_V$ lure] [$_D$ the] [$_A$ unsuspecting]
      [$_N$ politician] [$_P$ into] [$_D$ a] [$_A$ cunning] [$_N$ trap]

What (66) tells us is that the words *journalist/politician/trap* belong to the category N (= noun), *he/any/the/a* to the category D (= determiner), *experienced/unsuspecting/cunning* to the category A (= adjective), *sometimes* to the category ADV (= adverb), *into* to the category P (= preposition), *knows/manage/lure* to the category V (= verb), *can/to* to the category I/INFL (since *can* is a finite present-tense auxiliary and *to* an infinitive particle), and *that* to the category C (= complementizer). It is important to note, however, that the category labels used in (66) tell us only how the relevant words are being used in this particular sentence. For example, the N label on *trap* in (66) tells us that the item in question functions as a noun in this particular position in this particular sentence, but tells us nothing about the function it may have in other sentences. So, for example, in a sentence such as *Greed can trap careless politicians*, the word *trap* functions as a verb – as represented in (67) below:

(67) [$_N$ Greed] [$_I$ can] [$_V$ trap] [$_A$ careless] [$_N$ politicians]

Thus, a labelled bracket round a particular word is used to indicate the grammatical category which the word belongs to in the particular position which it occupies in the phrase or sentence in question, so allowing for the possibility that the same word may have a different categorial status in other positions in other structures.

To summarize: in this chapter, we have looked at the nature of grammatical categories. At the beginning of the chapter, we defined a *category* as a class of expressions which share a common set of grammatical properties; we argued that inflectional and derivational morphology provide us with evidence for categorizing words, in that certain types of inflectional or derivational affix attach only to certain categories of word. We also argued that there is syntactic evidence for categorization, in that different categories of word occur in a different range of positions within the phrase or sentence. We suggested that we can determine the categorial status of a word from its morphological and syntactic properties, with *substitution* being used as a test in problematic cases. For example, verbs have the morphological property that they can take a range of inflectional suffixes (+s/+d/+n/+ing), and have the syntactic property that they can be used after a word like *can*; nouns (= N) have the morphological property that they typically inflect for number (cf. *cat/cats*), and the syntactic property that they can be preceded by *a/the*; adjectives (= A) have the morphological property that they have +ly or +ness derivatives, and the syntactic property that they can be modified by words like *very* and occur after the verb *be*; adverbs have the morphological property that they end in +ly, and the distributional property that they can follow a verb like *behave*; and prepositions have the morphological property that they are invariable, and the distributional property that they can be modified by *right/straight*.

We went on to draw a distinction between *lexical categories* (whose members have descriptive content) and *functional categories* (whose members lack descriptive content and serve to mark grammatical properties such as number, person, tense, etc.). We looked at the different types of functional category found in English. We began with determiners (= D), arguing that they belong to a different category from adjectives since they precede (but don't follow) adjectives, they can't be stacked, and they impose grammatical restrictions on the types of expression they can modify (e.g. *a* can only modify a singular count noun expression). We noted that most determiners can be used both prenominally (i.e. to modify a following noun) and pronominally (i.e. without any following noun), and that so-called *pronouns* are in effect pronominal determiners. We then looked at the functional counterparts of verbs, namely *auxiliaries* (= AUX): we argued that these are functors in that (unlike verbs) they describe no specific action or event, but rather encode verb-related grammatical properties such as tense, mood and aspect; we noted that auxiliaries are syntactically distinct from verbs in that (for example) they undergo inversion. A further type of functor which we looked at was infinitival *to*: we showed that this is distinct from the preposition *to*, and shares a number of properties in common with finite auxiliaries (e.g. auxiliaries and infinitival *to* allow ellipsis of their complements, but prepositional *to* does not). We noted Chomsky's suggestion that finite auxiliaries and infinitival *to* are different exponents of the same category I (or INFL). We also argued that complementizers (= C or COMP) like *that/if/for* form a further category of functors which mark the illocutionary force of a complement clause (e.g. indicate whether it is a statement or question), and that (for example) *if* is distinct from interrogative adverbs like *how/when/whether* in that it can only introduce a finite clause, and cannot introduce a clause which is used as the complement of a preposition.

Exercises

Exercise III

Discuss the categorization of the highlighted words in each of the following examples, giving empirical arguments in support of your analysis:

1a Nobody *need/dare* say anything
 b Nobody *needs/dares* to ask questions
 c John *is* working hard
 d John *may* stay at home
 e John *has* done it
 f John *has* to go there
 g John *used* to go there quite often
2a It is important *for* parents to spend time with their children
 b He was arrested *for* being drunk
 c We are hoping *for* a peace agreement to be signed
 d Ships make *for* the nearest port in a storm
 e Congress voted *for* the treaty to be ratified
 f I would prefer *for* the lock to be changed
 g It would be unfortunate *for* the students to fail their exams
3a Executives like *to* drive *to* work
 b I look forward *to* learning *to* drive

c It's difficult *to* get him *to* work

d I've never felt tempted *to* turn *to* taking drugs

e Better *to* yield to temptation than to submit *to* deprivation!

f Failure *to* achieve sometimes drives people *to* drink

g Try *to* go *to* sleep.

Model answer for 1a, 2a and 3a

The problem raised by the examples in 1 is whether the highlighted items have the categorial status of verbs or auxiliaries as they are used in each example – or indeed whether some of the items in some of their uses have a dual verb/auxiliary status. The words *need/dare* in 1a resemble modal auxiliaries like *will/shall/can/may/must* in that they lack the third person singular +s inflection, and take a *bare* infinitive complement (i.e. a complement containing the infinitive verb form *say* but lacking the infinitive particle *to*). They behave like auxiliaries in that they undergo inversion in questions, can appear in tags, and can be negated by *not/n't*: cf.

(i) (a) *Need/Dare* anyone say anything?

     (b) He *needn't/daren't* say anything, *need/dare* he?

Conversely, they are not used with *do*-support in any of these three constructions in Standard English: cf.

(ii) (a) **Does* anyone need/dare say anything?

      (b) **He *doesn't* need/dare say anything, *does* he?

Thus, *need/dare* when followed by a bare infinitive complement seem to have the status of (modal) auxiliaries.

In 2a, *for* could be either a complementizer (introducing the infinitival clause *parents to spend time with their children*), or a preposition (whose complement is the noun *parents*). The possibility that *for* might be used here as a preposition is suggested by the fact that the string *for parents* (or an interrogative counterpart like *for how many parents?*) could be preposed to the front of its containing sentence, as in (iii) below:

(iii) (a) *For parents*, it is important to spend time with their children

       (b) *For how many parents* is it important to spend time with their children?

The alternative possibility that *for* might be used as a complementizer (with the infinitival clause *parents to spend time with their children* serving as its complement) is suggested by the fact that the *for*-clause here could be substituted by a *that*-clause, as in:

(iv)   It is important *that parents should spend time with their children*

Thus, 2a is structurally ambiguous as between one analysis on which *for* functions as a preposition, and a second on which it functions as a complementizer.

In 3a, the first *to* is an infinitive particle, and the second *to* is a preposition. Thus, the second *to* (but not the first) can be modified by the prepositional intensifier *straight* (cf. *Executives like to drive straight to work*, but not **Executives like straight to drive to work*). Moreover, the second *to* is a contentive preposition which has the antonym *from* (cf. *Executives like to drive from work*), whereas the first has no obvious antonym since it is a dummy infinitive particle (cf. **Executives like from drive/driving to work*). In addition, like a typical transitive preposition, the second *to* (but not the first) can be followed by an objective pronoun like *them* – cf. *Executives think the only way of getting to their offices is to drive to them*). Conversely, the first (infinitival) *to* allows ellipsis of its complement (cf. *Executives like to*), whereas the second (prepositional) *to* does not (cf. **Executives like to drive to*). Thus, in all relevant respects the first *to* behaves like a dummy infinitive particle, whereas the second *to* behaves like a contentive preposition.

Exercise IV

Parse the words in the sentences below, using the labelled bracketing technique to assign each word to a grammatical category which represents how it is being used in the position in which it occurs in the sentence concerned. Give reasons in support of your proposed categorization, highlight any analytic problems which arise, and comment on any interesting properties of the relevant words.

1   He was feeling disappointed at only obtaining an average grade in the morphology exercise

2   Student counsellors know that money troubles can cause considerable stress

3   Opposition politicians are pressing for election debates to receive better television coverage

4 Seasoned press commentators doubt if the workers will ever fully accept that substantial pay rises lead to runaway inflation

5 Students often complain to their high school teachers that the state education system promotes universal mediocrity

6 Some scientists believe that climatic changes result from ozone depletion due to excessive carbon dioxide emission

7 Linguists have long suspected that peer group pressure shapes linguistic behaviour patterns in very young children

8 You don't seem to be too worried about the possibility that many of the shareholders may now vote against your revised takeover bid

Model answer for 1

[$_D$ He] [$_I$ was] [$_V$ feeling] [$_A$ disappointed] [$_P$ at] [$_{ADV}$ only] [$_V$ obtaining] [$_D$ an] [$_A$ average] [$_N$ grade] [$_P$ in] [$_D$ the] [$_N$ morphology] [$_N$ exercise]

An issue of particular interest which arises here relates to the status of the words *average* and *morphology*. Are these nouns or adjectives – and how can we tell? Since nouns used to modify other nouns are invariable in English (e.g. we say *skate boards*, not **skates boards*), we can't rely on morphological clues here. However, we can use syntactic evidence. If (as we claim), the word *average* functions as an adjective in 1, we should expect to find that it can be modified by an adverb like *relatively* which can be used to modify adjectives (cf. *relatively good*); by contrast, if *morphology* serves as a noun in 1, we should expect to find that it can be modified by the kind of adjective (e.g. *inflectional*) which can be used to modify such a noun. In the event, both predictions are correct, as we see from (i) below:

(i) He was feeling disappointed at only obtaining a *relatively average* grade in the *inflectional morphology* exercise

Some additional evidence that *average* can function as an adjective comes from the fact that it has the *+ly* adverb derivative *averagely*, and (for some speakers at least) the noun derivative *averageness* (cf. *The very averageness of his intellect made him a natural choice for prime minister*).

Helpful hint

In structures such as *morphology exercises*, you will not always find it easy to determine whether the first word (in this case, *morphology*) is a noun or adjective. As a rule of thumb, where the item concerned is clearly a noun in other uses, assume that it has the categorial status of a noun in this type of structure as well, unless (as in the case of *average* in the expression *average grade*) you have clear evidence that it is an adjective.

❸ Structure

In this chapter, we are concerned with the *structure* of phrases and sentences – i.e. with the way in which words are combined together to form phrases and sentences. To put our discussion on a concrete footing, let's consider how an elementary two-word phrase such as that produced by speaker B in the following mini-dialogue is formed:

(1)   SPEAKER A: What are you trying to do?
      SPEAKER B: *Help you*

As speaker B's utterance illustrates, the simplest way of forming a phrase is by **merging** (a technical term meaning 'combining') two words together: for example, by merging the word *help* with the word *you* in (1), we form the phrase *help you*. The resulting phrase *help you* seems to have verblike rather than nounlike properties, as we can see from the fact that it can occupy the same range of positions as the simple verb *help*, and hence e.g. occur after the infinitive particle *to*: cf.

(2)   (a) We are trying **to** *help*
      (b) We are trying **to** *help you*

By contrast, *help you* cannot occupy the kind of position occupied by a pronoun such as *you*, as we see from (3) below:

(3)   (a) *You* are very difficult
      (b)* *Help you* are very difficult

So, it seems clear that the grammatical properties of a phrase like *help you* are determined by the verb *help*, and not by the pronoun *you*. We might say that the verb *help* is the **head** of the phrase *help you*, and conversely that the phrase *help you* is a **projection** of the verb *help*. Since the head of the resulting phrase is the verb *help*, the phrase *help you* is a **verb phrase**; and in the same way that we abbreviate category labels like *verb* to V, we can abbreviate the category label *verb phrase* to VP. If we use the traditional labelled bracketing technique to represent the category of the overall verb phrase *help you* and of its constituent words (the verb *help* and the pronominal determiner *you*), we can represent the structure of the resulting phrase as in (4) below:

(4)   [$_{VP}$ [$_V$ help] [$_D$ you]]

What (4) tells us is that the overall phrase *help you* is a verb phrase
(VP), and that it comprises the verb (V) *help* and the pronominal determiner (D) *you*. The verb *help* is the **head** of the overall phrase, and the
pronoun *you* is the **complement** (or **object**) of the verb *help*. The operation by which the two words are combined together is called **merger** (cf.
Chomsky 1995).

Although we have used the traditional labelled bracketing technique
to represent the structure of the verb phrase *help you* in (4), an alternative way of representing the structure of phrases is in terms of a *labelled
tree diagram* such as (5) below (which is a bit like a family tree diagram –
albeit for a small family):

(5)

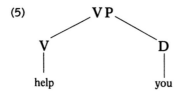

The tree diagram in (5) is entirely equivalent to the labelled bracketing
in (4), in the sense that the two provide us with precisely the same information about the structure of the phrase *help you*: so, (5) – like (4) –
tells us that *help* is a verb, *you* is a (pronominal) determiner, and *help
you* is a verb phrase. The differences between a labelled bracketing like
(4) and a tree diagram like (5) are purely notational: each category is
represented by a single *node* in a tree diagram, but by a *pair of brackets*
in a labelled bracketing.

We might generalize our discussion of (5) in an interesting way at
this point and hypothesize that all phrases are formed in essentially the
same way as the phrase in (5), namely by **merging** (i.e. combining) two
categories together to form a larger category. In the case of (5), the
resulting phrase is formed by merging two words. However, not all
phrases contain just two words – as we see if we look at the structure
of B's utterance in (6) below:

(6)   SPEAKER A: What's your main aim?
       SPEAKER B: *To help you*

The phrase in (6) would seem to be formed by merging the infinitive particle *to* with the verb phrase *help you*. What's the head of the resulting
phrase *to help you*? A reasonable guess would be that the head is the
infinitive particle *to*, so that the resulting string (i.e. sequence of words)

to help you is an **infinitive phrase**. This being so, we'd expect to find that infinitive phrases have a different distribution from verb phrases – and indeed this does seem to be the case, as sentences such as (7) and (8) below illustrate:

(7) (a) They *ought* **to help you**   (= *ought* + **infinitive phrase**)
     (b)*They *ought* **help you**   (= *ought* + **verb phrase**)

(8) (a) They *should* **help you**   (= *should* + **verb phrase**)
     (b)*They *should* **to help you**   (= *should* + **infinitive phrase**)

If we assume that *help you* is a verb phrase whereas *to help you* is an infinitive phrase, we can then account for the contrasts in (7) and (8) by saying that *ought* is the kind of word which requires an infinitive phrase after it as its complement, whereas *should* is the kind of word which requires a verb phrase as its complement.

   The infinitive phrase *to help you* is formed by merging the infinitive particle *to* with the verb phrase *help you*. Assuming that the verb phrase *help you* has the structure (5) above, the structure formed by merging the infinitive particle (= I) *to* with the VP in (5) will be the IP (= infinitive phrase) in (9) below:

(9)

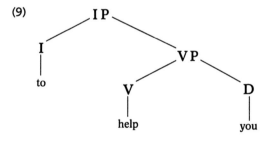

The resulting infinitive phrase is headed by the infinitive particle *to*, and the verb phrase *help you* is the complement of *to*.

   What is implicit in our discussion here is that we can build up complex structures in a pairwise fashion by merging successive pairs of categories to form ever larger phrases. For example, by merging the infinitive phrase *to help you* with the verb *trying* (here used in its progressive *+ing* form), we can form the phrase *trying to help you* – cf. speaker B's utterance in (10) below:

(10) SPEAKER A: What are you doing?
        SPEAKER B: *Trying to help you*

The resulting phrase would seem to be headed by the verb *trying*, as we see from the fact that it can be used after words like *be*, *start* or *keep* which require a complement containing an *+ing* verb form (cf. *They were/started/kept trying to help you*). This being so, the italicized phrase in (10) is a VP (= verb phrase) with the structure (11) below:

(11)

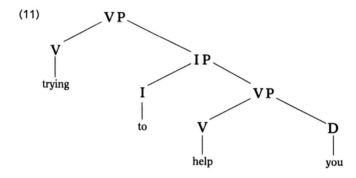

The head of the overall VP is the verb *trying*, and its complement is the IP *to help you*.

Having considered how *phrases* are formed, let's now turn to look at how *clauses* or *sentences* are formed. (See the *glossary* if you are not familiar with these traditional grammatical terms.) We might argue on theoretical grounds (in terms of our desire to develop a unified and internally consistent theory) that the optimum answer is to assume that clauses are formed by exactly the same **merger** operation (of combining two categories together) as phrases. To make our discussion more concrete, let's suppose that speaker B had chosen to use the *clause* italicized in (12) below to reply to speaker A, rather than the *phrase* in (10):

(12)   SPEAKER A: What are you doing?
      SPEAKER B: *We are trying to help you*

What's the structure of the clause produced by speaker B in (12)?

If we make the (unifying) assumption that clauses are formed in the same way as phrases, then it follows that the italicized clause in (12) must be formed by first merging the auxiliary *are* with the verb phrase *trying to help you*, and then subsequently merging the pronoun *we* with the string *are trying to help you*. If (as we argued in the previous chapter) auxiliaries like *are* belong to the same INFL (= I) category as the infinitive particle *to*, it might seem plausible to claim that the string *are trying to help you* is a projection of the auxiliary *are* and hence an IP (i.e. an auxiliary phrase), and that the whole clause *We are trying to help you* is a projection of the pronominal determiner *we*, and hence a DP (i.e. determiner phrase). But this can't be right, since it would provide us with no obvious way of explaining why speaker B's reply is ungrammatical in the dialogue in (13) below:

(13) SPEAKER A: What are you doing?

SPEAKER B: **Are trying to help you*

If we make the traditional assumption that complete phrases can be used to answer questions, and if *are trying to help you* is a complete auxiliary phrase (an IP), how come it can't be used to answer A's question in (13)?

The answer which we shall give to this question here is that *Are trying to help you* is an *incomplete* phrase. Why? Because auxiliaries require a subject, and the auxiliary *are* doesn't have a subject in (13). More specifically, let's assume that when we merge an auxiliary (= I) with a verb phrase (= VP), we form an incomplete auxiliary expression which is traditionally denoted as $\overline{\text{I}}$ (= I' = **I-bar**, in each case pronounced *eye-bar*); and that only when we merge the relevant I-bar with its subject do we form an **IP** (i.e. a complete auxiliary phrase). Given these assumptions, the italicized clause in (12) will have the structure (14) below:

(14)

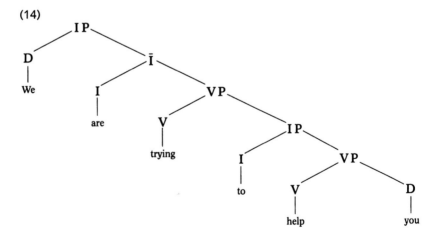

In a structure such as (14), the pronominal determiner *we* is said to be the **specifier** (and also the **subject**) of the auxiliary *are* (since it specifies who is trying to help you), and the VP *trying to help you* is the

complement of *are*. Thus, (14) illustrates the fact that a projection of a given head word may contain not only a complement, but also a specifier. An important assumption embodied in this analysis is that clauses are formed by essentially the same merger operation as phrases, and hence that (for example) a clause containing an auxiliary is in effect an *auxiliary phrase* (= IP).

A question which we haven't yet considered is what role is played in the structure of clauses by complementizers like *that*, *for* and *if*. In this connection, consider speaker B's reply in (15) below:

(15) SPEAKER A: What are you saying?
      SPEAKER B: *That we are trying to help you*

Where does the C (= complementizer) *that* fit into the sentence? A plausible answer is that C merges with the IP (14) *we are trying to help you* to form the **CP (complementizer phrase)** structure in (16) below:

(16)

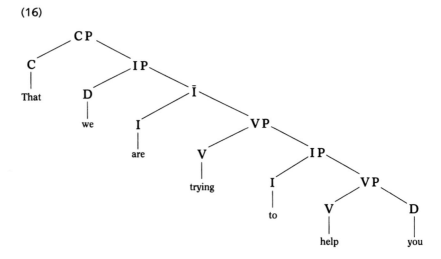

And indeed clauses introduced by complementizers have been taken to have the status of CP since the work of Stowell 1981 and Chomsky 1986b.

A tree diagram such as (16) provides a visual representation of the **categorial constituent structure** of the corresponding sentence – i.e. it tells us how the sentence is structured out of **constituents** (i.e. out of component words and phrases), and what category each constituent belongs to. For example, the tree diagram (16) tells us that the constituents of sentence (15) are the D *you*, the V *help*, the VP *help you*, the I *to*, the IP *to help you*, the V *trying*, the VP *trying to help you*, the I *are*, the I-bar *are trying to help you*, the D *we*, the IP *we are trying to help you*, the C *that* and the CP *that we are trying to help you*.

However, a tree diagram such as (16) provides only a partial representation of the overall grammatical structure of the corresponding sentence. For example, the only grammatical information which (16) provides us with for each of the words in the sentence is its categorial status (e.g. whether it is a verb or determiner etc.). There are numerous grammatical properties of words which are simply not captured by purely categorial representations like (16). We can illustrate this by looking at the grammatical properties of the auxiliary *are*. It has three sets of properties which any adequate account of its morphosyntax (i.e. morphology and syntax) must seek to describe: firstly, it is a present-tense form (the corresponding past-tense form being *were*); secondly, it requires a specific kind of subject as its specifier (e.g. a subject like *we, you* or *they*, but not a subject such as *us, I* or *he*). And thirdly, it requires a specific kind of complement (e.g. one containing a verb like *trying* in the +*ing* form, not one containing an infinitive verb like *try* or a perfective/past form like *tried*). How can we account for these three different sets of grammatical properties of the word *are*?

Phonetic and semantic properties are typically represented in terms of sets of **features**: for example, the fact that a consonant like /m/ (but not a consonant like /b/) is nasal is traditionally represented in terms of a phonetic feature such as [nasal]; and the fact that words like *boy, girl, kid, kitten, puppy* and *foal* (but not words like *man, woman, goat, cat, dog* and *horse*) represent the young of the relevant species is traditionally described in terms of a semantic feature such as [YOUNG]. (By convention, features are enclosed in square brackets, and semantic features are written in capital letters.) We might therefore extend the use of features to describe the kinds of grammatical properties illustrated by our discussion of *are* in (16). More specifically, let's suppose that words carry three sets of grammatical features: **head-features** (which describe their intrinsic grammatical properties), **complement-features** (which describe the kinds of complements they take) and **specifier-features** (which describe the kinds of specifier/subject they can have). Using simple abbreviations for grammatical features, we could then describe the grammatical properties of *are* (as it is used in (16) above) in the following terms. *Are* carries the head-feature [Pres], indicating that it is a present-tense form (its status as an auxiliary is indicated by the category label I attached to the node containing *are*). It carries the

complement-feature [+ing], used here as an informal abbreviation of the
fact that it **selects** (i.e. takes) a complement whose head word is a verb
carrying the participial inflection *+ing*: the complement of *are* in (16) is
the VP (verb phrase) *trying to help you*, and the head of this VP is the
verb *trying*, so the relevant requirement is met here. The specifier-features
of *are* include a case-feature (it requires a nominative subject like *we*, not
an objective subject like *us*), and (person/number) agreement-features (it
requires a subject which is either second person (like *you*) or plural (like
we/they): using simple abbreviations, we could say that the specifier-features of *are* are [2/PNom], meaning that *are* requires a second person or
plural subject carrying nominative case. What this means is that the *head
word* of the specifier of *are* must be nominative and either second person
or plural – a requirement satisfied in examples like (17) below:

(17)   [*We politicians*] are trying to better ourselves

Here, the subject/specifier of *are* is the bracketed DP (determiner
phrase) *we politicians*, and it is the head word of this phrase (i.e. the
determiner *we*) which is first person nominative plural. In (16), the subject of *are* is the single-word expression *we*, and since the head word of
this expression is *we*, the requirement for *are* to have a second person or
plural nominative subject is clearly met in (16). More generally, the complement-features of a word describe its **complement-selection** properties, and in effect say 'requires as its complement an expression whose
head word carries the head-features [. . .]'; and the specifier-features
of a word in effect say 'requires as its subject an expression whose head
word carries the head-features [. . .].'

Having shown how the grammatical properties of a word like *are*
can be characterized in terms of a set of **head-, complement- and specifier-features**, let's look briefly at how we might characterize the properties of the other words in (16). The head-features of the complementizer
that include a feature such as [Decl], indicating that it introduces
declarative (statement-making) clauses: its specifier-features indicate
that it cannot have a specifier; and its complement-features indicate that
it requires a complement headed by a finite I constituent (not e.g. by
infinitival *to*): since the complement of *that* is the IP *we are trying to
help you* in (16), and the head word of this complement is the finite auxiliary *are*, this requirement is met here.

The head-features of the pronoun *we* indicate that it is a first person
plural nominative pronoun; its specifier-features indicate that it doesn't

take a specifier; its complement-features indicate that it can either be used without any complement (as in (16)), or can be used with a plural noun complement (such as *politicians* in (17)).

The head-features of the word *trying* (as it is used in (16) above) indicate that it is a progressive *ing*-participle; its specifier-features allow it to be used in a verb phrase which doesn't have any specifier; and its complement-features indicate that it requires a complement headed by the infinitive particle *to*: since the complement of *trying* in (16) is the IP *to help you* and this is headed by infinitival *to*, this requirement is met here.

The head-features of infinitival *to* indicate that it is an infinitive particle; its specifier-features allow it to be used without any overt specifier/subject; and its complement-features indicate that it selects a complement headed by a verb in its (uninflected) infinitive form. Since the complement of *to* here is the VP *help you* and this is headed by the infinitival verb form *help*, the complement-selection requirements of *to* are met here.

The head-features of the word *help* (as used here) indicate that it is an infinitival verb form; its specifier-features are such that it can be used in a verb phrase without any specifier of its own; its complement-features indicate that it can either be used without any complement (as in *We are trying to help*), or with a complement whose head word carries objective case. Since the pronoun *you* can serve either as a nominative form (e.g. in *You are lying*) or as an objective form (e.g. in *I hate you*), the relevant requirement is met here.

The head-features of the pronoun *you* indicate that it is a second person singular or plural, nominative or objective pronoun. Its specifier-features allow it to be used (as here) without any specifier; its complement-features specify that when plural it can take a plural noun like *politicians* as its complement (cf. *You politicians are liars*), but when singular it doesn't normally allow a complement (cf. **You politician are a liar*).

An interesting question raised by our discussion here is how we ensure that the grammatical features carried by the different words in a sentence are compatible with those of other words in the same sentence. Chomsky (1995) develops a theory of feature-checking designed to answer this kind of question. Let's briefly explore some of the key concepts of **checking theory**.

Let's assume that the syntactic structures generated (i.e. produced) by merging pairs of categories together are used as the basis for computing two types of structural representation for a sentence: a representation of its phonetic form (= a **PF-representation**), and a representation of its logical form (= an **LF-representation**). In simple terms, the PF-representation of a sentence tells us how it is pronounced, and its LF-representation describes linguistic aspects of its meaning. Let us further suppose that some grammatical features are **interpretable** (at LF) by virtue of having semantic content, whereas others are **uninterpretable** (at LF) by virtue of having no semantic content, and that LF-representations may contain only (semantically) interpretable features. If a derivation (i.e. a set of grammatical operations used to form a given type of structure) gives rise to an LF-representation which contains only (semantically) interpretable features, the relevant derivation is said to **converge** (at LF); if it gives rise to an LF-representation containing one or more (semantically) uninterpretable features, the derivation is said to **crash** (at LF), and the corresponding sentence is ill formed. Finally, let us also suppose that grammatical features are **checked** in the course of a derivation, and that uninterpretable features are erased once checked (in much the same way as you cross items off a shopping list once you have bought them).

To make our discussion more concrete, let's look at how grammatical features are checked in a simple sentence such as:

(18)   She has gone

Consider first the grammatical features carried by each of the three words in the sentence. (Here, we are concerned only with grammatical features: hence, we ignore phonetic and semantic features.) The head-features of *she* indicate that it is third person nominative singular; those of *has* that it carries present tense; and those of *gone* that it is an *n*-participle (i.e. a perfective/past participle). The specifier-features of *has* tell us that it requires a third person singular nominative subject; and its complement-features indicate that it requires a complement headed by a verb in the *n*-participle form. Since neither *she* nor *gone* has a specifier or complement here, we can assume that in the relevant uses their head- and complement-features specify that they can be used without any specifier or complement. Accordingly, (18) *She has gone* will have the structure (19) below:

(19)

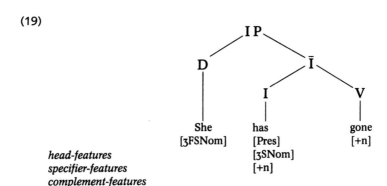

(3 = third person, F = feminine, S = singular, Nom = nominative case, Pres = present tense, +n = *n*-participle; the blank entries for the specifier- and complement-features of *she* and *gone* mean that (in this use) they don't have a specifier or complement). The features within square brackets provide an informal indication of the fact that *she* carries the head-features 'third person feminine singular nominative'; *has* carries the head-feature 'present-tense', the specifier-features 'requires third person singular nominative subject', and the complement-features 'takes an *n*-participle complement'; and *gone* carries the head-feature '*n*-participle'.

Let's assume that the only (semantically) interpretable features in (19) are the [3FS] person/number/gender head-features of *she* (since these tell us e.g. that *she* can refer to an expression like *the girl*, but not to an expression like *the men*), and the [Pres] present-tense head-feature of *has* (since *has* clearly has a different interpretation from the corresponding past-tense form *had*). By contrast, let's suppose that case-features are uninterpretable, since e.g. the pronouns *he/him* carry the same interpretation (as subject of *will win/to win*) in sentences such as:

(20) (a) I expect *he* will win
      (b) I expect *him* to win

even though they have different case properties (*he* is nominative and *him* is objective). In addition, let's assume that all verb inflections other than tense inflections are uninterpretable – hence that the [+n] head-feature carried by *gone* is uninterpretable. Let's also assume that only (some) head-features are interpretable, and that all complement- and specifier-features are uninterpretable (since they have no semantic content, but simply tell us what kind of complement or specifier a given item requires).

Finally, let's assume that the specifier-features of a head must be checked against the head-features of (the head word of) its specifier; and likewise, the complement-features of a head must be checked against the head-features of (the head word of) its complement. If there is a match between *checker* and *checked* in respect of any given feature, the relevant specifier- or complement-feature is erased (because specifier- and complement-features are uninterpretable), and the corresponding head-feature is erased if it is uninterpretable (but is not erased if interpretable). If there is a mismatch between *checker* and *checked* in respect of some feature, the relevant feature cannot be erased from either.

Given these assumptions, consider how checking works in (19). Let's look first at what happens when the specifier-features of *has* are checked against the head-features of *she* in (19). The [3] (third person) and [S] (singular) specifier-features of *has* exactly match the [3S] head-features of *she*: since the relevant features play a role in the interpretation of *she* but not in that of *has*, the [3S] specifier-features of *has* are erased, but the [3S] head-features of *she* are not. The [Nom] (nominative-case) specifier-feature of *has* exactly matches the [Nom] head-feature of *she*, and since case-features play no role in semantic interpretation, both [Nom] features are erased. Thus, checking the specifier-features of *has* against the head-features of *she* in (19) erases all the specifier-features of *has*, together with the nominative case-feature of *she*, but leaves the interpretable features [3FS] on *she*.

Now consider what happens when the complement-features of *has* are checked against the head-features of *gone*. These match exactly, since the [+n] complement-feature of *have* tells us that it requires a complement headed by an *n*-participle, and the [+n] head-feature of *gone* tells us that it is an *n*-participle. If we assume that the inflectional properties of nonfinite verbs (like the case properties of pronouns) play no role in semantic interpretation, both [+n] features will be erased.

So, checking in (19) will mean that the only grammatical features which survive in the corresponding LF-representation are those in (21) below:

(21)

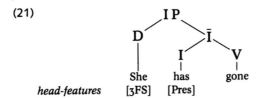

	She	has	gone
head-features	[3FS]	[Pres]	

All specifier- and complement-features have been erased (because they play no role in semantic interpretation). Likewise, uninterpretable head-features (e.g. the nominative case-feature of *she* and the [+n] inflectional feature of *gone*) have also been erased, because they too are uninterpretable. The only grammatical features which survive at LF are *interpretable head-features*. Now let's turn to consider how checking breaks down in an ungrammatical structure such as:

(22)

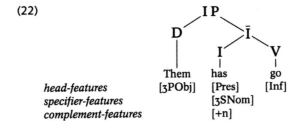

	Them	has	go
head-features	[3PObj]	[Pres]	[Inf]
specifier-features		[3SNom]	
complement-features		[+n]	

(3 = third person, P = plural, S = singular, Obj = objective case, Nom = nominative case, Pres = present tense, Inf = infinitival, +n = *n*-participle.) Here, the [3] specifier feature of *has* (requiring it to have a third person subject) can be erased because its specifier *them* is a third person pronoun. But the [S] specifier feature of *has* (requiring it to have a singular subject) cannot be erased because the subject of *has* is the plural pronoun *them*, and so remains unchecked. Similarly, the [Nom] specifier-feature of *has* (requiring it to have a nominative subject) remains unchecked because it is incompatible with the objective case-feature [Obj] carried by *them*. In addition, the [+n] complement-feature of *has* (requiring it to have an *n*-participle complement) cannot be checked because of a mismatch with the [Inf] head-feature carried by *go*. Checking therefore results in the (partial) LF-representation (23) below (*partial* because we are concerned here only with grammatical features, and so do not represent purely semantic features):

(23)

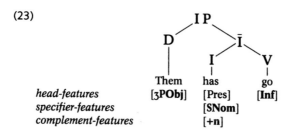

head-features	Them [3PObj]	has [Pres]	go [Inf]
specifier-features		[SNom]	
complement-features		[+n]	

Since numerous (**bold-printed**) uninterpretable features remain in (23) (viz. the [Obj] case-feature of *them*, the [Inf] inflectional feature of *go*, the [SNom] specifier-feature of *has*, and the [+n] complement-feature of *has*), the resulting LF-representation violates the requirement (termed the **principle of full interpretation** by Chomsky) that LF-representations should contain only semantically interpretable features, and the corresponding sentence *Them has go* is ungrammatical.

Our discussion of features here has shown us how to deal with restrictions which words impose on their choice of subject and complement. But now consider the rather different type of restrictions illustrated by the sentences below:

(24) (a) He can feel proud of *himself*
       (b)*She can feel proud of *himself*
       (c)**Himself* help me?! You've got to be kidding!

Words like *himself* are termed (reflexive) **anaphors**, and have the property that they cannot be used to refer directly to an entity in the outside world, but rather must be **bound** by and hence take their reference from an **antecedent** elsewhere in the same phrase or sentence. Where an anaphor is **unbound** (i.e. has no suitable antecedent to bind it), the resulting sentence is ungrammatical. In (24a), the third person masculine singular anaphor *himself* is bound by a suitable third person masculine singular antecedent (*he*), with the result that (24a) is grammatical. But in (24b), *himself* has no suitable antecedent (the feminine pronoun *she* is obviously not a suitable antecedent for the masculine anaphor *himself*), and so is *unbound* (with the result that (24b) is ungrammatical). In (24c), there is no potential antecedent of any kind for the anaphor *himself*, with the result that the anaphor is again unbound (and the sentence ungrammatical).

There seem to be structural restrictions on the binding of anaphors by their antecedents, as we can illustrate in terms of the following contrast:

(25) (a) **The president** can congratulate *himself*

   (b)*Supporters of **the president** can congratulate *himself*

As a third person masculine singular anaphor, *himself* must be bound by a third person masculine singular antecedent like *the president*. However, it would seem from the contrast in (25) above that the antecedent must occupy the right kind of position within the structure in order to bind the anaphor, or else the resulting sentence will be ungrammatical. The question of what is the *right position* for the antecedent can be defined in terms of the following structural condition:

(26) C-COMMAND CONDITION ON BINDING
A bound constituent must be c-commanded by an appropriate antecedent.

(The term **c-command** is a conventional abbreviation of *constituent-command*.) Somewhat inaccurately, we can think of (26) as requiring that the antecedent should occur higher up in the structure than the constituent which it binds. A simple (and more accurate) way of visualizing the relation **c-command** is to think of tree diagrams as networks of train stations, with each node in the tree (i.e. each point in the tree which carries a category label) representing a different station in the network. We can then say that a node X c-commands another node Y if you can get from X to Y by catching a northbound train, getting off at the first station and then catching a southbound train on a different line (i.e. you can't travel south on the line you travelled north on).

   Returning now to the contrast in (25), let's suppose that (25a) has the structure (27) below, and that the DP (determiner phrase) *the president* is the antecedent of the anaphoric determiner *himself* (as is indicated below by the fact that the two carry the same subscript letter index *i*):

(27)

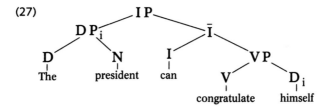

If the **c-command condition on binding** (26) is to be satisfied, it follows that the DP node containing *the president* must c-command the D node containing *himself*. Thinking of nodes as train stations, we can say that the DP *the president* does indeed c-command the D *himself* because if we catch a northbound train from DP and get off at the first station (IP), we can then catch a southbound train to D (via I-bar and VP). We therefore correctly predict that (25a) is grammatical, with *the president* interpreted as the antecedent of *himself*.

But now consider why *the president* can't be the antecedent of *himself* in the structure (28) below (cf. (25b) above):

(28)

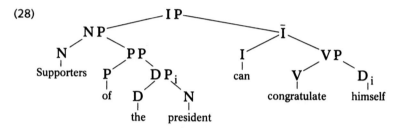

The answer is that the DP *the president* doesn't c-command the D *himself*: if you take a northbound train from DP and get off at the first station, you arrive at PP; but you can't get to the D node containing *himself* by taking a southbound train from PP. Since there is no other c-commanding antecedent for *himself* within the sentence (e.g. although the NP *supporters of the president* c-commands *himself*, it is not a suitable antecedent because it is a plural expression, and *himself* requires a singular antecedent), the anaphor *himself* remains *unbound* – in violation of the **c-command condition on binding** (26). Thus, (25b) is correctly predicted to be ungrammatical.

Our discussion of **binding** here provides crucial evidence in support of the assumption that sentences have the kind of syntactic structure represented by tree diagrams like (27) and (28). The reason is that the restriction on binding described in (26) is one which crucially involves the structural relation **c-command** – and this relation is defined in terms of the relative structural positions occupied by the anaphor and its antecedent. The fact that restrictions on the binding of anaphors can be given a straightforward characterization in structural terms provides strong support for our claim that sentences have a hierarchical constituent structure.

To summarize: in this chapter, we have looked at how words are combined together to form phrases and sentences. We hypothesized that phrases and sentences are formed by a binary **merger** operation which combines pairs of categories to form larger and larger structures, and that the structures thereby formed can be represented in terms of tree diagrams. We suggested that the grammatical properties of words can be described in terms of sets of **head-features** (which describe the intrinsic grammatical properties of words), **complement-features** (which describe the types of complement which they allow) and **specifier-features** (which determine the kinds of specifier/subject they allow). We argued that restrictions on the use of anaphors like *himself* can be given a structural characterization in terms of the **c-command condition on binding** (which requires that a bound constituent should be c-commanded by an appropriate antecedent).

Exercises

Exercise V

Discuss the derivation of the following sentences, showing how their structure is built up in a pairwise fashion by successive merger operations.

1 He was getting cross with Mary
2 You must feel proud of yourself
3 He may need to ask for help
4 Inflation is threatening to undermine the recovery
5 They are expecting to hear from you
6 You should try to talk to her
7 They might think Sam was cheating at syntax
8 I would imagine that they have arrested him

In addition, in relation to any one of these sentences, show how the features of each of the words it contains are checked.

Helpful hints

Assume that the sentences are derived by first merging the last two words in the sentence to form a constituent, then merging the constituent thereby formed with the third-from-last word to form an even larger constituent, then merging this even larger constituent with the fourth-from-last word . . . and so on. (It should be noted, however, that while this simple parsing procedure will work for the sentences in this exercise, it requires modification to handle more complex sentences.) Also assume that just as (for example) a verb/V can merge with a following complement to form a verb phrase/VP, so too a preposition/P can merge with a following complement to form a prepositional phrase/PP, an adjective/A can merge with a following complement to form an adjectival phrase/AP, and a determiner/D can merge with a following complement to form a determiner phrase/DP.

Model answer for 1

Merging the preposition *with* and the noun *Mary* derives the PP (prepositional phrase) in (i) below:

(i)
```
        PP
      /    \
     P      N
     |      |
   with    Mary
```

Merging the PP in (i) with the adjective *cross* immediately to its left forms the AP (adjectival phrase) (ii) below:

(ii)
```
          AP
        /    \
      A       PP
      |      /   \
    cross   P     N
            |     |
          with   Mary
```

Merging the AP in (ii) with the verb *getting* derives the VP (verb phrase) in (iii) below:

(iii)
```
          VP
        /    \
      V        AP
      |      /    \
   getting  A      PP
            |     /   \
          cross  P     N
                 |     |
               with   Mary
```

Merging the VP in (iii) with the auxiliary (i.e. I constituent) *was* forms the string *was getting cross with Mary*: since this is an incomplete phrase (in that it can't stand on its own as a complete sentence, but rather requires a subject like *he*), it has the status of an I-bar, with the structure (iv) below:

(iv)

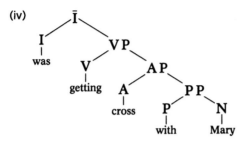

Merging the I-bar in (iv) with the subject pronoun *he* will in turn derive the IP (i.e. inflected auxiliary phrase) (v) below:

(v)

On this view, syntactic structures are derived in a *bottom–up* fashion, i.e. by building up trees in successive layers from bottom to top.

Consider now the features carried by each of the words in (v), and how they are checked. The head-features of the pronoun *he* indicate that it is a third person masculine singular nominative pronoun; its specifier- and complement-features indicate that it doesn't allow a specifier or complement. The head-features of *was* indicate that it is past tense. Its specifier-features indicate that it requires a first or third person singular nominative subject, and these are checked against the head-features of *he*, so resulting in erasure of the specifier-features of *was* (since all specifier-features are uninterpretable), and of the nominative case-feature of *he* (since case features are also uninterpretable) – but not of the third person masculine singular head-features of *he*, since these are interpretable. The complement-features of *was* (in its use as a progressive auxiliary) specify that it requires a complement headed by a verb in the *ing*-participle form: since the complement of *was* is the VP *getting cross with Mary* and the head of this VP is the verb *getting* whose head-features tell us that it is an *ing*-participle, the relevant requirements are met here. The complement-features of the verb *get* indicate that it allows a complement headed by an adjective; and since its complement is the phrase *cross with Mary* and this is headed by the adjective *cross*, this requirement is met here. (The complement-selection properties of *get* thus seem to be essentially categorial in nature, in that *get* requires the head of its complement to be a word belonging to the category adjective.) The complement-features of the adjective *cross* specify that it requires a complement headed by the specific preposition *with* (not one headed by a preposition such as *on*, or *by*, or *from*): thus, the complement-selection properties of *cross* seem to be essentially *lexical* in nature (in that *cross* requires a complement headed by a particular lexical item – i.e. the word *with*). The complement-features of the preposition *with* indicate that (by virtue of being transitive) it requires a complement headed by an item with an objective-case head-feature (e.g. a pronoun like *me*). The fact that the noun *Mary* can be used as the complement of *with* suggests that *Mary* must carry covert case (e.g. *Mary* must be objective in *He doesn't like Mary* and nominative in *Mary doesn't like him*).

Exercise VI
It might be suggested that children generally have more problems in acquiring *uninterpretable* grammatical features than in acquiring *interpretable* ones. To what extent do sentences such as the following (produced by different children aged 2–4 years) support this claim? Discuss the derivation of the relevant sentences, identifying the nature of the errors made by the children.

1 I can building a tower
2 She didn't goed home
3 My can make a pie
4 Mummy is help me
5 Me'll have that
6 Him don't want it
7 He doesn't likes me
8 He haven't got to do it

Helpful hints

Treat negative forms like *don't/doesn't/didn't/haven't* as single-word
auxiliary forms (like e.g. *has* or *will*). Note that different children make
different errors; hence, don't assume all the children make all the errors.

Model answer for 1

Example 1 appears to be derived as follows. The determiner *a* is merged
with the noun *tower* to form the DP (determiner phrase) *a tower*; this is
merged with the verb *building* to form the VP (verb phrase) *building a
tower*. This VP is merged with the auxiliary *can* to form the I-bar *can
building a tower*; and the resulting I-bar is merged with the pronominal
determiner *I* to form the IP (auxiliary phrase) (i) below:

(i)
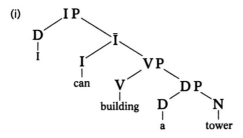

The child would seem to have acquired the interpretable features of
the relevant items, and (for example) seems to know (tacitly) that *a*
is a singular determiner (since it has the singular complement *tower*).
However, the child appears not to have acquired the complement-
features of *can* (which require it to have a complement headed by a verb
in the uninflected infinitive form), since the complement of *can* is the
VP *building a tower* and this is headed by the +*ing* form *building*, not by
the infinitive form *build*. Since complement-features and the inflectional head-features of nonfinite verbs are *uninterpretable* features, sentences like 1 are consistent with the view that children have problems
in acquiring uninterpretable features. It may be that this particular child
is treating *can* like *be* (i.e. as an auxiliary taking an +*ing* complement).

❹ Empty categories

So far, our discussion of syntactic structure has tacitly assumed that all constituents in a given structure are *overt*. However, we now turn to argue that syntactic structures may also contain *empty* (= covert = null) categories – i.e. categories which have no overt phonetic form, and hence which are inaudible or silent. As we shall see, **empty categories** play a central role in the theory of grammar which we are outlining here.

We begin by looking at clauses which might be argued to contain an empty subject. In this connection, compare the structure of the bracketed infinitive clauses in the (a) and (b) examples below:

(1) (a) We would like [*you* to stay]
      (b) We would like [to stay]

(2) (a) We don't want [*anyone* to upset them]
      (b) We don't want [to upset them]

Each of the bracketed infinitive complement clauses in the (a) examples in (1–2) contains an overt (italicized) subject. By contrast, the bracketed complement clauses in the (b) examples appear to be subjectless. However, we shall argue that apparently subjectless infinitive clauses contain an understood *null subject*. (By saying that a constituent is *null* or *empty* or *covert*, we mean that it has no overt phonetic form and so is silent.) The kind of null subject found in the bracketed clauses in the (b) examples has much the same grammatical and referential properties as pronouns, and hence is conventionally designated as **PRO**. (The fact that English allows infinitives to have null subjects does not mean that English is a *null subject language*, since null subject languages are languages which allow *finite* clauses to have a null subject.)

Given this assumption, sentences such as (1a) and (1b) have essentially the same structure, except that the bracketed IP has an overt pronominal determiner *you* as its subject in (1a), but a covert pronominal determiner **PRO** as its subject in (1b) – as represented in (3a–b) below:

(3)

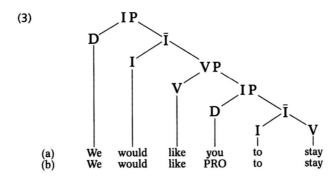

(a)	We	would	like	you	to	stay
(b)	We	would	like	PRO	to	stay

Using the relevant technical terminology, we can say that the null subject PRO in (3b) is **controlled** by (i.e. refers back to) the subject *we* of the matrix (= containing = next highest) clause – or, equivalently, that *we* is the **controller** or **antecedent** of PRO. Verbs (such as *like*) which allow an infinitive complement with a PRO subject are said to function (in the relevant use) as **control verbs**.

An obvious question to ask at this juncture is why we should posit that apparently subjectless infinitive complements like those bracketed in (1b–2b) above have a null PRO subject. Part of the motivation for positing PRO is semantic in nature. In traditional grammar it is claimed that subjectless infinitive clauses have an *understood* or *implicit* subject – and positing a PRO subject in such clauses is one way of capturing the relevant intuition. The implicit subject becomes explicit if the relevant clauses are paraphrased by a finite clause, as we see from the paraphrases for the (a) examples given in the (b) examples below:

(4) (a) I am sorry [to have kept you waiting]
    (b) I am sorry [*I* have kept you waiting]

(5) (a) Dumbo has promised [to come to my party]
    (b) Dumbo has promised [*he* will come to my party]

The fact that the bracketed clauses in the (b) examples contain an overt (italicized) subject makes it plausible to suppose that the bracketed clauses in the synonymous (a) examples have a covert PRO subject.

There is also a considerable body of syntactic evidence in support of claiming that subjectless infinitive clauses have a covert PRO subject. Part of the relevant evidence comes from the syntax of reflexive anaphors (i.e. *self/selves* forms such as *myself/yourself/himself/themselves* etc.). As examples such as the following indicate, reflexives generally require a *local* antecedent:

(6) (a) They want [**John** to help *himself*]
     (b)***They** want [John to help *themselves*]

In the case of structures like (6), a *local* antecedent means *an antecedent contained within the same [bracketed] clause as the reflexive*. Example (6a) is grammatical because it satisfies this *locality* requirement: the antecedent of the reflexive *himself* is the noun *John*, and *John* is contained within the same [bracketed] *help*-clause as *himself*. By contrast, (6b) is ungrammatical because the reflexive *themselves* does not have a local antecedent (i.e. it does not have an antecedent within the bracketed clause containing it); its antecedent is the pronoun *they*, and *they* is an immediate constituent of the *want*-clause, not of the [bracketed] *help*-clause. In the light of the requirement for reflexives to have a *local* antecedent, consider now how we account for the grammaticality of the following:

(7) John wants [**PRO** to prove *himself*]

Given the requirement for reflexives to have a local antecedent, it follows that the reflexive *himself* must have an antecedent within its own [bracketed] clause. This requirement is satisfied in (7) if we assume that the bracketed complement clause has a PRO subject, and that PRO is the antecedent of *himself*. Since PRO in turn is controlled by *John* (i.e. *John* is the antecedent of PRO), this means that *himself* is coreferential to (i.e. refers to the same person as) *John*.

  We can formulate a further argument in support of positing a PRO subject in apparently subjectless infinitive clauses in relation to the syntax of *predicate nominals*: these are nominal (i.e. noun-containing) expressions used as the complement of a *copular* (i.e. linking) verb such as *be, become, remain* (etc.) in expressions such as *John was/became/ remained **my best friend***, where the predicate nominal is *my best friend*, and the property of *being/becoming/remaining my best friend* is predicated of *John*. Predicate nominals in copular constructions have to agree with the subject of their own clause, as we see from examples such as the following:

(8) (a) They want [**their son** to become *a millionaire/ *millionaires*]
     (b) He wants [**his sons** to become *millionaires/ *a millionaire*]

As examples like (8) illustrate, the italicized predicate nominal has to agree with the (bold-printed) subject of its own [bracketed] *become*-clause, and cannot agree with the subject of the *want*-clause. In the light of this clause-internal agreement requirement, consider now how we account for the agreement pattern in (9) below:

(9) (a) They want [**PRO** to become *millionaires/*a millionaire*]
     (b) He wants [**PRO** to become *a millionaire/*millionaires*]

If we posit that the *become*-clause has a PRO subject which is controlled by the subject of the *want* clause, the relevant agreement facts can be accounted for straightforwardly: we simply posit that the predicate nominal (*a*) *millionaire(s)* agrees with PRO (since PRO is the subject of the *become*-clause), and that PRO in (9a) is plural because its controller/antecedent is the plural pronoun *they*, and conversely that PRO in (9b) is singular because its antecedent/controller is the singular pronoun *he*. It goes without saying that it is far from obvious how we would handle the relevant agreement facts if we didn't posit a PRO subject for the bracketed infinitive complements in sentences such as (9).

The conclusion which our discussion here leads us to is that just as infinitive complements like *you to stay* in (1a) have an overt subject (*you*), so too apparently subjectless infinitive complements like *to stay* in (1b) have a covert PRO subject – as shown in (3) above. It is interesting to compare the case properties of these two types of subject, and how they are checked. An overt infinitive subject carries *objective* case, as we see from the fact that *you* in (3a) can be substituted by an objective pronoun like *him/them* (not by a nominative pronoun like *he/they*). But what of a covert PRO subject? If we assume that it is a defining characteristic of personal pronouns that they carry case, then PRO too must carry case. Chomsky and Lasnik (1995, pp. 119–20) suggest that PRO carries **null case**, and that its case is checked by infinitival *to*. What this implies is that infinitival *to* (in this use) carries a null-case specifier-feature (indicating that it requires a PRO subject with null case) which is checked against the null-case head-feature of PRO. This would suggest interesting parallels with the way in which nominative case is checked: just as the null case carried by PRO in (3b) is checked by the head I constituent *to* of the IP containing PRO, so too the nominative case carried by *we* is checked by the head I constituent *would* of the IP containing *we*. In both cases, checking involves a spec–head relation – more specifically, a relation between the head I constituent of IP and its specifier.

But how is the objective case carried by the overt infinitive subject *you* in (3a) checked? There are good reasons for thinking that it is checked by the immediately preceding verb *like*. For one thing, the verb *like* is transitive (as we see from structures like *I like him*, where *like* checks the objective case of *him*), and objective case can only be checked by a transitive item. Secondly, such an analysis would correctly predict that infinitives with objective subjects can only be used as the complement of an immediately preceding transitive verb (or an immediately preceding transitive complementizer like *for*), so accounting for the ungrammaticality of structures such as those below:

(10) (a) *[*Them* to abandon syntax] would be a mistake
      (b) *He may be anxious [*them* to make amends]
      (c) *Brigadier Blunderbuss gave the order [*them* to cease fire]

Sentences like (10) are ungrammatical because the case of the italicized objective subject *them* cannot be checked (so causing the derivation to crash at LF, because case-features are uninterpretable). The case of *them* cannot be checked because in none of the relevant examples is the bracketed infinitive clause the complement of a transitive verb or complementizer: in (10a), the bracketed IP is the subject of *would*; in (10b) it is the complement of the adjective *anxious* (adjectives are intransitive); and in (10c) it is the complement of the noun *order* (nouns too are intransitive).

What we are suggesting here is that the case of a null PRO subject is checked in a different way from the case of an objective subject. More specifically, the null case of a PRO subject is internally checked (from within IP) by the null-case infinitive particle *to*; but the case of an objective subject is externally checked (from outside IP) by an immediately preceding transitive verb or transitive complementizer. Since it is exceptional for a subject to have its case externally checked from outside its containing IP, the relevant phenomenon is generally known as **exceptional case-marking** (conventionally abbreviated to **ECM**): hence, an infinitive complement with an objective subject is referred to as an **ECM complement**; and a verb which selects an infinitive complement with an objective subject is referred to as an **ECM verb**. As we shall see, the different ways in which the case properties of null and objective subjects are checked are reflected in systematic asymmetries between control infinitives with PRO subjects and ECM infinitives with objective subjects.

One such asymmetry relates to the behaviour of the relevant complements in active and passive structures. A verb like *decide* (when used as a control verb) allows an infinitival IP complement with a PRO subject irrespective of whether (as in (11a) below) it is used as an active verb or (as in (11b) below) as a passive participle:

(11) (a) They had *decided* [**PRO** to postpone the meeting]
       (b) It had been *decided* [**PRO** to postpone the meeting]

By contrast, a verb like *believe* can function as an ECM verb taking an infinitive complement with an objective subject only when used actively (as in (12a) below), not when used passively (as in (12b) below):

(12) (a) People genuinely *believed* [**him** to be innocent]
       (b)*It was genuinely *believed* [**him** to be innocent]

Why should this be? If (as we suggest) the null case of PRO in control structures like (11) is checked by infinitival *to*, it makes no difference whether the verb *decide* is used in an active or passive form. By contrast, if (as we also suggest) the objective case carried by the subject of an ECM infinitive clause is externally checked by an immediately preceding transitive verb or transitive complementizer, we can account for the contrast in (12) straightforwardly: in (12a) the bracketed IP is immediately preceded by the active (and transitive) verb form *believed* (which can check the objective case of *him*); but in (12b) the immediately preceding verb is the passive participle form *believed*, and passive participles are intransitive (as is shown by the fact that the passive participle *arrested* doesn't allow an objective complement like *them* in a sentence such as *It was arrested **them***).

   A second asymmetry between control infinitives and ECM infinitives relates to adverb position. An adverb modifying a control verb can be positioned between the control verb and its IP complement, as we see from (13) below (where the adverb *hard* modifies the verb *tried*):

(13) He tried *hard* [**PRO** to convince her]

By contrast, an adverb modifying an ECM verb cannot be positioned between the ECM verb and its IP complement, as we see from (14) below (where the adverb *sincerely* modifies the verb *believes*):

(14) *She believes *sincerely* [**him** to be innocent]

How come? If we suppose that the case of PRO in control structures like (13) is checked by infinitival *to*, we correctly predict that an adverb positioned between the preceding verb and its IP complement will not prevent the case of PRO from being checked. By contrast, if we posit that the case of an objective subject is checked by an *immediately preceding* transitive verb or transitive complementizer, it follows that the presence of the intervening adverb *sincerely* prevents the transitive verb *believes* from checking the objective case of the infinitive subject *him*.

So far, all the clauses we have looked at in this chapter and the last have contained an IP projection headed by a finite auxiliary or infinitival *to*. The obvious generalization suggested by this is that all clauses are IPs. An important question begged by this assumption, however, is how we are to analyse finite clauses which contain no overt auxiliary. In this connection, consider the construction illustrated in (15) below:

(15)   He could have seen her, or [she have seen him]

Both clauses here (viz. the *he*-clause and the *she*-clause) appear to be finite, since both have nominative subjects (*he/she*). If all finite clauses contain an IP projection headed by a finite INFL, it follows that both clauses in (15) must be IPs containing a finite I (= INFL) constituent. This is clearly true of the *he*-clause, which contains the finite modal auxiliary *could*; however, the *she*-clause doesn't seem to contain any finite auxiliary constituent, since *have* is an infinitive form (the corresponding finite form being *has*). How can we analyse finite clauses as projections of an INFL constituent when clauses like that bracketed in (15) contain no finite auxiliary?

An intuitively plausible answer is to suppose that the string *she have seen him* in (15) is an elliptical (i.e. abbreviated) variant of *she **could** have seen him*, and that the I constituent *could* undergoes head ellipsis (alias **gapping**) in the second clause. If this is so, then the second clause will have the structure (16) below (where e marks the ellipsed auxiliary *could*):

(16)

```
            I P
          /     \
         D       I
         |      /  \
        she    I    VP
               |   /   \
               e  V     VP
                  |    /   \
                have  V     D
                      |     |
                    seen   him
```

The head I position of IP would then be filled by an ellipsed auxiliary *e*. We can think of ellipsis as a process by which a constituent (in this case, *could*) is given a null phonetic form, but retains its grammatical and semantic properties (so that *e* in (16) is a silent counterpart of *could*). The *null INFL* analysis in (16) provides a principled account of three sets of facts. Firstly, the bracketed clause in (15) is interpreted as an elliptical form of *she could have seen him*: this can be straightforwardly accounted for under the analysis in (16), given that *e* is an elliptical form of *could*. Secondly, the subject is in the nominative case form *she*: this can be attributed to the fact that the I position in (16) is filled by a null counterpart of *could* and so is finite (and thereby requires a nominative specifier). Thirdly, the perfective auxiliary *have* is in the uninflected infinitive form: this is because *e* (being an elliptical form of *could*) has the same grammatical properties (hence the same complement-selection properties) as *could*, so that *e* (like *could*) requires a complement headed by a word (like *have*) in the infinitive form.

A further argument in support of the analysis in (16) comes from facts relating to *cliticization* (a process by which one word attaches itself in a leechlike fashion to another). Perfective *have* has a range of different variant forms in the spoken language. When unstressed, it loses its initial /h/ segment and has its vowel reduced to schwa /ə/, and so is pronounced as /əv/ e.g. in sentences such as *You should have been there*. (Because *of* is also pronounced /əv/ when unstressed, some people write this as *You should of been there* – not *you*, of course!) However, when *have* is used with a subject ending in a vowel or diphthong (e.g. a subject pronoun like *I/we/you/they*), it can lose its vowel entirely and be contracted down to /v/; in this form, it is phonetically too insubstantial to survive as an independent word, and *cliticizes* (i.e. attaches itself) to its subject, e.g. in structures such as:

(17) (a) *You've* done your duty
      (b) *We've* seen the Mona Lisa
      (c) *I've* forgotten to lock the door
      (d) *They've* shown no interest in my idea

However, note that *have* cannot cliticize onto *she* in (18) below:

(18) *He could have seen her or *she've* seen him

Why should cliticization of *have* onto *she* be blocked here? The *null auxiliary* analysis in (16) provides us with an obvious answer, if we make the reasonable assumption that *have* can only cliticize onto an *immediately preceding* word ending in a vowel or diphthong. We can then say that *have* is blocked from cliticizing onto *she* in (18) by the presence of the null auxiliary which intervenes between *have* and *she*. Thus, the *null INFL* analysis seems entirely appropriate for elliptical finite clauses like the *she*-clause in (15) – i.e. clauses which contain an ellipsed auxiliary.

Our analysis of apparently auxiliariless clauses like that bracketed in (15) as IPs headed by an empty (ellipsed) INFL suggests an interesting analysis of finite clauses such as the following which contain a finite verb, but no auxiliary:

(19) (a) He hates syntax
      (b) He failed syntax

Why not treat auxiliariless finite clauses in much the same way as we analysed structures like (15) which contain an ellipsed auxiliary – namely as IP structures headed by a null I constituent? More specifically, let's suppose that auxiliariless finite clauses like those in (19) above are IP constituents which have the structure (20) below:

(20)

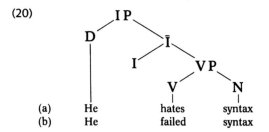

(a)	He	hates	syntax
(b)	He	failed	syntax

The fact that the INFL node in (20) contains no overt or covert item is meant to represent the assumption that the head I position of IP is simply *unfilled*. However, one apparent problem posed by the analysis in (20) is that of how we account for the fact that *he* agrees with *hates* in (20a). After all, agreement (e.g. between *he* and *has* in *He has gone*) typically involves a local (phrase-internal) spec(ifier)–head relation between INFL and its specifier: but since *hates* and *he* are contained within different phrases (*hates* being the head of VP, and *he* being the subject of IP), the two are clearly not in a local specifier–head relation, so would not be expected to agree. How can we solve this problem? One way would be to suppose that when INFL is unfilled, the tense and agreement properties of the head V of VP **percolate** up to INFL. Since *hates* is a third person singular present-tense verb form, the features of INFL (inherited from *hates*) will indicate that it has the features *third person singular present tense*, and so will require it to have a third person singular nominative subject. (We return to consider *percolation* in rather more detail in the next chapter, so for the time being we say no more about it here.)

'But why on earth would we want to pretend that clauses which obviously don't contain an auxiliary actually contain an unfilled auxiliary position?' you might wonder. Well, from a theoretical point of view, an obvious advantage of the IP analysis is that it provides a unitary characterization of the syntax of clauses, since it allows us to say that all clauses contain an IP projection, and that the subject of a clause is always in spec-IP (i.e. always occupies the specifier position within IP), that INFL in a finite clause always has a nominative subject, and always agrees with its subject. Lending further weight to theory-internal considerations such as these is a substantial body of empirical evidence. A direct consequence of the *unfilled INFL* analysis (20) of auxiliariless finite clauses is that finite auxiliaries and finite verbs occupy different positions within the clause: finite auxiliaries occupy the head I position of IP, whereas finite nonauxiliary verbs occupy the head V position of VP. An interesting way of testing this hypothesis is in relation to the behaviour of items which have the status of auxiliary verbs in some uses, but of nonauxiliary verbs in others. One such word is *have*. In the kind of use illustrated in (21) below, it functions as a perfective auxiliary:

(21) (a) She *has* gone to Paris
     (b) I *have* been working on my assignment
     (c) They *had* been warned about syntax

However, in the uses illustrated in (22) below, *have* functions as a causative or experiential verb (i.e. a verb carrying much the same meaning as *cause* or *experience*):

(22) (a) The doctor *had* an eye-specialist examine the patient
     (b) The doctor *had* the patient examined by an eye-specialist
     (c) The teacher *had* three students walk out on her
     (d) I've never *had* anyone send me flowers

By traditional tests of auxiliarihood, perfective *have* is an auxiliary, and causative/experiential *have* is a lexical (i.e. nonauxiliary) verb: e.g. perfective *have* can undergo inversion (*Has she gone to Paris?*) whereas causative/experiential *have* cannot (*Had the doctor an eye-specialist examine the patient?*). In terms of the assumptions we are making here, this means that finite forms of *have* are positioned in the head I position of IP in their perfective use, but in the head V position of VP in their causative or experiential use.

Evidence in support of this claim comes from facts about *cliticization*. We noted earlier in relation to our discussion of (17) and (18) above that *have* can cliticize onto an immediately preceding word ending in a stressed vowel or diphthong, provided that no (overt or covert) constituent intervenes between the two. In the light of this, consider contrasts such as the following:

(23) (a) *They've* seen a ghost   (= perfective *have*)
      (b) * *They've* their car serviced regularly   (= causative *have*)
      (c) * *She'd* three students walk out on her   (= experiential *have*)

How can we account for this contrast? If we assume that perfective *have* in (23a) is a finite auxiliary which occupies the head I position of IP, but that causative *have* in (23b) and experiential *had* in (23c) are nonauxiliary verbs occupying the head V position of a VP complement of an unfilled I, then prior to cliticization the three clauses will have the respective (simplified) structures indicated by the labelled bracketings in (24a–c) below (where [$_I$ ___] denotes an INFL position which is unfilled):

(24) (a) [$_{IP}$ They [$_I$ have] [$_{VP}$ [$_V$ seen] a ghost]]
      (b) [$_{IP}$ They [$_I$ ___] [$_{VP}$ [$_V$ have] their car serviced regularly]]
      (c) [$_{IP}$ She [$_I$ ___] [$_{VP}$ [$_V$ had] three students walk out on her]]

If *have*-cliticization is subject to an *adjacency* condition (to the effect that cliticization is only possible when *have* immediately follows the expression to which it cliticizes and is blocked by the presence of an intervening constituent), it should be obvious why *have* can cliticize onto *they* in (24a) but not *have/had* onto *they/she* in (24b–c): after all, *have* is immediately adjacent to *they* in (24a), but *have/had* is separated from *they/she* by a null INFL constituent in (24b–c). A crucial premise of this account is the assumption that (in its finite forms) *have* is positioned in the head I of IP in its perfective use, but in the head V of VP in its causative and experiential uses. Thus, *have*-cliticization facts suggest that finite clauses which lack a finite auxiliary are IPs headed by an unfilled I constituent.

A further piece of empirical evidence in support of the IP analysis comes from *tag questions*. As we see from the examples below, sentences containing (a finite form of) perfective *have* are tagged by *have*, whereas sentences containing (a finite form of) causative *have* are tagged by *do*:

(25) (a) She has gone to Paris, *has/*does* she?
      (b) She has her hair styled by Vidal Sassoon, *does/*has* she?

Given the I analysis of perfective *have* and the V analysis of causative *have* and the assumption that all clauses are IP constituents, the main clauses in (25a–b) will have the respective (simplified) structures indicated in (26a–b) below (where ___ denotes an unfilled position):

(26) (a) [$_{IP}$ She [$_I$ has] [$_{VP}$ [$_V$ gone] to Paris]]
      (b) [$_{IP}$ She [$_I$ ___] [$_{VP}$ [$_V$ has] her hair styled by Vidal Sassoon]]

If we assume that the I constituent which appears in the tag must carry the same semantic and grammatical properties as the I constituent in the main clause, the contrast in (25) can be accounted for in a principled fashion. In (26a), the head I position of IP is filled by the perfective auxiliary *has*, and so the tag contains a copy of this auxiliary. In (26b), however, the head I position of IP is unfilled (and hence contains no meaning-bearing constituent), and so can only be tagged by the meaningless *dummy* auxiliary *does* (which carries the same present-tense feature as the unfilled I constituent in the main clause). Note, incidentally, that the assumption that auxiliaries in tags carry the same grammatical properties as the I constituent in the main clause provides us with evidence for positing that the unfilled I constituent in a structure such as (26b) carries tense-features (since these are copied in the auxiliary in the tag); the relevant tense-features percolate up from V to I when I is unfilled, so that I in (26b) inherits the present-tense feature carried by *has*.

Thus, we have substantial empirical evidence that auxiliariless finite clauses are IP constituents headed by an unfilled INFL. Since clauses containing a finite auxiliary are also IPs, the natural conclusion to draw is that all finite clauses are IPs. Since *to* infinitive clauses are also IPs, we might generalize still further and say that all finite and infinitival clauses are IPs. This in turn has implications for how we analyse *bare* (i.e. *to*-less) infinitive complement clauses such as those bracketed below:

(27) (a) I have never known [*Tom criticize him*]

(b) A reporter saw [*Senator Sleaze leave Benny's Bunny Bar*]

(c) You mustn't let [*the pressure get to you*]

If (as we are suggesting) all finite and infinitival clauses are indeed IPs, bare infinitive clauses like those in (27) will be IPs headed by an abstract INFL constituent. More specifically, we might suppose that the relevant clauses are IPs headed by a null counterpart of infinitival *to* (below denoted as ø), so that the bracketed IP in (27a) would have the structure (28) below:

(28)

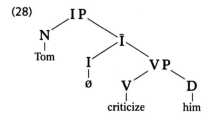

We have assumed in (28) that rather than being unfilled, INFL is filled by a null variant of infinitival *to*. One reason for thinking this is that the head V in a bare infinitive complement is always in the *infinitive* form – i.e. the same form as is required after infinitival *to*: we can account for this if we assume that the null infinitive particle ø has the same complement-selection properties as infinitival *to*, and thus selects a complement headed by a verb like *criticize* in the infinitive form. We could then say that verbs like *know/hear/let/watch/see* as used in (27) above select an IP complement headed by the null infinitive particle ø, whereas verbs like *expect, judge, report, consider, want*, etc. select an IP complement headed by *to*, as in (29) below:

(29) (a) I expect [him *to* win]

(b) I judged [him *to* be lying]

(c) They reported [him *to* be missing]

It would then follow that all infinitive clauses contain an IP headed by *to* or by its covert counterpart ø.

Empirical evidence in support of the IP analysis comes from cliticization facts in relation to sentences such as:

(30) (a) % I wouldn't let [*you* have done it] (% = OK in some varieties)

(b) * I wouldn't let [*you've* done it]

If we suppose that the bracketed infinitive complement in (30b) is an IP headed by the null infinitive particle ø, as in (31) below:

(31) I wouldn't let [$_{IP}$ you [$_I$ ø] [$_{VP}$ [$_V$ have] done it]]

we can account for the fact that *have* cannot cliticize onto *you* by positing that the presence of the null infinitive particle ø between *you* and *have* blocks cliticization.

Having arrived at a unitary characterization of clauses as IPs, we now turn our attention to the syntax of *nominal* structures. (We shall use the term *nominal* here to describe any structure containing a noun or pronoun.) Let's begin by considering the structure of the italicized nominals below:

(32) *We* don't expect *students* to enjoy *the course*

Given our existing assumptions, (32) will have the structure (33) below:

(33)

However, (33) presupposes a curiously asymmetric analysis of the status of nominals. Some (like *we*) have the status of D; others (like *students*) have the status of N; and others (like *the course*) are DPs. Given our earlier arguments that clauses have a uniform status as IP constituents, it would seem natural to ask whether we can attain a uniform characterization of the syntax of nominals. But how? What we shall suggest here (following ideas developed by Abney 1987 and Longobardi 1994) is that nominals are projections of a head D constituent (and hence have the status of D or DP constituents).

What this implies in the case of *bare* noun expressions (i.e. noun expressions used without any modifying determiner) is that such nominals are DPs headed by a null determiner (below symbolized as Ø). This means (for example) that the bare noun *students* in (32) is not simply an N, but rather a DP of the form (34) below:

(34)

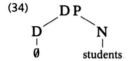

The assumption that bare nominals contain a null determiner is a traditional one – for example, Chomsky (1965, p. 108) suggests that the noun *sincerity* in a sentence such as *Sincerity may frighten the boy* is premodified by a null determiner. If this is so, then empty categories play just as central a role in the syntax of nominals as they do in the syntax of clauses: in the same way as auxiliariless finite clauses are IPs headed by an empty INFL, so too bare nominals are DPs headed by an empty determiner. As we shall see, this empty determiner has specific semantic and grammatical properties of its own.

The semantic properties of the null determiner Ø can be illustrated in relation to the interpretation of the italicized bare nominals in sentences such as:

(35) (a) *Eggs* are fattening   (b) *Bacon* is fattening

(36) (a) I had *eggs* for breakfast   (b) I had *bacon* for breakfast

The nouns *eggs/bacon* in (35) have a *generic* interpretation, and hence are interpreted as meaning 'eggs/bacon in general'. In (36) they have an *existential* (= partitive) interpretation, roughly paraphraseable as 'some eggs/bacon'. If we say that bare nominals are DPs headed by a null generic/existential determiner Ø, we can say that the semantic properties of Ø determine that bare nominals will be interpreted as generically or existentially quantified.

Moreover, there is evidence to suggest that the null determiner Ø carries *person* properties – in particular, it is a third person determiner. In this respect, consider sentences such as:

(37) (a) We syntacticians take **ourselves/*yourselves/*themselves** too
           seriously, don't *we/*you/*they*?
      (b) You syntacticians take **yourselves/*ourselves/*themselves** too
           seriously, don't *you/*we/*they*?
      (c) Syntacticians take **themselves/*ourselves/*yourselves** too
           seriously, don't *they/*we/*you*?

The examples in (37a) show that a first person expression such as *we syntacticians* can only bind a first person reflexive like *ourselves*, and can only be tagged by a first person pronoun like *we*. The examples in (37b) show that a second person expression like *you syntacticians* can only bind a second person reflexive like *yourselves*, and can only be tagged by a second person pronoun like *you*. The examples in (37c) show that a bare nominal like *syntacticians* can only bind a third person reflexive like *themselves* and can only be tagged by a third person pronoun like *they*. One way of accounting for the relevant facts is to suppose that the nominals *(we/you) syntacticians* in (37) are DPs of the form (38) below:

(38)

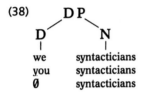

and that the person properties of the DP are determined by those of its head determiner. If we suppose that *we* is a first person determiner, *you* is a second person determiner and *Ø* is a third person determiner, the facts in (37) above are precisely as the analysis in (38) would lead us to expect.

In addition to having quantificational properties and person properties, the null determiner *Ø* also has specific *complement-selection* properties – as can be illustrated by the following set of examples:

(39) (a) I write *poems*
      (b) I write *poetry*
      (c) *I write *poem*

If we suppose that each of the italicized bare nouns in (39) is the complement of the null determiner *Ø*, the restrictions in (39) would seem to suggest that *Ø* can select as its complement an expression headed by a plural count noun like *poems*, or by a singular mass noun like *poetry* – but not by a singular count noun like *poem*. The complement-selection properties of the null determiner *Ø* would seem to be parallel to those of the overt determiner *enough:* cf.

(40) (a) I've read *enough poetry*
      (b) I've read *enough poems*
      (c) *I've read *enough poem*

The fact that the null generic/existential determiner Ø has much the same quantificational, person and complement-selection properties as a typical overt determiner such as *enough* strengthens the case for positing the existence of a null determiner Ø, and for analysing bare nominals as DPs headed by a null determiner.

The assumption that *bare nominals* are DPs headed by a null determiner leads us towards our goal of attaining a unitary characterization of the syntax of nominals. We can then say that nominals modified by an overt determiner are DPs, bare nominals are DPs headed by a null determiner and pronouns are determiners used without a complement. This means that all nominal and pronominal arguments are projections of an (overt or covert) D constituent – an assumption widely referred to as the **DP hypothesis**. Given this assumption, sentence (32) *We don't expect students to enjoy the course* will no longer have the asymmetrical analysis (33) above, but rather the more uniform structure (41) below:

(41)

in which the three nominals *we*, *students* and *the course* are all analysed as D projections (in accordance with the *DP hypothesis*).

The analysis we have presented here points to significant potential parallels between the internal structure of clauses and that of nominals. Just as clauses are projections of an overt or covert I constituent, so too nominals are projections of an overt or covert D constituent. Using the terminology suggested by Jane Grimshaw (1991), we can say that V has an **extended projection** into IP in the same way as N has an extended projection into DP (so that IP is an extended projection of V, and DP is an extended projection of N). The parallels between IP and DP may go even further – as we can illustrate in terms of the following examples:

(42) (a) We can arrange [for the accountants to audit the books]
      (b) We can arrange [for an audit of the books]

In (42a), the verb *audit* has a direct projection into the VP *audit the books*, an extended projection into the IP *the accountants to audit the books*, and a further extended projection into the CP (complementizer phrase) *for the accountants to audit the books*. In (42b) the noun *audit* has a direct projection into the NP *audit of the books*, an extended projection into the DP *an audit of the books*, and a further extended projection into the PP (prepositional phrase) *for an audit of the books*. Thus, CP and PP might be analysed as (secondary) extended projections of V and N respectively.

To summarize: in this chapter, we have seen that **empty categories** (i.e. categories which have no overt phonetic form) play a central role in the grammar of English. We began by arguing that apparently subjectless clauses have an empty PRO subject controlled by an antecedent in a higher clause. We suggested that PRO has null case, and has its case checked by infinitival *to*; by contrast, objective infinitive subjects (e.g. *him* in *I expect **him** to win*) have their case checked by an immediately preceding transitive verb (like *expect*) or transitive (*for*) complementizer. We went on to argue that elliptical clauses like that bracketed in *He could have seen her or [she have seen him]* are IPs headed by a null (ellipsed) finite auxiliary. We then extended this analysis to auxiliariless clauses like *He hates syntax*, arguing that they are IPs headed by a null INFL constituent, and that the tense/agreement properties of the verb *hates* percolate from V to INFL. We concluded that all clauses are IP constituents, headed by an overt or covert INFL constituent. We then turned to look at the syntax of nominals, arguing that bare noun expressions should be analysed as DPs headed by a null determiner Ø which has a generic or existential interpretation, and which has the complement-selection property that it can only be used to quantify a singular mass noun or plural count noun. We concluded that all nominals are D-projections, comprising either an overt or covert pronominal determiner (like *he* or *PRO*) used without a complement, or an overt or covert prenominal determiner (like *the* or Ø) used with a noun expression as its complement. We suggested that there are significant parallels between the syntax of clauses and that of nominal arguments, in that just as verbs have an extended projection into IP (and in some structures may have a further extended projection into CP) so too nouns have an extended projection into DP (and in some structures may have a further extended projection into PP).

Exercise VII

Draw tree diagrams to represent the structure of the following sentences, presenting arguments in support of key assumptions made in your analysis. Discuss the features carried by the italicized items, and say how they are checked.

1   Students *hate* the lectures
2   He *had* a breakdown
3   The suspect denied that he had *stolen* the jewels
4   He seems keen for you to *help* us
5   I feel sure she will try *to* come to the meeting
6   I imagine that journalists *may* want him to talk about corruption
7   %He wouldn't let me *have* done it
8   It is *getting* harder to gain admission to university

Model answer

Given the assumptions made in the text, both nominal expressions containing an overt determiner (like *the lectures*) and bare nominals like *students* are determiner phrases, and they differ only in respect of whether they are headed by the overt third person determiner *the* or the covert third person determiner Ø. Thus, *the lectures* is a DP formed by merging the determiner *the* with the noun *lectures*, and *students* is a DP formed by merging the null determiner Ø with the noun *students*. So, 1 is formed by merging the verb *hate* with the DP *the lectures* to form the VP (verb phrase) *hate the lectures*; merging this VP with an abstract INFL constituent to form the I-bar *INFL hate the lectures*; and then merging this I-bar with the DP Ø *students* to form the IP (i) below:

(i)

```
                        ___IP___
               ___DP___          ___Ī___
              D        N        I        ___VP___
              |        |                V        ___DP___
              Ø      students         hate     D        N
                                               |        |
                                              the     lectures
```

Evidence in support of positing a null third person determiner Ø comes from the fact that a sentence like I can only be tagged by a third person pronoun like they:

(ii) **Students** hate the lectures, don't *they/*we/*you*?

The fact that we also find the use of the dummy present-tense auxiliary *don't* in the tag (i.e. in the part of the sentence following the comma) supports the claim in (i) that the sentence is an IP headed by a null present-tense INFL (hence is tagged by the dummy present-tense auxiliary *don't*).

However, this raises the question of how INFL comes to acquire a present-tense head-feature if INFL is unfilled. The answer is that the relevant present-tense head-feature percolates up from the verb *hate* (which occupies the head V position of VP) to INFL. It seems reasonable to assume that this is because INFL must contain a tense-feature in order to be interpretable at LF: hence, an unfilled INFL *attracts* the tense-feature carried by the head verb of the verb phrase (in this case, *hate*).

The complement-features of the verb *hate* indicate that (by virtue of being transitive) it requires a complement whose head carries an objective-case head-feature. The complement of *hate* in (i) is the DP *the lectures*, and the head word of this DP is the determiner *the*. It therefore follows that (even though it doesn't overtly inflect for case), the determiner *the* must carry covert case-features (indicating that it can be either nominative or objective – e.g. nominative in *The door opened* and objective in *Open the door!*). Thus, the objective complement-feature of *hate* can be checked against the nominative/objective head-feature of *the*, and both case-features thereby erased (since case-features and complement-features are uninterpretable).

The specifier-features of *hate* indicate that it requires a specifier whose head is nominative and either first/second person or plural. However, there is no specifier within the VP headed by *hate*; hence, the only way in which *hate* can check its specifier-features is if the relevant features percolate up to INFL (in the same way as the head-features of *hate* do). The specifier of INFL is the DP Ø *students*, whose head is the null determiner Ø. The head-features of Ø indicate that it is third person (cf. (ii) above), that it can be singular or plural in number (though here it is clearly plural, since it has the plural complement *students*), and that (like *the*) it can carry nominative or objective case. It follows, therefore, that the head-features of Ø satisfy the requirements imposed by the specifier-features of INFL (which in turn are inherited from *hate*), so the specifier-features of *hate* can be checked and erased (along with the nominative case-feature carried by Ø).

Exercise VIII

Account for the (un)grammaticality of the following sentences:

1a   They had planned to escape
 b *They had planned him to escape (intended as synonymous with 'They had planned that he should escape')

2a   We consider him to be right
 b *We consider to be right (intended as synonymous with 'We consider ourselves to be right')

3a   He would like me to retire
 b   He would like to retire

4a *He said her to like oysters (intended as synonymous with 'He said she liked oysters')
 b *He said to like oysters (intended as synonymous with 'He said he liked oysters')

5a   She seems keen for them to participate
 b *She seems keen for to participate

6a   He received a request to help the refugees
 b *He received a request they/them to help the refugees

7a   It was agreed to review the policy

  b *It was agreed them to review the policy

8a   Congress decided to ratify the treaty

  b *Congress decided for the president to ratify the treaty

9a   He felt himself to be ageing

  b *He felt himself was ageing

10a   You must let yourself have a break

  b *You must let have a break (intended as synonymous with 10a)

Pay particular attention to how grammatical properties of the subjects are checked.

Helpful hints
You may find it useful to suppose that different words (or different kinds of word) select different types of complement, e.g. some selecting a CP headed by *for*, others selecting an IP headed by *to*, others selecting an IP headed by the null infinitive particle ø (etc.), and yet others selecting more than one type of complement.

Model answer for 1 and 2
Given the IP analysis of subjectless infinitive complements presented in the text of this chapter, 1a–b will have the respective syntactic structures (i) (a–b) below:

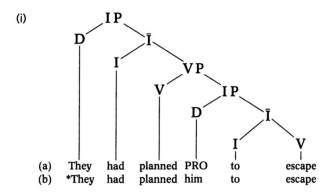

(i)

(a)   They   had   planned PRO   to   escape
(b)   *They had   planned him   to   escape

If we assume that it is a complement-feature of the verb *plan* that it can take an IP complement headed by infinitival *to*, and a specifier-feature of infinitival *to* that it can check null case, the grammaticality of (i)

(a) can be accounted for straightforwardly (the null-case head-feature carried by PRO being checked by *to*).

Less straightforward to account for is why (i) (b) should be ungrammatical. One possibility would be to say that the verb *plan* is intransitive when it takes an infinitive complement (though transitive e.g. in structures such as *The rooms are the way we planned **them***), and hence can't check the objective case carried by the infinitive subject *him* in (i). A very different possibility would be to posit that there are two types of infinitive particle *to*: one which can check null case, and one which is caseless (i.e. doesn't check the case of its subject). We could then say that when the verb *plan* takes an infinitive complement, it requires a complement headed by null-case *to* (i.e. by the kind of *to* which requires a null-case PRO subject).

Given the assumptions made in the text, 2a–b will have the respective structures indicated below:

(ii)

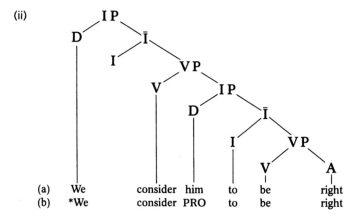

(a)	We	consider him	to	be	right
(b)	*We	consider PRO	to	be	right

In relation to (ii) (a), we can say that *consider* selects an IP complement headed by infinitival *to*, and that *consider* is a transitive verb in this use, and hence can check the objective case of the infinitive subject *him* (since *consider* immediately precedes *him*). But how can we account for the ungrammaticality of (ii) (b)? One way is to suppose that *consider* is (obligatorily) transitive when it selects an infinitival IP complement, and hence must check the objective case-feature which it carries: the relevant feature can clearly only be checked if the infinitive complement has an *objective* subject, not if it has a null-case PRO subject. A different approach to the same problem would be to say that there are two different types of infinitive particle (null-case *to* and caseless *to*), and that *consider* selects an IP complement headed by caseless *to*, not one

headed by null-case *to*. If *consider* doesn't allow an infinitive complement headed by null-case *to*, it follows that it doesn't allow a complement with a null-case PRO subject (since if it had a complement with
a PRO subject, the case of PRO could not be checked).

⑤ Head movement

So far, we have assumed that syntactic structures are derived by a series of **merger** operations. We now go on to argue that derivations may involve not only merger, but also **movement** operations. In this chapter, we look at two main types of movement operation, one which affects auxiliaries in present-day English, and another which affected verbs in earlier stages of English. We shall argue that both types of movement involve essentially the same **head movement** operation, involving movement from one head position to another. We begin by looking at the syntax of so-called *auxiliary inversion* in English.

In chapters 3 and 4, we saw that complementizers are positioned in front of subjects in the clauses they introduce. More specifically, we suggested that complementizers head a separate layer of functional super-structure in clauses, which we termed a *complementizer phrase* (= CP), with the head C (= COMP) position of CP being filled by complementizers like *that/for/if*. However, complementizers are not the only kinds of constituent which can precede subjects in clauses. After all, in our brief discussion of *auxiliary inversion* in chapter 1, we saw that auxiliaries can also precede subjects in inversion structures (e.g. in yes–no questions such as *Can you help me?*). In this respect, inverted auxiliaries seems to resemble complementizers – as the following (love-struck, soap-operesque) dialogue illustrates

(1) SPEAKER A: Honey-buns, there's something I wanted to ask you
     SPEAKER B: What, sweetie-pie?
     SPEAKER A: **If you will marry me**
     SPEAKER B *(pretending not to hear)*: What d'you say, darlin'?
     SPEAKER A: **Will you marry me?**

What's the structure of the two bold(-printed) proposals which speaker A makes in (1)? The answer is straightforward enough in the case of *If you will marry me*: it's a clause introduced by the complementizer *if*, and so is a **CP** (complementizer phrase) constituent, with the structure (2) below:

(2)

```
        C P
      /    \
    C       I P
    |      /    \
   if    D       Ī
         |      /  \
        you    I    VP
               |   /  \
             will V    D
                  |    |
                marry  me
```

But now consider the more problematic question of the structure of the second proposal, *Will you marry me?* Here we have an auxiliary inversion structure, in which the auxiliary *will* appears in front of the subject *you*. What position is being occupied by the inverted auxiliary *will*? Since *will* appears to occupy the same presubject position that the complementizer *if* occupies in (2), a natural suggestion to make is that the inverted auxiliary actually occupies the head C position of CP. If this is so, then we'd expect to find that *will* and *if* are mutually exclusive (on the assumption that we can only insert *one* word in a given head position like C, not *two* words): in other words, if both complementizers and inverted auxiliaries occupy the head C position of CP, we'd expect to find that a clause can be introduced *either* by a complementizer *or* by a preposed auxiliary – but not by the two together. This is indeed the case, as we see from the ungrammaticality of speaker B's reply in (3) below:

(3) SPEAKER A: What d'you want to ask me?
    SPEAKER B: *If *will* you marry me

The fact that no clause can contain both a complementizer and an inverted auxiliary provides us with strong empirical evidence that inverted auxiliaries occupy the same structural position as complementizers – i.e. that both occupy the head COMP position in CP.

But how can it be that a finite auxiliary (which normally occupies the head INFL position within IP) comes to be positioned in the head COMP position of CP? The answer provided by descriptive grammarians is that auxiliaries move out of their normal postsubject position into presubject position by an operation traditionally referred to as *inversion*. In terms of the framework being used here, this would mean that an inverted auxiliary moves from the head I position in IP into the head C position in CP, as in (4) below:

(4)

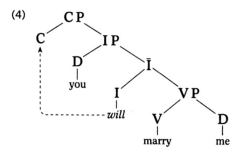

This type of *inversion* operation involves movement of a word from the head position in one phrase into the head position in another phrase (in this case, from the head I position of IP into the head C position of CP), and so is known more generally as **head-to-head movement** (or **head movement**).

An obvious question which is begged by the head movement analysis is *why* auxiliaries should undergo inversion in questions. Using a metaphor developed by Chomsky (1995), let's say that COMP in an interrogative clause is a **strong** head, and that a strong head has to be filled. In a complement-clause yes–no question like that bracketed below, COMP can be filled by the complementizer *if*:

(5)   He asked [*if* I would marry him]

(Speaker A's first proposal in (1) can be regarded as an elliptical form of *I wanted to ask you* [*if you will marry me*], with *if* introducing the bracketed complement clause.) However, complementizers can't be used to introduce main clauses in English, so some other way has to be found of filling the strong COMP node in main-clause questions. A strong COMP node has the power to lure an auxiliary from INFL to COMP (as in (4) above), thereby satisfying the requirement for a strong COMP to be filled.

An obvious question raised by this analysis is what it means to say that COMP is a *strong* node in questions. One way of visualizing this (suggested by Chomsky 1995) is to say that COMP in questions contains an abstract question affix **Q**: and since it is in the nature of affixes that they must be affixed (i.e. attached) to an appropriate kind of word, we could then say that Q must be affixed either to an interrogative complementizer like *if* or to an auxiliary like *will*. On this account, speaker A's

question *Will you marry me?* would have the derivation (6) below
(where *Q* is an affixal question particle):

(6)

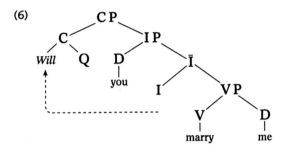

The auxiliary *will* moves into COMP in order to satisfy the requirement
for the question affix *Q* to be affixed to an appropriate kind of item. The
question affix analysis is far from implausible from a cross-linguistic
point of view: for example, yes–no questions in Latin were formed using
the overt question affix +*ne*. If we adopt the question affix analysis, we
can then say that it is a morphological property (viz. the fact that *Q* is
an affix) which triggers the syntactic operation of auxiliary inversion.
However, in order to simplify exposition, we shall simply assume (in
subsequent discussion) that an interrogative COMP is *strong* and hence
can lure an auxiliary from INFL to COMP, leaving open the question of
whether a strong interrogative COMP does or doesn't contain an affixal
question particle *Q*.

   The assumption that some categories are **strong** (and conversely
others are **weak**) provides us with an interesting account of an otherwise puzzling property of questions in English – namely the fact that
the question counterpart of a statement which contains no auxiliary
requires the use of the (dummy or expletive) auxiliary *do*, as we can
see from sentences such as the following:

(7) (a) They know him
     (b) *Do* they know him?

Why should this be? One answer would be to suppose that an interrogative COMP is strong in present-day (and so has to be filled) whereas
INFL is weak (and so doesn't have to be filled). Since INFL is weak, it
can be left empty in sentences such as (7a), which has the structure (8)
below:

(8)

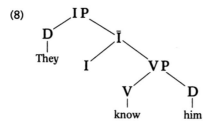

However, if we assume that interrogative clauses are CPs headed by a strong C, and that complementizers can't be used to fill COMP in main clauses, the only way of filling COMP is to resort to generating the auxiliary *do* in INFL and then raising it from INFL to COMP (to satisfy the requirement for a strong COMP to be filled) as in (9) below:

(9)

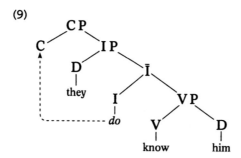

The auxiliary *do* can't be directly generated in COMP here because *do* requires a VP complement, and will only have a VP complement if it originates in INFL. Chomsky (1995) suggests that dummy *do* is only used as a **last resort** – i.e. only where needed in order to satisfy some grammatical requirement which would not otherwise be satisfied (the relevant requirement in (9) being the need to fill a strong COMP). The *last resort* condition follows from a more general **economy principle** banning the use of superfluous constituents and operations: from this principle it follows that a dummy item like *do* or an operation like *inversion* are used only when there is no other way of satisfying some grammatical requirement (e.g. the need to fill a strong interrogative COMP).

An interesting question which arises from the assumption that auxiliaries in questions move from I to C is what happens to the head I position in IP once it is vacated by movement of the inverted auxiliary into C. What we shall argue here is that the head I position of IP remains in place, but in the form of an **empty category**. What properties does this empty category have? It seems clear that the empty category left behind in the head I position of IP in a structure such as (4) must have the same head-features as *will*, since (like *will* in (2) above) it occupies the head I position of IP. Likewise, the empty I in (4) must have the same specifier-features as *will*, since (like *will*) it requires a nominative specifier (cf. *Will **she/ *her** marry me?*). Moreover, the empty I must have the same complement-features as *will*, since the head V constituent of the VP has to be in the infinitive form *marry* (and cannot e.g. be in the +*ing* form, cf. **Will you **marrying** me?*).

So, it would seem that the empty category left behind in I by movement of *will* from I to C in (4) has the same head, specifier and complement-features as *will*. The empty category would therefore seem to be a silent copy of *will* – i.e. a constituent which has the same grammatical properties as *will*, and which differs from *will* only in that it has no phonetic content. To use the relevant terminology, we can say that when the auxiliary *will* moves, it leaves behind (in the position out of which it moves) an empty **trace** of itself, and that this trace (by virtue of being a silent copy of *will*) has precisely the same grammatical features as *will*. (The romantics among you can think of *traces* as being like the footprints you leave behind in the sand when you walk along the beach in Mallorca or Malibu.) Given this assumption, our earlier question *Will you marry me?* will have the simplified structure (10) below:

(10)

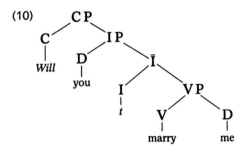

where *t* is a trace of the moved auxiliary *will*. The assumption that moved constituents leave behind a (silent) trace of themselves is the cornerstone of what became known in the 1970s as **trace theory**. Using the relevant terminology, we might say that a moved constituent is the **antecedent** of its trace, and that the antecedent of an empty trace serves to **bind** the trace – i.e. to determine its properties. (This involves a slightly extended use of the terms *antecedent/bind* compared with our use of them at the end of chapter 3.) We might further posit that a moved constituent and its trace together form a (movement) **chain**, so that C and I form a chain in (10). Extending the chain analogy still further (to

gratify the bikers among you), let's say that the moved auxiliary *will* in C
and its empty trace *t* in I are the two different **links** of the relevant movement chain. Let's also say that the moved constituent is the **head** of the
associated movement chain, and the trace is the **foot** of the chain. In
our ensuing discussion, we shall adopt the convention of using the same
type-face to denote a trace and its antecedent (hence both the trace *t*
and its antecedent *will* are printed in italics in (10) above); the general
convention used in the literature is to mark the binding relation
between a trace and its antecedent by attaching identical subscript
letters – called **indices** – to them (e.g. $will_i$ and t_i).

'Why on earth should we want to assume that moved constituents
leave behind an invisible empty category *trace*?' you might wonder at
this point. There is both theoretical and empirical evidence in support
of this assumption. The relevant theoretical evidence comes from the fact
that trace theory enables us to explain an otherwise puzzling property
of movement operations. It will become more evident as our exposition
unfolds that moved constituents always move from a lower to a higher
position in any given structure, never from a higher to a lower position:
for example, the moved auxiliary *will* in (10) moves from the head I
position in IP into the head C position in CP, and thereby moves from
a lower to a higher position in the structure. Why should movement
always be from a lower to a higher position? Trace theory provides
us with a natural explanation for the fact that movement is always
upwards, never *downwards*. If we assume that a moved constituent
leaves behind a trace which it binds, then the *upward* nature of movement is a direct consequence of the **c-command condition on binding**
which we posited in our brief discussion of anaphors in chapter 3 (where
we saw that a reflexive anaphor like *himself* must be c-commanded by
its antecedent). If a moved constituent has to bind its trace, and if a
bound constituent has to be c-commanded by its antecedent, it follows
that a moved constituent must always move into a position where it c-
commands (and hence occurs higher up in the structure than) its trace:
hence, movement will always be in an *upwards* direction. For example,
in (10) above the moved auxiliary *will* in C c-commands its trace in I by
virtue of the fact that (using our train analogy) if you travel one stop
on a northbound train from C you arrive at CP, and from there you can
catch a southbound train to I (via IP and Ī). So, one theoretical argument in support of trace theory is that it explains the *upward* nature
of movement.

A second theoretical reason for positing that a moved constituent leaves behind an empty category trace (and hence e.g. that there is an empty I constituent in inversion structures such as (10) above) relates to the *headedness* property of projections. If all phrases and clauses are projections of a head word category (as we argued in chapters 3 and 4), then IP must be headed by an I constituent; and if there is no overt I constituent in (10), there must be a *covert* one.

In addition to theory-internal considerations such as these, there is also empirical evidence for claiming that a moved constituent (e.g. the moved auxiliary *will* in (10) above) leaves behind an empty category trace. Part of this evidence comes from familiar facts about *have-* cliticization. In this connection, note that *have* cannot cliticize onto the immediately preceding pronoun *we/I/you/they* in inversion structures such as the following:

(11) (a) Will *we have/*we've* finished the rehearsal?
      (b) Should *I have/*I've* called the police?
      (c) Would *you have/*you've* wanted to come with me?
      (d) Could *they have/*they've* done something to help?

(*'ve* represents the vowel-less clitic form /v/ here.) The sequence *we've* in (11a) doesn't rhyme with *weave* (in careful speech styles), since *we have* can be reduced to /wiəv/ but not /wiv/: similarly, *I've* doesn't rhyme with *hive* in (11b), nor *you've* with *groove* in (11c), nor *they've* with *grave* in (11d). Why should cliticization of *have* onto the pronoun be blocked here? We can give a straightforward answer to this question if we posit that inverted auxiliaries move from I to C, and leave behind an empty category trace *t* in the I position out of which they move. Given this assumption, a sentence such as (11a) will have the structure (12) below. (To simplify exposition, details not of direct relevance to the discussion at hand are omitted – e.g. all features have been omitted, and the internal structure of the VP *finished the rehearsal* is not shown.)

(12)

It would seem natural to suggest that the fact that there is an empty trace *t* intervening between *have* and *we* prevents *have* from cliticizing onto *we* in structures such as (12), since cliticization is subject to an **adjacency condition** (in that the clitic must be immediately adjacent to its host in order for cliticization to be possible). More generally, cliticization facts lend empirical support to the claim that auxiliary inversion results in an IP headed by an I constituent which is filled by a trace of the moved auxiliary.

Our discussion of auxiliary inversion here has interesting implications for the derivation of sentences (i.e. the way in which they are formed). More specifically, it implies that derivations may involve both **merger** and **movement** operations. For example, our earlier sentence *Will you marry me?* is formed by merging *marry* with *me* to form the VP *marry me*; merging this VP with the auxiliary *will* to form the I-bar *will marry me*; merging the resulting I-bar with *you* to form the IP *you will marry me*; and finally merging this IP with a C constituent into which the auxiliary *will* moves, forming the CP *Will you marry me?* (and leaving a trace behind in I, as in (10) above).

Having looked briefly at *auxiliary inversion* in English, we now turn to look at another type of **head movement** operation, which we shall refer to simply as **verb movement** or **V movement**, since it involves movement of a finite nonauxiliary verb from the head V position of VP into the head I position of IP. We shall see that this kind of V movement operation was productive in the Early Modern English (= EME) period when Shakespeare was writing (around the year 1600), but is no longer productive in Modern Standard English (= MSE). Since part of the evidence for V movement involves negative sentences, we begin with a brief look at the syntax of negation in EME.

In Shakespearean English, clauses containing a finite auxiliary are typically negated by positioning *not* between the auxiliary and the verb: cf.

(13) (a) You may *not* deny it   (Princess, *Love's Labour's Lost*, V.ii)
      (b) I would *not* lose you   (Portia, *Merchant of Venice*, III.ii)
      (c) Thou shalt *not* die for lack of a dinner   (Orlando, *As You Like It*, II.vi)
      (d) I will *not* hear thy vain excuse   (Duke, *Two Gentlemen of Verona*, III.i)

It would seem plausible to suppose that *not* in EME is a VP-adverb (i.e. an adverb which occupies some position internally within VP). If so, (13a) will have a structure along the lines of (14) below:

(14)

```
            IP
        D         Ī
        |      I      VP
      You     |    ADV        V̄
             may    |      V         D
                   not     |         |
                         deny       it
```

An analysis such as (14) accounts for the position which *not* occupies in front of the verb *deny*. It also enables us to provide a straightforward account of interrogatives such as:

(15) (a) Didst thou not hear somebody?   (Borachio, *Much Ado About Nothing*, III.iii)

     (b) Will you not dance?   (King, *Love's Labour's Lost*, V.ii)

     (c) Have I not heard the sea rage like an angry boar?

                              (Petruchio, *Taming of the Shrew*, I.ii)

If interrogatives involve movement from INFL to COMP, then a sentence such as (15a) will have the derivation (16) below:

(16)

```
            CP
        C         IP
        |      D       Ī
      Didst  thou   I       VP
              ↑     |    ADV        V̄
              └---------t  |     V         D
                         not   |         |
                             hear    somebody
```

As (16) shows, the auxiliary *didst* originates in I and moves to C, leaving behind a trace *t* in the position out of which it moves. The assumption that *not* is contained within VP provides a straightforward account of the fact that *not* remains positioned in front of the verb *hear* when *didst* is preposed.

However, what is particularly interesting about negative sentences in Shakespearean English is that in auxiliariless finite clauses, the (boldprinted) main verb is positioned in front of the negative *not*: cf.

(17) (a) He **heard** *not* that   (Julia, *Two Gentlemen of Verona*, IV.ii)

(b) I **care** *not* for her   (Thurio, *Two Gentlemen of Verona*, V.iv)

(c) My master **seeks** *not* me   (Speed, *Two Gentlemen of Verona*, I.i)

(d) I **know** *not* where to hide my head   (Trinculo, *The Tempest*, II.ii)

(e) Thou **thinkest** *not* of this now   (Launce, *Two Gentlemen of Verona*, IV.iv)

(f) She **lov'd** *not* the savour of tar   (Stephano, *The Tempest*, II.ii)

(g) My charms **crack** *not*   (Prospero, *The Tempest*, V.i)

(h) Demetrius loves her and he **loves** *not* you

(Lysander, *Midsummer Night's Dream*, III.ii)

If we assume that *not* in EME occupied a preverbal position internally within VP, how can we account for the fact that the verb (which would otherwise be expected to follow the negative *not*) ends up positioned in front of *not* in sentences like (17)? An obvious answer is to suggest that when INFL is not filled by an auxiliary, the verb moves out of the head V position in VP into the head I position in IP. If this is so, (17a) *He heard not that* will have the derivation (18) below:

(18)

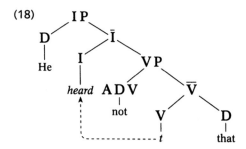

Thus, the verb *heard* originates in the head V position within VP, and then moves across *not* into the head I position in IP, so accounting for the fact that *heard* is positioned in front of *not*.

There would seem to be significant parallels between between **V-to-I movement** in (18) and **I-to-C movement** in (16). For one thing, in both cases movement is from one head position to another, and so is an instance of the more general operation of **head movement**. Moreover, in both cases movement is from a *lower* to a *higher* position, and so results in a structure in which the moved head c-commands its trace (thereby satisfying the **c-command condition on binding**). Furthermore, in both cases movement is **local**, with the moved head being moved into the head position in the next-highest phrase within the structure; and in both cases, the moved head can move across an intervening nonhead constituent. Thus, *didst* in (16) moves from the head I position in IP into the head position within the next-highest phrase in the structure (into the head C position of CP), and in doing so moves across its specifier *thou*; likewise, *heard* in (18) moves from the head V position in VP into the head position in the next-highest phrase in the structure (= the head I position of IP), and in doing so moves across the adverb *not*. Since both **V-to-I movement** and **I-to-C movement** are local operations, it seems reasonable to suppose that their *locality* property is not accidental, but rather reflects the operation of some principle of Universal Grammar. Lisa Travis (1984) suggested that the relevant principle is a **head movement constraint** (= HMC) to the effect that a head can only move from the head position in one phrase to the head position in the immediately containing (i.e. next-highest) phrase in the structure.

As we see from the examples in (15) above, questions in EME (= Early Modern English) involved the same *inversion* operation as in MSE (= Modern Standard English). Given our assumption that *inversion* involves movement from I to C, an obvious prediction made by the assumption that verbs move from V to I in EME is that they can subsequently move from I to C, so resulting in sentences such as:

(19) (a) *Saw* you my master?   (Speed, *Two Gentlemen of Verona*, I.i)
      (b) *Heard* you this, Gonzalo?   (Alonso, *The Tempest*, II.I)
      (c) *Speakest* thou in sober meanings?   (Orlando, *As You Like It*, V.ii)
      (d) *Call* you this gamut?   (Bianca, *Taming of the Shrew*, III.i)
      (e) *Came* you from the church?   (Tranio, *Taming of the Shrew*, III.ii)
      (f) *Know* you not the cause?   (Tranio, *Taming of the Shrew*, IV.ii)
      (g) *Spake* you not these words plain?   (Grumio, *Taming of the Shrew*, I.ii)

If so, a typical Early Modern English question such as (19f) *Know you not the cause?* would be derived in the manner represented in (20) below:

(20)

The fact that the verb *know* is positioned to the left of the subject *you* suggests that it is raised first from V to I and then from I to C by two successive applications of head movement (numbered (1) and (2) respectively). In structures like (20), head movement is said to apply in a **successive cyclic** fashion, moving the verb *know* (in successive steps) first into INFL, then into COMP. Each separate movement operation is local (in that it moves *know* only into the head position in the next-highest phrase containing it in the tree).

It is interesting to reflect on the significance of the fact that negatives like (17) and interrogatives like (19) are no longer grammatical in MSE (Modern Standard English). What is the nature of the change that has taken place in the course of the evolution of the language? The answer seems to be that it was possible for finite (nonauxiliary) verbs to move to INFL in EME, but that this is no longer possible in MSE; hence (for example) nonauxiliary verbs could move to INFL in EME sentences such as (17), and from INFL subsequently move to COMP, so giving rise to interrogatives such as (19) – but no movement to INFL (and thence to COMP) is possible for nonauxiliary verbs in MSE.

Why should finite nonauxiliary verbs be able to move to INFL in Early Modern English, but not in present-day English? Using Chomsky's *strength* metaphor, we might suggest that finite verbs carried *strong* agreement-features (i.e. strong person/number specifier-features) in EME, whereas their counterparts in MSE carry *weak* agreement-features. And we might further suppose that only verbs which carry strong agreement-features are strong enough to move into INFL – hence that verbs carrying weak agreement-features are too weak to move into INFL.

One question raised by this account is 'What determines whether finite verbs carry strong or weak agreement-features?' A plausible answer is that this is correlated with the relative *richness* of the agreement inflections carried by finite verbs, in that finite verbs have strong agreement-features in languages in which they carry rich agreement inflections, and weak agreement-features in languages in which they carry relatively impoverished agreement inflections. In this connection, it is interesting to note that whereas third person singular +*s* is the only regular agreement inflection found on (present-tense) verbs in Modern Standard English, in Shakespearean English we find three present-tense inflections, viz. second person singular +*st* and third person singular +*th* and +*s*: cf.

(21) (a) Thou see*st* how diligent I am   (Petruchio, *Taming of the Shrew*, IV.iii)
      (b) Thou say*st* true   (Petruchio, *Taming of the Shrew*, IV.iii)
      (c) The sight of love feed*eth* those in love   (Rosalind, *As You Like It*, III.v)
      (d) She tak*eth* most delight in music, instruments and poetry
                                                              (Baptista, *Taming of the Shrew*, I.i)
      (e) Winter tame*s* man, woman and beast   (Grumio, *Taming of the Shrew*, IV.i)
      (f) It looks ill, it eats drily   (Parolles, *All's Well That Ends Well*, I.i)

Accordingly, we might argue that finite verbs have strong agreement-features in EME by virtue of the relatively rich system of agreement inflections they carry; and conversely that finite verbs have weak agreement-features in MSE by virtue of their relatively impoverished agreement morphology in present-day English. (See Rohrbacher 1994 and Vikner 1995 for interesting attempts to explore the correlation between the strength of agreement-features and the relative richness of agreement inflections in a range of different languages.)

The different strength of the agreement-features carried by finite verbs in EME on the one hand and MSE on the other is reflected in a further syntactic difference between them. Early Modern English was a **null subject language**, as we see from sentences such as the following:

(22) (a) Hast any more of this?   (Trinculo, *The Tempest*, II.ii)
      (b) Sufficeth, I am come to keep my word   (Petruchio, *Taming of the Shrew*, III.ii)
      (c) Would you would bear your fortunes like a man   (Iago, *Othello*, IV.i)
      (d) Lives, sir   (Iago, *Othello*, IV.i, in reply to 'How does Lieutenant Cassio?')

Since the null subject in sentences like (22) occurs in a nominative position (by virtue of being the subject of a finite clause), it has different case properties from the PRO subject of infinitives (which has null case), and hence is generally taken to be a different kind of null subject conventionally designated as **pro** (affectionately known as *little pro*, whereas its big brother is affectionately known as *big PRO*). By contrast, MSE is a **non-null subject language**, as we see from the fact that the present-day counterparts of (22) require (italicized) overt subjects: cf.

(23) (a) Have *you* any more of this?
      (b) *It* is enough that I have come to keep my word
      (c) *I* wish you would bear your fortunes like a man
      (d) *He* is alive, sir

It would seem, therefore, that finite verbs can have a null *pro* subject in a language like EME where they carry strong agreement-features, but not in a language like MSE where they carry weak agreement-features. Why should this be? An obvious suggestion is that in a language with a rich system of agreement inflections, the agreement inflections on the verb serve to **identify** the null subject (e.g. the +*st* inflection on *hast* in (22a) is a second person singular inflection, and hence allows us to identify the null subject as a second person singular subject with the same properties as *thou*). But in a weak agreement language like MSE, agreement morphology is too impoverished to allow identification of a null *pro* subject (e.g. if we asked **Can help?*, we'd have no way of telling from the agreementless form *can* whether the missing subject is *I, you, he, they* or whatever).

What our discussion here suggests is that there is parametric variation across languages in respect of whether finite verbs carry strong or weak agreement-features, and that the relative strength of these features determines whether nonauxiliary verbs can raise to INFL, and whether null subjects are permitted or not. However, this still poses the question of why finite verbs should raise out of V into I in languages like EME where they carry strong agreement-features. One answer to this question is provided by **checking theory**: let us suppose that movement checks *strong* features which would otherwise remain unchecked. As we have seen, finite verbs in EME carry strong agreement-features; hence a finite verb raises to INFL in order to *check* its strong agreement-features (i.e. its person/number specifier-features) against those of the subject occupying the specifier position within IP. To see how this might work, consider the syntax of a sentence such as *Thou thinkest not of this* (cf. (17e) above). The verb *thinkest* originates in the head V position of VP, and (because it contains strong agreement-features) then raises to INFL as in (24) below. (The [2SNom] features of *thou* mark the second person singular nominative head-features of *thou*, the [Pres] feature of *thinkest* marks its present-tense head-feature, and the [2SNom] features carried by *thinkest* are specifier-features which mark the fact that it requires a second person singular nominative subject as its specifier; all other features are omitted, to simplify exposition.)

(24)

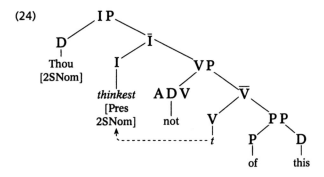

Since subject–verb agreement involves a local checking relation between INFL and its specifier, an obvious consequence of moving *thinkest* from V into I in (24) is that it enables the specifier-features of *thinkest* to be checked: this is because *thinkest* ends up in INFL, and from there can check its [2SNom] specifier-features against the corresponding [2SNom] head-features of *thou*. Since the two sets of features match, the specifier-features of *thinkest* are erased along with the nominative case-feature of *thou* (because the relevant features are uninterpretable), so ensuring that the derivation does not crash. Movement of *thinkest* to INFL also ensures that INFL carries a tense-feature (viz. the present-tense head-feature of *thinkest*), thereby ensuring that INFL will be interpretable at the level of logical form (if we assume that INFL must carry a tense-feature in order to be interpretable at LF).

As we have seen, the agreement properties of finite nonauxiliary verbs in EME are checked by moving the verb into INFL, so that the verb is in a local spec–head relation with its subject, and its person/number/case specifier-features can be checked. But recall (from our discussion in the previous chapter) that the specifier-features of finite nonauxiliary verbs are checked in a rather different way in MSE – as we can illustrate in relation to a simple sentence such as:

(25) She mistrusts him

Example (25) is an IP headed by an empty INFL constituent, with the verb *mistrusts* occupying the head V position of VP, and the subject *she* occupying the specifier position within IP. We suggested in the previous chapter that the head- and specifier-features of finite nonauxiliary verbs percolate from V to INFL in English, to satisfy the requirement that INFL carry a tense-feature (in order to be interpretable at LF), and to enable the specifier-features of the verb to be checked. In the case of (25), percolation will work in the manner indicated in (26) below. (To simplify exposition, we show only the features directly relevant to our discussion here.)

(26)

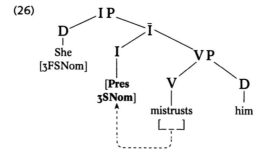

Once the bold-printed head- and specifier-features of *mistrusts* have percolated up to INFL, its [3SNom] specifier-features (requiring it to have a third person singular nominative subject) can then be checked for compatibility with the [3FSNom] head-features of *she*, and thereby erased (along with the uninterpretable nominative head-feature of *she*). Chomsky (1995) refers to the relevant process of feature-percolation as **attraction**. (The idea is that INFL in structures like (26) *attracts* the relevant features carried by *mistrusts*.)

So, it would appear that EME and MSE make use of two very different ways of checking the agreement properties of finite (nonauxiliary) verbs: EME makes use of **movement** of the verb from V to INFL; MSE makes use of **attraction** of the head- and specifier-features of the verb from V to INFL. These two different ways of checking the relevant features of finite verbs correlate directly with the relative **strength** of the agreement-features carried by the verbs. In a language like EME in which verbs carry strong agreement-features, agreement is checked by movement; in a language like MSE where verbs carry weak agreement-features, agreement is checked by attraction (= percolation). Since the ultimate goal of any theory is to *explain* why things are the way they are, an important question for us to ask is *why* strong features should be checked by movement, and weak features by attraction. The answer to this question may lie in the nature of the two different operations. We have described movement informally as 'movement of a word', and attraction as 'movement of a set of features'. But if (following Chomsky) we take words to be *sets of phonetic, grammatical and semantic features*, it is clear that movement too involves 'movement of a set of features'. So what is the difference between the two? The answer is that movement is an operation which affects the complete set of (phonetic, grammatical and semantic) features carried by a word, whereas attraction affects only the *grammatical* features carried by an item (more specifically, those grammatical features which can't be checked otherwise). We might conjecture that what it means for a word like *thinkest* in (24) to carry strong agreement-features is that these strong agreement-features cannot be separated from the other (phonetic, grammatical and semantic) features carried by the relevant word; hence, the only way of checking the strong agreement-features of *thinkest* is to move the whole word (i.e. the whole set of phonetic, grammatical and semantic features carried by the word). Conversely, what it means to say that a verb like *mistrusts* in (26) has weak grammatical features is that the relevant grammatical features can be moved on their own, with the other (phonetic and semantic) features carried by the word being left behind.

We might further suppose that in consequence of the **economy principle**, only the minimal set of features needed to satisfy some grammatical requirement undergo movement in a given structure. Thus, because INFL requires a tense-feature and the [3SNom] specifier-features of *mistrusts* cannot be checked unless they move to INFL, the relevant tense/agreement-features percolate to INFL in (26); because these features are weak, they can be separated from the other features carried by *mistrusts*, and hence the economy principle requires that only these features should move. By contrast, the verb *thinkest* in (24) carries strong [2SNom] agreement-features, with the result that not just these features but all the other features carried by *thinkest* move to INFL (so that in effect the whole word *thinkest* moves to INFL). So, attraction is more economical than movement, since movement affects all the (phonetic, grammatical and semantic) features carried by a word, whereas attraction involves movement of grammatical features alone: hence, the economy principle will ensure that attraction will be preferred to movement wherever possible (e.g. in structures like (26)), with movement only being forced where the relevant features being checked are strong.

To summarize: in this chapter, we have been concerned with the syntax of **head movement**. We began by looking at auxiliary inversion in questions in English, arguing that this involves an **I movement** operation whereby an auxiliary moves from INFL to COMP. We suggested that auxiliaries move to COMP because an interrogative COMP is strong (perhaps by virtue of containing an abstract question affix **Q**), and a strong head position must be filled. We argued that an inverted auxiliary leaves behind a trace (i.e. a silent copy of itself) in the INFL position out of which it moves when it moves to COMP. We went on to show that finite verbs in Early Modern English (EME) could move from V to INFL by an operation of **V movement** (as is shown by word-order facts in negative sentences like *I care not for her*), but that this kind of movement is generally no longer possible in Modern Standard English (MSE). We argued that **I movement** and **V movement** are two different reflexes of a more general **head movement** operation, and that head movement is subject to a strict locality constraint (the **head movement constraint**) which requires it to apply in a successive cyclic (stepwise) fashion. We suggested that verbs in EME had strong agreement-features (by virtue of the relatively rich agreement inflections they carried) and consequently allowed a null *pro* subject, whereas their counterparts in MSE have weak agreement-features (by virtue of their impoverished agreement morphology) and so do not allow a *pro* subject. We argued that the strong agreement-features of finite verbs in EME were checked by movement of the verb (along with its features) from V to INFL, whereas the weak agreement-features of finite verbs in MSE are checked by **attraction** (i.e. percolation) of the relevant agreement-features from V to INFL (with the verb itself remaining *in situ* in the head V position of VP).

Exercises

Exercise IX

Discuss the derivation of each of the following (adult) sentences, drawing a tree diagram to represent the structure of the overall sentence and saying why the relevant derivation crashes or converges.

1 He smokes cigars

2 *He d's smoke cigars (*d's* = unstressed does, /dəz/)

3 *Smokes he cigars?

4 *If he smokes cigars?

5 Does he smoke cigars?

6 Would he have smoked cigars?

7 I wonder if he smokes cigars

8 *I wonder if does he smoke cigars

In addition, discuss the derivation of each of the following child sentences produced by children aged 2–4 years (the name of the child producing each sentence is given in parentheses), and identify the nature of the child's error in each case:

9 Is the clock is working? (Shem)

10 Does it doesn't move? (Nina)

11 Do she don't need that one? (Adam)

12 Did we went to somebody's house? (Adam)

13 Does it opens? (Adam)

Finally, discuss the derivation of the following questions produced by an unnamed 3-year-old girl (reported by Akmajian and Heny 1975, p. 17):

14 Is I can do that?

15 Is you should eat the apple?

16 Is the apple juice won't spill?

Helpful hints

Assume in relation to 6 that *have* occupies the head V position of VP here (since the head I position of IP is filled by another constituent – which?), and that *have* takes a VP complement of its own. In relation to 12, assume that *somebody's house* has the structure 17 below:

17
```
            D P
          /      \
        Q          D̄
        |        /     \
    somebody    D       N
                |        |
               's      house
```

– i.e. that it is a DP headed by a possessive determiner *'s* whose complement is the noun *house* and whose specifier is the pronoun (i.e. pronominal quantifier/determiner) *somebody*.

Model answer for 1

Given the assumptions made in the text, 1 will be derived by merging the null determiner Ø with the noun *cigars* to form the DP Ø *cigars*; then merging this DP with the verb *smokes* to form the VP *smokes* Ø *cigars*; then merging this VP with a null INFL to form the I-bar *INFL smokes* Ø *cigars*, which in turn is merged with the pronoun *he* to form the IP in (i) below:

(i)

The pronoun *he* carries the head-features [3MSNom] indicating that it is third person masculine singular nominative. The verb *smokes* carries the head-feature [Pres] indicating that it is a present-tense form. This feature is attracted to INFL, in order to ensure that INFL will be interpretable at LF (by virtue of carrying a tense-feature). The verb *smokes* also carries the specifier-features [3SNom], indicating that it requires a third person singular nominative subject. However, since the specifier-features of a head can only be checked in relation to the specifier of the phrase containing the head, clearly we cannot check the specifier-features of *smokes* against the head-features of *he* in (i) because the two are contained in different phrases (*smokes* is the head V of VP, and *he* is the specifier of IP). Since finite verbs carry weak agreement-features in present-day English (as we see from the fact that they don't allow null subjects), the verb *smokes* cannot move from V to INFL in (i), since only verbs with strong agreement-features can move to INFL. Instead, the weak agreement-features carried by the verb *smokes* are checked by **percolation** (alias **attraction**) to INFL. Thus, the bold-printed head- and specifier-features of *smokes* percolate up to the INFL node in the manner represented by the dotted arrow in (ii) below:

(ii)

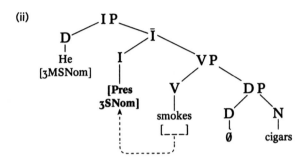

The [3SNom] specifier-features of INFL can then be checked against
the corresponding [3SNom] person/number/case head-features of *he*,
and thereby be erased (along with the uninterpretable nominative-case
head-feature of *he*). The analysis in (ii) correctly predicts that since
INFL contains no overt item (but carries a present-tense head-feature),
sentence 1 will be tagged by a present-tense form of the dummy auxiliary
do: cf.

(iii) (a) He smokes cigars, *does* he/*smokes he?
       (b) He smokes cigars, *doesn't* he/*smokesn't he?

(Other features here are ignored, since they are of no immediate interest.)

Exercise X
Discuss the derivation of the following Shakespearean sentences:

1 Thou marvell'st at my words   (Macbeth, *Macbeth*, III.ii)

2 Macbeth doth come   (Third Witch, *Macbeth*, I.iii)

3 He loves not you   (Lysander, *Midsummer Night's Dream*, III.ii)

4 You do not look on me   (Jessica, *Merchant of Venice*, II.vi)

5 Wilt thou use thy wit?   (Claudio, *Much Ado About Nothing*, V.i)

6 Wrong I mine enemies?   (Brutus, *Julius Caesar*, IV.ii)

7 Do you fear it?   (Cassius, *Julius Caesar*, I.ii)

8 Knows he not thy voice?   (First Lord, *All's Well That Ends Well*, IV.i)

9 Didst thou not say he comes?   (Baptista, *Taming of the Shrew*, III.ii)

10 Can'st not rule her?   (Leontes, *Winter's Tale*, II.iii)

Model answer for 1–2
If we assume that finite verbs in EME carry strong agreement-features
and raise to INFL to check their agreement properties with the subject

(which occupies the specifier position in IP), 1 will have the derivation
in (i) below (simplified by not showing the internal structure of the
prepositional phrase *at my words*, since this is of no direct relevance
to the syntax of the verb *marvell'st*):

(i)

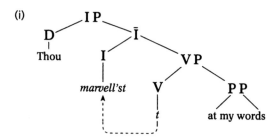

Sentence 2 differs from 1 in that it contains the auxiliary *doth* (which is
a variant of *does*). If we make the standard assumption that auxiliaries
occupy the head I position of IP, 2 will have the structure (ii) below:

(ii)

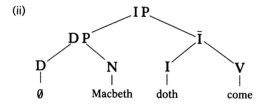

(Given our arguments in chapter 4 that *bare* nominals are DPs headed
by a null determiner, we assume here that the bare noun *Macbeth* is a
DP headed by a null determiner: and indeed, proper names in many
languages are premodified by an overt determiner – cf. e.g. Italian *la
Callas*, literally *the Callas*.)

A potential problem posed by sentences like 2 is that they might
seem to call into question the assumption that dummy verbs like *do* are
used purely as a last resort. We might suppose that if *do*-support were
purely a last resort, sentences like 2 would be ungrammatical, since they
have the *do*-less counterpart *Macbeth cometh* (which involves raising
cometh from V to INFL). However, one way of maintaining the last
resort account would be to suppose that the use of *do* here is determined
by the need to satisfy *metrical* requirements. This becomes clearer if we
look at the context in which 2 was uttered, viz.

(iii) A drum! A drum!
       Macbeth doth come

Since the second line must contain four syllables and end in a word rhyming with *drum*, and since the three-syllable utterance *Macbeth cometh* satisfies neither requirement, the four-syllable utterance *Macbeth doth come* (which satisfies both) is used instead.

An alternative possibility would be to suppose that *do* in EME was not a dummy auxiliary at all, but rather had independent semantic content of some kind. One possibility is that *do* in EME served the function of marking *aspect*. After all, there are varieties of present-day English in which *do* is an aspectual auxiliary: for example, in Caribbean creoles (according to Harris 1986 and Rickford 1986) we find the auxiliary *do* being used in sentences like:

(iv)   He does be sick

to mark habitual aspect (so that (iv) has much the same meaning as *He is usually sick*). Likewise, *do* functions as a habitual aspect marker in Irish English (cf. Guilfoyle 1983, Harris 1986), and in south-western varieties of British English (cf. Wakelin 1977, pp. 120–1). However, since sentence 2 *Macbeth doth come* doesn't have the habitual sense of *Macbeth usually comes*, it's implausible that *doth* functions as an aspectual auxiliary here. An alternative possibility is that *do* in EME had a *performative* sense, and thus meant something like *perform the action of . . .* This performative use of *do* in EME may be connected to its use in present-day British English in sentences such as:

(v)   He can read books quicker than I can *do*

where *do* might be glossed as *perform the relevant action* (i.e. of reading books). If *do* had independent semantic content in EME, it would clearly not be subject to the last resort condition (since the latter applies only to dummy or expletive items with no semantic content of any kind). However, the precise function and content of *do* in EME is anything but clear. As noted by Tieken-Boon van Ostade (1988, p. 1) the origin of *do* 'may truly be called one of the great riddles of English linguistic history'.

⑥ Operator movement

In the previous chapter, we looked at the syntax of **head movement**. In this chapter, we look at a very different kind of movement operation, known as **operator movement** because it applies to expressions which contain an (e.g. interrogative or negative) **operator** of some kind.

So far, we have implicitly assumed that CP comprises a head C constituent (which is filled by a complementizer in some structures and by a preposed auxiliary in others) and an IP complement. However, one question which such an analysis begs is where the bold-printed pre-auxiliary constituents are positioned in structures such as (1) below:

(1) (a) **What languages** *can* you speak?
     (b) **No other colleague** *would* I trust

Each of the sentences in (1) contains an inverted auxiliary (*can/would*) occupying the head C position of CP, preceded by a bold-printed phrase of some kind (viz. *what languages* and *no other colleague*). Each of the pre-auxiliary phrases contains a word which is sometimes classed as an **operator**: more precisely, *what* is an **interrogative operator** (or **wh-operator**) and *no* is a **negative operator**. Expressions containing (e.g. interrogative or negative) operators are – for obvious reasons – called **operator expressions** (hence *what languages* and *no other colleague* in (1) are operator expressions).

It seems clear that each of the operator expressions in (1) functions as the complement of the verb at the end of the sentence. One piece of evidence leading to this conclusion is the fact that each of the examples in (1) has a paraphrase in which the operator expression occupies complement position after the relevant verb: cf.

(2) (a) You can speak *what languages*?
     (b) I would trust *no other colleague*

Structures like (2a) are sometimes referred to as *wh-in-situ* questions, since the interrogative wh-operator expression *what languages?* does not get preposed, but rather remains *in situ* (i.e. 'in place') in the canonical (i.e. 'usual') position associated with its grammatical function (e.g. *what languages* in (2a) is the complement of *speak*, and complements are canonically positioned after their verbs, so *what languages* is positioned after the verb *speak*). Structures like (2a) are used primarily as *echo questions*, to echo and question something previously said by someone else (e.g. if a friend boasts 'I just met Lord Lickspittle', you could reply – in an air of incredulity – 'You just met *who*?'). Sentences such as (2) make it seem plausible to suppose that the operator phrases in (1) originate as complements of the relevant verbs, and subsequently get moved to the front of the overall sentence. But what position do they get moved into?

The answer is obviously that they are moved into some position preceding the inverted auxiliary. Now, if inverted auxiliaries occupy the head C position of CP, we might suppose that preposed operator phrases are moved into some prehead position within CP. Given that *specifiers* are typically positioned before heads, an obvious suggestion to make is that preposed operator phrases occupy the **specifier position within CP** (abbreviated to **spec-CP**). If indeed it is the case that preposed operator phrases are moved into spec-CP, the sentences in (1) will be derived as in (3) below:

(3)

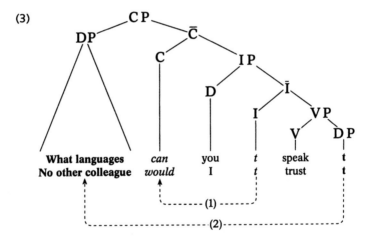

(We have assumed in (3) that *what* and *no* are both determiners of some kind, and that the phrases *what languages* and *no other colleague* are DPs, i.e. determiner phrases.) Two different kinds of movement operation (indicated by the arrows) are involved in (3): (1) involves movement of a *head* (the italicized auxiliary *can/would*) from I to C, and – as noted in the previous chapter – this type of movement operation is referred to as **head movement**; (2) involves movement of an operator expression into the specifier position within CP, and this very different kind of movement operation is known as **operator movement** or **O movement**.

When operator movement applies to expressions containing an operator beginning with *wh* (e.g. *who, what, which, when*, etc.), it is sometimes referred to more specifically as **wh-movement**. In the rest of this chapter, we shall focus on the syntax of interrogative operators.

A tacit assumption made in our analysis of operator movement in (3) is that just as a moved head (e.g. an inverted auxiliary) leaves behind a *trace* in the position out of which it moves, so too a moved operator expression leaves behind a trace at its *extraction site* (i.e. in the position out of which it is extracted/moved). The assumption that moved operator expressions leave a trace behind can be defended on empirical grounds. One piece of evidence comes from facts relating to a phenomenon generally known as *wanna-contraction*. In colloquial English, the string *want to* can sometimes contract to *wanna*, so that alongside (4a) below we find (4b):

(4) (a) I *want to* go home
     (b) I *wanna* go home

In nonsloppy speech styles, however, the sequence *want to* cannot contract to *wanna* in a sentence such as (5a) below, as we see from the ungrammaticality of (5b):

(5) (a) Who would you want to help you?
     (b)*Who would you wanna help you?

Why should this be? Well, let's assume that *who* originates as the subject (and specifier) of the IP (infinitive phrase) *to help you* – as seems plausible in view of the fact that (5a) has the echo question counterpart:

(6) You'd want *who* to help you?

Let's also assume that the wh-pronoun *who* (being an interrogative operator) undergoes movement from its underlying spec-IP position to the spec-CP position at the front of the clause, and that it leaves behind a trace in spec-IP. Assuming that auxiliary inversion also takes place, the resulting structure will then be along the lines of (7) below (where *t* is the trace of *who* and we omit the trace of *would* for simplicity):

(7) *Who* would you want *t* to help you?

Why should *wanna*-contraction then be blocked in a structure such as (7)? Since we have already seen in earlier chapters that cliticization is subject to an adjacency condition (and hence is only possible when the two words involved are immediately adjacent), the presence of the intervening trace *t* between *to* and *want* will prevent *to* from cliticizing onto *want*, and hence blocks *wanna-contraction*. (We might suppose that in sloppy speech styles, intervening traces are ignored, and so do not suffice to block contraction.)

A similar kind of argument in support of claiming that moved operator expressions leave behind a trace comes from facts about *have-cliticization*. The perfective auxiliary form *have* has the clitic variant /v/ and can cliticize to an immediately preceding word which ends in a vowel or diphthong. Significantly, however, cliticization is not possible (in nonsloppy speech styles) in sentences such as (8a) below, as we see from the fact that the sequence *say have* in (8a) cannot contract to *say've* in (8b):

(8) (a) Which students would you say *have* got most out of the course?
     (b)*Which students would you say*'ve* got most out of the course?

(Hence the sequence *say've* is not homophonous with *save*.) Why should *have* be prevented from cliticizing onto *say* here? We might assume that prior to being moved to the front of the sentence by operator movement, the operator phrase *which students?* was the subject of *have* – as in the echo question counterpart (9) below:

(9) You would say *which students* have got most out of the course?

If the moved phrase *which students* leaves behind a trace (= *t*) in the position out of which it moves, the superficial structure of (8b) will be (10) below (simplified by not showing the trace of the inverted auxiliary *would*):

(10) *Which students* would you say *t* have got most out of the course?

This being so, we can say that *have* cannot cliticize onto *say* in (10) because it is not immediately adjacent to *say*, the two words being separated by the intervening trace *t* in (10) – so accounting for the ungrammaticality of (8b).

The analysis presented here correctly predicts that while *have-cliticization* is not possible in structures like (8b) above, it is indeed possible in structures like (11b) below:

(11) (a) *Who have* they arrested?
      (b) *Who've* they arrested?

Given our twin assumptions that preposed operators move into spec-CP and inverted auxiliaries move to COMP, (11a) will have the derivation (12) below (where movement (1) is **head movement**, and (2) is **operator movement**):

(12)

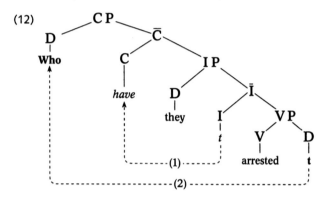

Since *who* is immediately adjacent to *have* here, our analysis correctly predicts that *have* should be able to cliticize onto *who*: the fact that the resulting sentence (11b) is grammatical makes it all the more plausible to posit that spec-CP is the **landing-site** for preposed operator expressions (i.e. spec-CP is the position into which they move).

Additional support for the claim that operator expressions move into spec-CP comes from the fact that in some varieties of English, preposed wh-expressions can precede a complementizer like *that*. This is true, for example, of Belfast English structures such as the following (from Henry 1995, p. 107):

(13) (a) I wonder [**which dish** *that* they picked]
      (b) They didn't know [**which model** *that* we had discussed]

If we assume that the complementizer *that* occupies the head C position in the bracketed CP, it seems reasonable to suppose that the wh-expressions *which dish?/which model?* that precede the complementizer *that* occupy the specifier position within CP, and this is what Alison Henry argues.

Given that our ultimate goal is *explanation*, an important question to ask is *why* interrogative operator expressions should move to spec-CP. The answer is that operator movement is driven by Lasnik's (1995) principle of **enlightened self-interest** (which specifies that constituents move in order to check features carried by other constituents, so that movement is motivated by a form of **altruism**). A natural extension of the altruism analysis would be to suppose that the head COMP constituent of CP (in questions) carries an interrogative specifier-feature, and that (correspondingly) wh-operators like *who?* carry an interrogative head-feature. We could then say that wh-operators move to spec-CP in order to check the interrogative specifier-feature carried by COMP (which needs to be checked and erased, since specifier-features are uninterpretable). Since interrogative operators in English typically begin with *wh* (cf. *who?, what?, which?, where?, when?, why?,* etc.), let's use [**wh**] to designate the relevant interrogative feature.

To see how this works, consider how we might derive a sentence such as:

(14)   What was he doing?

Let's assume that the inverted auxiliary *was* originates in INFL, and that the pronominal determiner *what?* originates as the complement of *doing* – as in the corresponding echo question (15) below:

(15)   He was doing *what?*

Let's also assume that COMP in questions is a strong (perhaps affixal) head, so the auxiliary *was* moves from INFL to COMP in order to fill COMP. Let's further assume that an interrogative COMP carries a [wh] specifier feature (indicating that it requires a specifier with a [wh] head-feature), and that *what?* moves to spec-CP as in (16) below:

(16)
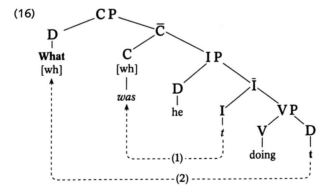

Since *what?* and COMP are contained within the same CP projection in the resulting structure (16), the [wh] specifier-feature of COMP can be checked against the [wh] head-feature of its specifier *what?* Checking here involves a local spec–head relation between a wh-COMP and its wh-specifier; it will result in erasure of the specifier-feature of COMP (since specifier-features are uninterpretable). We can assume that the [wh] head-feature of *what?* is interpretable at LF (since the fact that *what* is an interrogative operator plays a role in determining the semantic interpretation of the sentence), and so is not erased.

The assumption that **wh-movement** (i.e. movement of wh-operator expressions) is motivated by the need to check the [wh] specifier-feature of COMP in questions provides an interesting account of why in multiple wh-questions (i.e. questions containing more than one wh-operator) such as (17) below, only one wh-operator can be preposed, not both:

(17) (a) **Who** do you think will say *what?*
          (b)* *What* **who** do you think will say?

Example (17a) has the derivation (18) below:

(18)

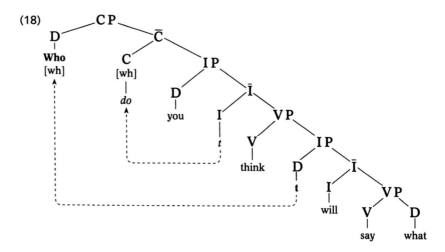

The [wh] specifier-feature of COMP is erased once it has been checked by movement of *who* into spec-CP. This means that no other wh-operator expression can subsequently move to spec-CP because the [wh] specifier-feature of COMP has now been erased (and movement only take places where a grammatical feature needs to be checked). Thus, checking theory provides a neat account of why only one wh-operator is preposed in multiple wh-questions in English.

However, a question not answered by our account is why it should be possible to prepose *who* on its own in a multiple wh-question like (17a), but not *what* – i.e. why we can't say:

(19) *****What** do you think *who* will say?

Example (19) would be derived as in (20) below:

(20)

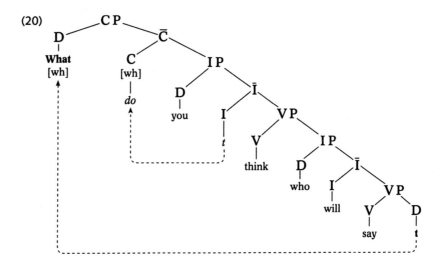

Since movement of *what* into spec-CP would enable the [wh] specifier-feature of COMP to be checked, why does the derivation in (20) crash? Why should *who* be able to move to spec-CP in (18), but not *what* in (20)?

A natural suggestion to make is that this is because *who* is closer to COMP than *what*, and **economy** considerations favour shorter movements over longer ones. So, COMP lures the *nearest* wh-operator into spec-CP: since *who* is nearer to COMP in (18/20) than *what*, it is *who* which must move to spec-CP, not *what*. The relevant condition (favouring shorter moves over longer ones) is known as the principle of **shortest movement**. Since the effect of the principle is to favour the formation of movement chains with minimal (i.e. the smallest/shortest possible) links, the relevant principle is also referred to as the **minimal link condition** (or the **minimality condition**). It should be obvious that the head movement constraint discussed in the previous chapter (which holds that a head can only move into the next highest head position in the structure containing it) can be subsumed under the principle of shortest movement (or the equivalent minimal link/minimality condition).

Thus far, most of the instances of wh-movement which we have looked at have involved movement of a wh-determiner (a pronominal wh-determiner such as *who?* or *what?*) on its own into spec-CP.

However, in sentences such (21–2) below, we find movement of a whole DP headed by a wh-determiner (*which?/what?*) into spec-CP, with movement of the determiner alone leading to ungrammaticality:

(21) (a) *Which film* did you see?
      (b)* *Which* did you see *film*?

(22) (a) *What reason* did he give?
      (b)* *What* did he give *reason*?

To use a **pied-piping** metaphor familiar from nursery stories (What! You've forgotten how the pied-piper lured all the rats out of the village of Hamelin by playing his pipe?), it would seem that when the wh-operator *which?/what?* moves to spec-CP in (21–2), its complement (*film/reason*) has to be **pied-piped** along with the moved wh-operator. Why should this be?

Consider first why moving the wh-determiner without its complement leads to ungrammaticality. Sentence (21b) will have the derivation (23) below:

(23)

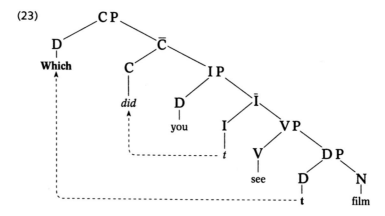

Why should the derivation in (23) crash? One possibility is that movement of *which* on its own into spec-CP results in the formation of a chain *which . . . t* which is *nonuniform*, in that *which* and its trace differ in respect of their phrase structure status. To see why, consider the immediate structures containing *which?* and its trace, given in (24a–b) below:

(24)(a)

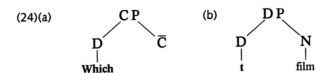

In (24a) the D node containing *which?* is a maximal projection (i.e. it is the largest category headed by *which?*), whereas in (24b) the D node containing its trace *t* is not a maximal projection since the maximal projection of the D node containing *t* is the DP *t film*). If (following Chomsky 1995) we posit the following constraint on chains:

(25) CHAIN UNIFORMITY PRINCIPLE
A chain must be uniform with regard to phrase structure status.

the ungrammaticality of the (b) examples in (21–2) above can be accounted for in a principled fashion, since the (b) examples all result in a nonuniform chain whose head (= the preposed wh-word *which?/what?*) is a maximal projection, but whose foot (= the trace of the preposed wh-word) is not.

But now consider what happens if we prepose the whole DP *which film?* in (21a), in the manner indicated in (26) below:

(26)

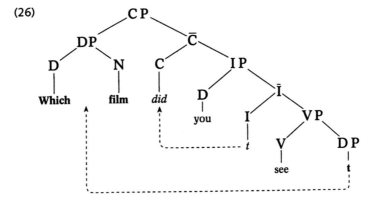

Here the resulting chain is uniform, since its head is the DP *which film?* (which is a maximal projection) and its foot is a DP-trace (hence also a maximal projection). Thus, it would seem that operator movement moves a D alone wherever possible (e.g. in structures like (20) above), but moves a DP when movement of D alone would violate the **chain**

uniformity principle (e.g. in structures like (26) above). The more general principle which this suggests is that movement operations move only the *minimal* (i.e. smallest) constituent required to satisfy UG principles: this can be argued to be a particular instance of the more general **economy principle**, which in effect tells us to move features rather than constituents whenever possible, and (when moving constituents) to move the smallest constituent possible the smallest distance possible.

We can extend the account given here from contrasts such as (21–2) above to those such as (27) below:

(27) (a) *Whose car* did you borrow?
     (b)* *Whose* did you borrow *car?*
     (c) * *Who* did you borrow *'s car?*

Following a suggestion attributed to Richard Larson in Abney 1987, we might conjecture that genitive *'s* in English is a head determiner which takes a D projection as its specifier, and an N projection as its complement, so that *whose car* has the structure (28) below:

(28)

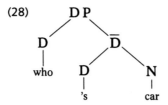

(We can assume that *'s* attaches to *who*, forming *who's*, written as *whose.*) We cannot prepose *who* on its own in (27c) since this will result in the suffix *'s* being stranded (*'s* is unable to attach to *who*, since *who* has been moved to the front of the sentence and is no longer adjacent to *'s*). Nor can we move the sequence *who's* (= *whose*) in (27b), since this is not a constituent (and only constituents can undergo movement operations). So, the minimal constituent which can be preposed is the whole DP *whose car* – as in (27a).

The **economy principle** might also be argued to have a central role to play in accounting for contrasts such as the following in colloquial English:

(29) (a) *Who* were you talking to?
     (b)* *To who* were you talking?
     (c) * *Talking to who* were you?

Each of the sentences in (29) is derived by preposing a wh-expression (*who*, *to who*, or *talking to who*) into the spec-CP position indicated by the question-mark in (30) below (and moving the auxiliary *were* from INFL into COMP):

(30)

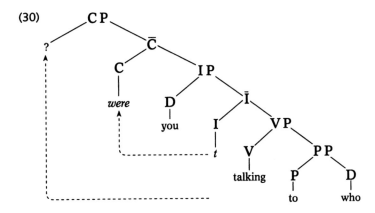

Since an interrogative COMP has a [wh] specifier-feature, some constituent containing a wh-operator must move into the spec-CP position indicated by ? in (30), in order to check this [wh] feature. If we move the determiner *who* on its own, the resulting chain *who . . . t* will be uniform, since both its head and foot will be D constituents which do not project into DP (and so are maximal projections). Of course, this will also be true if the PP *to who* moves into spec-CP, since the result will be a uniform chain whose head and foot are both maximal (PP) projections; and the same is likewise true if the VP *talking to who* moves into spec-CP, since this will again result in a uniform chain whose head and foot are both maximal (VP) projections. So, since preposing the D *who*, the PP *to who* and the VP *talking to who* all result in the formation of a uniform chain, why should preposing D be preferred to preposing PP, or preposing VP? The obvious answer is that the D *who* is smaller than the PP *to who*, which in turn is smaller than the VP *talking to who*. And if we assume that (for **economy** reasons) operator movement moves only the minimal (i.e. smallest) constituent needed to check the strong [wh] specifier-feature of COMP, the relevant facts fall out as we expect.

However, our discussion here overlooks an important *stylistic* variable. In formal styles of English (where the objective form of the relevant pronoun is *whom* rather than *who*), the facts are rather different, as we see from the sentences below:

(31) (a) ** Whom were you talking to?*
      (b) *To whom were you talking?*
      (c) ** Talking to whom were you?*

As these examples show, in formal English, the wh-pronoun *whom* cannot be preposed on its own; rather, the preposition *to* must be pied-piped along with *whom* (though the verb *talking* cannot be pied-piped in the same way). What is going on here?

Consider first why (31a) is ungrammatical. What's happened here is that the preposition *to* has been **stranded** or **orphaned** (i.e. separated from its complement *whom*); the fact that (31a) is ungrammatical suggests that there is a constraint (i.e. prohibition) against **preposition-stranding** in formal styles of English – a constraint rather inaccurately encapsulated in the traditional rule of prescriptive grammar: 'Never end a sentence with a preposition.' (The precise nature of this constraint need not concern us here; for a technical account within the minimalist framework, see Salles 1995.)

Given the **no-preposition-stranding** constraint, we can begin to make sense of the data in (31). Movement of *whom* alone will violate the **no-preposition-stranding** constraint, and so leads to ungrammaticality in (31a). The minimal constituent which can be preposed without violating the constraint is the PP *to whom*, in which *to* is pied-piped along with *whom*: hence, (31b) is grammatical. In (31c), the whole VP *talking to whom* has been preposed, with the verb *talking* being pied-piped as well; but this violates the **economy principle** (which requires that only the *minimal* constituent required to ensure that the [wh] specifier-feature of COMP can be checked should be preposed). So, the contrasting patterns of grammaticality found in colloquial English sentences like (29) on the one hand and formal English sentences like (31) turn out to be reducible to the fact that the constraint against preposition-stranding holds in formal English (and many other languages – e.g. French, Italian, Spanish, etc.), but not in colloquial English. Everything else about the relevant data follows from UG principles.

The analysis we have presented here suggests that it is a defining characteristic of wh-questions that they contain a wh-specifier (i.e. a wh-operator in spec-CP). This assumption raises interesting questions about sentences such as (32) below:

(32) Who helped him?

If we assume (as we have done hitherto) that all wh-questions are CPs containing a wh-operator which moves into spec-CP, (32) will involve movement of *who* from its underlying position in spec-IP into its superficial position in spec-CP, and so will have the (simplified) derivation (33) below:

(33)

But what is problematic about the derivation in (33) is that an interrogative COMP is strong in English, and so triggers auxiliary inversion in root clauses. If (33) were the right analysis for (32), we would expect to find *do*-support required as a last resort here. But in fact it is neither necessary nor possible to use an unstressed form of *do* (e.g. the clitic form *'d* of *did* which we find in sentences like *Where'd he go?*), as we see from the ungrammaticality of:

(34)   *Who'd help him (*'d* = *did*)

(Irrelevantly, (34) is grammatical on an alternative interpretation whereby *'d* is a contracted form of *would*. Equally irrelevant is the fact that we could use a stressed form of *do* here, e.g. in *Who* DID *help him?*; since stressed forms mark contrast or emphasis, they can be assumed to have semantic content and hence not to be subject to the last resort condition.) The absence of any inverted auxiliary in (32) calls into question the assumption made in (33) that the subject *who* moves into spec-CP.

   If *who* doesn't move to spec-CP, it must remain *in situ* in spec-IP. Thus, it may well be (as suggested by Grimshaw 1993) that a sentence like (32) is simply an IP with a structure along the lines of (35) below:

(35)

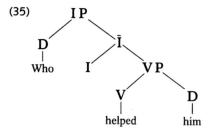

This would mean that interrogative clauses with interrogative subjects have the status of IPs (cf. (35) above), but other types of interrogative clause have the status of CPs (cf. (12) above). Why should there be such a curious asymmetry in the structure of questions, with some clauses projecting up to CP, and others projecting only as far as IP?

We can offer an interesting answer to this question in terms of the **economy principle**. Let's suppose that (in consequence of the economy principle) we project only the minimal structure required to ensure that a given expression is interpreted in the appropriate way at the level of LF (logical form). Let's also suppose that a clause can only be interpreted as a question at LF if it contains an interrogative specifier, and that COMP is strong when it has an interrogative specifier, but that INFL is always weak in Modern Standard English. In a wh-subject question like (32) *Who helped him?* the requirement for a question to have an interrogative specifier can be satisfied by simply projecting the clause as far as IP (as in (35) above), since the relevant IP has the interrogative operator *who?* as its specifier: hence, the IP (35) is interpretable as a question at LF without the need to project the structure any further into a CP. However, in other types of question (e.g. (11a) *Who have they arrested?*), the clause has to project beyond IP into CP (and the operator *who?* move into spec-CP as in (12) above) in order to generate a structure containing an interrogative operator as its specifier (i.e. a structure which is interpretable as a question at LF). The **economy principle** determines that only one wh-operator will be moved into spec-CP in a multiple wh-question structure like (18), since (on this account) we move only the minimal constituents required to ensure that the resulting structure is interpreted as a question at LF, and this can be achieved by moving only one wh-operator to the front of the sentence.

Our assumption that clauses are only interpretable as interrogative at LF if they contain an interrogative operator raises interesting questions about the syntax of yes–no questions such as:

(36) Is it raining?

If all questions contain an interrogative specifier, what kind of specifier do yes–no questions contain? Perhaps (as suggested in Grimshaw 1993 and Roberts 1993) they contain an abstract question operator of some kind which is directly generated in spec-CP (i.e. which is positioned in spec-CP by merger rather than movement). If so, a question like (36) will have the structure (37) below (where **Op** denotes a null yes–no question operator which is merged with the C-bar *is it raining* to form the CP *Op is it raining?*; I have not made any assumptions about what category *Op* belongs to here – perhaps it is an adverb of some kind):

(37)

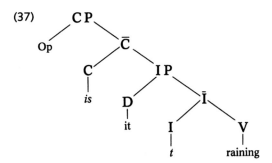

From a historical perspective, the null-operator analysis is by no means implausible, since in Early Modern English we found yes–no questions introduced by the overt yes–no question operator *whether* – as illustrated by the following Shakespearean examples:

(38) (a) *Whether* had you rather lead mine eyes or eye your master's
          heels?   (Mrs Page, *Merry Wives of Windsor*, III.ii)
      (b) *Whether* dost thou profess thyself a knave or a fool?
                                          (Lafeu, *All's Well That Ends Well*, IV.v)

Given the null operator analysis, we could posit that yes–no questions have essentially the same syntax in present-day English as in Early Modern English, save that yes–no questions could be introduced by the overt operator *whether* in Early Modern English, but are introduced by a covert operator *Op* in present-day English.

A second piece of evidence in support of positing a null yes–no question operator comes from the fact that yes–no questions can be introduced by *whether* when they are transposed into reported speech (and so occur in a complement clause), as we see from the examples below:

(39) (a) 'Are you feeling better?', he asked
      (b) He asked *whether* I was feeling better

A third piece of evidence is that yes–no questions with auxiliary inversion resemble *whether* questions in that in both cases *yes/no* are appropriate answers: cf.

(40) (a) When he asked 'Did you vote for Larry Loudmouth?', I said 'Yes' and you said 'No'
      (b) When he asked *whether* we voted for Larry Loudmouth, I said 'Yes' and you said 'No'

A fourth argument is that main-clause yes–no questions can be tagged by *or not* in precisely the same way as complement-clause *whether* questions: cf.

(41) (a) Has he finished *or not*?
      (b) I can't say whether he has finished *or not*

If yes–no questions are indeed CPs containing an abstract null yes–no question operator (a null counterpart of *whether*) in spec-CP, our hypothesis that a clause is only interpretable as a question at LF if it contains an interrogative specifier becomes all the more plausible.

To summarize: we began this chapter by arguing that wh-questions are CPs headed by a COMP constituent with a [wh] specifier-feature, and that this specifier-feature is checked by moving a wh-expression containing an interrogative operator with a [wh] head-feature into spec-CP (i.e. into the specifier position within CP). We pointed out that such an analysis would correctly predict that in multiple wh-questions, only one of the wh-expressions moves to spec-CP; and we argued that the **shortest movement principle** determines which of the wh-expressions moves. We noted that in structures where the wh-operator has a complement (e.g. in expressions like *which film?* where *film* is the complement of *which?*), the complement is **pied-piped** along with the wh-operator, in order to avoid violation of the **chain uniformity principle**. We suggested that (in consequence of the **economy principle**), only the minimal material necessary is pied-piped along with a moved

wh-operator. We went on to argue that questions with wh-subjects
(e.g. *Who helped him?*) are IPs (and hence have no requirement for *do*-
support), and that the interrogative operator in such cases is in spec-IP.
We then suggested that it is a general property of interrogative clauses
that they contain an interrogative specifier (in spec-IP in sentences like
Who said that?, and in spec-CP in sentences like *What did he say?*),
perhaps because a clause can only be interpreted as interrogative if it
contains an interrogative specifier. We noted that one consequence of
this assumption would be that yes–no questions like *Are you enjoying
syntax?* contain an abstract yes–no question operator (**Op**) in spec-CP.

Exercises

Exercise XI

Account for the (un)grammaticality of the examples in 1–5 below
in Modern Standard English:

1a   Which prisoners did they say have escaped?
 b *Which prisoners did they say've escaped?
2a   What did he think would happen to who?
 b *Who did he wonder what would happen to?
3a   What colour did you choose?
 b *What did you choose colour?
4a   Who've they been talking to?
 b *To who've they been talking?
5a   Do you feel better?
 b *Feel you better?

In addition, discuss the derivation of the following wh-questions
in Jamaican Creole (cf. Bailey 1966):

6a Homoch   kuoknat im   en   sel?
     How-much coconut him been sell
     'How many coconuts did he sell?'
 b *Homoch   kuoknat en   im sel?
     How-much coconut been him sell? (intended as synomymous with 6a)
7a Huu yu   a   taak bout?
     Who you does talk about
     'Who are you talking about?'

b *Bout   huu yu   a   taak?

About who you does talk? (intended as synonymous with 7a)

Finally, discuss the syntax of the italicized interrogative complement clauses below in (one variety of) Belfast English (cf. Henry 1995):

8a They wondered *which one that he chose*

 b They wondered *which one did he choose*

 c *They wondered *which one that did he choose*

9a They wondered *if/whether (*that) we had gone*

 b *They wondered *if/whether had we gone*

 c They wondered *had we gone*

Helpful hints

In relation to 6 and 7, note that auxiliaries/verbs don't inflect for agreement in Jamaican Creole, and pronouns don't inflect for case (i.e. they are invariable in form): according to Rickford (1986) and Harris (1986), *a* is a contracted form of *does* (which has the reduced forms *da* and *a*). In relation to 9, consider the possibility that *whether* functions as a complementizer in Belfast English (even though it doesn't function as such in Modern Standard English, for the reasons given in chapter 2).

Model answer for 1

The DP *which prisoners?* here functions as the subject of *have escaped*, as we see from its position in the corresponding echo question *They said which prisoners have escaped?* Accordingly, 1a has the derivation (i) below:

(i)

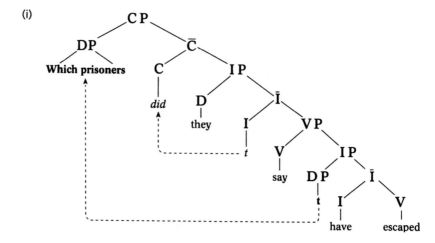

COMP is strong (perhaps because it contains a *Q* affix) in an interrogative clause, and so has to be filled; to satisfy this requirement, the dummy auxiliary *did* is generated in INFL, and then moved to COMP, as a last resort. The wh-operator *which* moves into spec-CP in order to check the [wh] specifier-feature carried by an interrogative COMP (or, alternatively, in order to ensure that the clause has an interrogative specifier and so can be interpreted as a question at LF). However, *which* cannot move on its own, as we see from the ungrammaticality of:

(ii)   *Which* did they say *prisoners* have escaped?

This is because movement of *which* on its own leads to violation of the **chain uniformity principle**, since it results in a chain whose head (*which?*) is a maximal projection, but whose foot (the trace of *which?*) is a minimal projection (cf. our discussion of (24) in the main text). Consequently, the noun *prisoners* is pied-piped along with the wh-operator *which?*, and the whole DP *which prisoners?* is moved into spec-CP by **operator movement**. Since a moved constituent leaves behind a trace in the position out of which it moves, preposing of *which prisoners?* leaves a trace as the subject of *have*. Because this trace intervenes between *say* and *have*, it blocks *have* from cliticizing onto *say* – hence the ungrammaticality of 1b.

Exercise XII
Discuss the syntax of the following Early Modern English (= EME) questions taken from various plays by Shakespeare:

1	What sayst thou?	(Olivia, *Twelfth Night*, III.iv)
2	What dost thou say?	(Othello, *Othello*, III.iii)
3	Whom overcame he?	(Boyet, *Love's Labour's Lost*, IV.i)
4	What didst not like?	(Othello, *Othello*, III.iii)
5	What think you he hath confessed?	(First Lord, *All's Well That Ends Well*, IV.iii)
6	Who comes with him?	(Baptista, *Taming of the Shrew*, III.ii)
7	Who knows not that?	(Curtis, *Taming of the Shrew*, IV.i)
8	Saw you my daughter?	(Duke, *Two Gentlemen of Verona*, V.ii)
9	Didst thou not say he comes?	(Baptista, *Taming of the Shrew*, III.ii)
10	Can'st not rule her?	(Leontes, *Winter's Tale*, II.iii)

Model answer for 1

Sentence ı has the derivation (i) below:

(i)

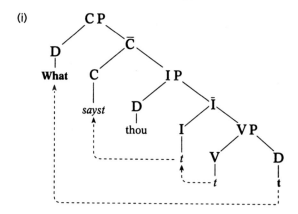

The verb *sayst* in ı originates as the head V of VP. Since verbs carry strong agreement inflections in EME (as we see from the fact that second person singular verbs carry the inflection +*st* which is no longer used in present-day English), the verb *sayst* moves out of the head V position in VP into the head I position of IP, by **head movement**. This enables agreement between *sayst* and *thou* to be checked, and also ensures that INFL will be interpretable at LF (since INFL thereby acquires the present-tense head-feature of *sayst*). Since C is strong in interrogative clauses (perhaps by virtue of containing an abstract interrogative affix Q), *sayst* then moves from I to C, again by **head movement**: thus, head movement applies in a successive cyclic (one-step-at-a-time) fashion.

    The wh-operator *what?* originates as the complement of the verb *sayst* (and in this position, checks its objective case-feature against the corresponding case-feature carried by the transitive verb *sayst*). It then moves into the specifier position within CP, and thereby comes to be positioned in front of the inverted verb *sayst*. Why should *what* move? One possible answer is provided by checking theory. We might suppose that an interrogative COMP carries a [wh] specifier-feature, and that *what?* moves to spec-CP in order to check (and erase) this feature against the [wh] head-feature carried by *what?* An alternative account is to suppose that *what?* moves to spec-CP in order to satisfy the requirement that a clause can only be interpreted as interrogative if it has an interrogative specifier.

❼ Subjects

In this chapter, we look rather more closely at the syntax of *subjects*. So far, we have assumed that subjects occupy the specifier position within IP and remain *in situ* (except where the subject is an interrogative operator which undergoes operator movement, e.g. in sentences like **Who** *did he say was coming?*). However, we shall now argue that subjects originate in the specifier position within VP, and are subsequently raised to spec-IP for checking purposes by a movement operation known as **(subject) raising**.

Let's begin by looking at the structure of *expletive* sentences such as (1) below:

(1) (a) *There* is nobody living **there**
    (b) *There* is someone knocking at the door
    (c) *There* are several patients waiting to see the doctor

Sentence (1a) contains two different occurrences of *there*. The second (bold-printed) *there* is a locative pronoun paraphraseable as 'in that place', and contains the diphthong /eə/; the first (italicized) *there* is an *expletive* (i.e. *dummy* or *pleonastic*) constituent which contains the unstressed vowel /ə/ and does not have a locative interpretation (i.e. it is not paraphraseable as 'in that place'), but rather has no intrinsic reference (as we see from the fact that its reference can't be questioned – hence the ungrammaticality of **Where is nobody living there?*). Expletive *there* seems to have the categorial status of a pronominal determiner, since (like other pronominal determiners – e.g. personal pronouns such as *he/she/it/they*) it can occur in sentence *tags*, as we see from examples like those in (2) below (where the part of the sentence following the comma is the *tag*):

(2) (a) Don Quickshot has been arrested, has *he?*
    (b) Peggy Prim buys her clothes at Marks and Spencer, does *she?*
    (c) Randy Rabbit is a regular at Benny's Bunny Bar, is *he?*
    (d) Bill and Ben are a happily unmarried couple, aren't *they?*
    (e) It always rains in Manchester, doesn't *it?*
    (f) There's nobody living there, is *there?*
    (g) There's someone knocking at the door, isn't *there?*
    (h) There are several patients waiting to see the doctor, are *there?*

It seems clear that the pronoun *there* in sentences such as (1) occupies the specifier position within IP. Some evidence in support of this claim comes from the fact that the auxiliary *is/are* can be moved in front of it (into COMP) in yes–no question structures such as (3) below:

(3) (a) **Is** *there* nobody living there?
     (b) **Is** *there* someone knocking at the door?
     (c) **Are** *there* several patients waiting to see the doctor?

where *is/are* originates in the head I position of IP and moves across expletive *there* (which occupies the specifier position in IP) into the head C position of CP. Given that auxiliary inversion typically moves an auxiliary across a subject in spec-IP, the fact that the auxiliary *is* moves across the expletive pronoun *there* in getting from its position in (1) into its position in (3) suggests that *there* must be in spec-IP.

Moreover, given that auxiliaries select a VP complement, it seems likely that the complement of the auxiliary *is/are* in (1) is a verb phrase. If this is so, then (1b) will be an IP with the simplified structure (4) below:

(4)

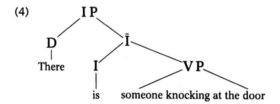

An analysis such as (4) would enable us to provide a straightforward account of the fact that the verb *knocking* surfaces in the +*ing* form, and not (for example) in the infinitive form *knock*. Given the structure in (4), we should expect that the head I constituent (= *is*) of IP will determine the morphological form of head V constituent (= *knocking*) of the complement VP: since the progressive auxiliary *be* selects a complement headed by a verb in the +*ing* form, the fact that *knocking* is in the +*ing* form can be accounted for straightforwardly.

But what is the internal structure of the VP constituent in (4)? It seems clear that the V *knocking* is the head of the VP, and it is plausible to assume that *at the door* is its complement. But what role does *someone* play within the VP? A natural suggestion to make is that *someone* is the subject of *knocking at the door*; if we assume that the canonical position for the subject of a particular constituent is the specifier position within the relevant projection, we might suggest that *someone* in

(4) occupies **spec-VP** (i.e. the specifier position within VP). If so, (4) will have the structure (5) below:

(5)

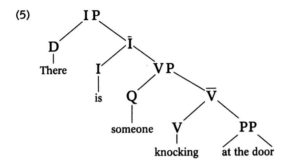

What (5) claims is that the head V constituent (= *knocking*) of the VP merges with its PP complement (= *at the door*) to form a verbal expression which is conventionally termed a $\bar{\text{V}}$ (= V' = **V-bar**, in each case pronounced vee-bar), and the resulting V-bar constituent *knocking at the door* is then predicated of the pronominal quantifier/determiner *someone*, so forming the overall VP *someone knocking at the door*.

An interesting variant of a sentence like (1b) is the type of sentence illustrated in (6) below:

(6) Someone is knocking at the door

Here, *someone* is clearly the subject of the auxiliary *is*, and hence would appear to be positioned in spec-IP. And yet, in our earlier structure (5), *someone* was instead the subject of *knocking*, and occupied the specifier position in VP. The obvious question to ask is how we can account for the fact that subjects like *someone* are in spec-VP in expletive structures like (5), but in spec-IP in nonexpletive structures like (6). In this connection, recall our suggestion in chapters 5 and 6 that constituents can *move* from a lower to a higher position within the sentence containing them (e.g. auxiliaries can move from I to C, and operator expressions can move e.g. from VP-complement position to CP-specifier position). This opens up the possibility of a movement account of the dual position of *someone* in sentences like (1b) and (6). More specifically, let us suppose that *someone* originates in spec-VP and remains *in situ* in expletive structures such as (5), but is *raised* into spec-IP in nonexpletive structures such as (6). If this is so (and if we assume that a moved subject leaves behind a trace in the position out of which it moves), then (6) will be derived as in (7) below:

(7)

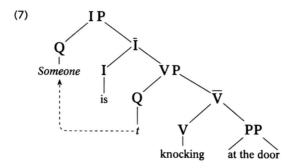

Since the arrowed movement operation which applies in (7) has the effect of raising *someone* from being the subject of VP to becoming the subject of IP, it is traditionally referred to as **subject-to-subject raising** (usually abbreviated to **subject raising**, or more simply **raising**). The more general claim underlying the analysis in (7) (known as the **VP-internal subject hypothesis**) is that subjects originate in spec-VP, and are subsequently raised into spec-IP in all but a few constructions (e.g. not in existential structures like (5) above in which the spec-IP position is filled by a *dummy* or *expletive* constituent).

An interesting piece of evidence in support of the VP-internal subject hypothesis comes from cliticization facts. As we saw in our discussion of forms like *they've* and *wanna* in the previous chapter, cliticization (e.g. of *have* onto *they*, or of *to* onto *want*) is blocked by the presence of an intervening empty category. In the light of this, consider the fact that *to* can cliticize onto *want* (forming *wanta/wanna*) in sentences such as (8) below:

(8) (a) We *want* to help you
     (b) We *wanna* help you

We argued in chapter 4 that apparently subjectless infinitive complements (like *to help you* in (8a) above) have a null-case PRO subject in spec-IP. If this were so, (8a) would have the simplified structure (9) below:

(9)

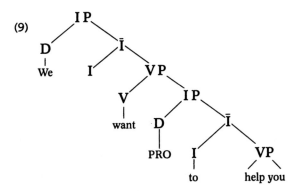

But then we should expect that the intervening empty category PRO would prevent *to* from cliticizing onto *want*, thereby wrongly predicting that (8b) is ungrammatical. What's gone wrong here? Baltin (1995, p. 244) suggests that the VP-internal subject hypothesis provides us with an answer. If we assume that PRO subjects originate (and remain) in spec-VP, then (8a) will no longer have the structure (9) above, but rather that in (10) below:

(10)

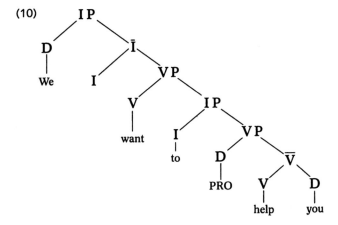

Since there is no (overt or covert) category intervening between *want* and *to* in (10), we correctly predict that *to* can cliticize onto *want*, forming (8b) *We wanna help you*. But note that a crucial premise in the argument is that PRO is positioned in spec-VP, not in spec-IP. (Of course, Baltin's analysis raises questions about how the null case carried by PRO is checked: if it is checked by *to* rather than by *help*, we are going to have to say that the case of PRO is checked from outside its containing VP by infinitival *to*, in much the same way as in exceptional case-marking structures like *We expect* **him** *to resign*, the case of *him* is checked from outside its containing phrase by the verb *expect*.)

The core assumption of the **VP-internal subject hypothesis** is that subjects originate in spec-VP; in control structures like (10) and in expletive structures like (5), the subject remains in spec-VP; but in other structures, the subject raises from spec-VP into spec-IP. Given that a moved constituent leaves behind a trace in any position out of which it moves, it follows that subjects which move from spec-VP to spec-IP will leave behind a trace in the spec-VP position out of which they move. Empirical motivation for positing that moved subjects leave behind traces in spec-VP comes from evidence which is essentially similar in character to that which we used to support the postulation of a PRO subject in *control* structures in chapter 4. Consider, for example, how we account for the syntax of the italicized reflexive pronouns contained within the bracketed verb phrases in the sentences below:

(11) (a) He certainly has [compromised *himself/ *themselves*]
      (b) [Compromised *himself/ *themselves*], he certainly has

Reflexives generally require a *local* c-commanding antecedent within the phrase containing them. This being so, it follows that the reflexives in (11) must have an antecedent within the bracketed verb phrase containing them. This will obviously be the case if we assume that a sentence such as (11a) is derived in the manner indicated informally in (12) below:

(12) [$_{IP}$ He certainly [$_I$ has] [$_{VP}$ *t* [$_V$ compromised] himself]]

The derivation in (12) claims that the subject *he* originates in spec-VP as the subject of *compromised*, and is then raised into spec-IP, where it becomes the subject of *has* – leaving a trace *t* behind in the spec-VP position which it vacates. The trace *t* of the moved subject *he* provides an appropriate phrase-internal antecedent for *himself* in (12), since both *himself* and the trace are immediate constituents of the bracketed VP, and since both are third person masculine singular (the trace carrying the same grammatical properties as its antecedent *he*). By contrast, *themselves* could not be used in place of *himself* in (12) because it would lack an antecedent within the bracketed VP (the trace *t* cannot be its antecedent since the trace is third person masculine singular, and *themselves* is third person plural). If we suppose (following Chomsky 1995) that a trace is a *silent copy* of the relevant moved constituent, it follows that traces will have the same syntactic and semantic properties as their antecedents, and will differ from their antecedents only in that they have no overt phonetic form: this assumption accounts for the fact that the trace *t* in (12) has the same *third person masculine singular* features as its antecedent *he*.

We can derive the structure associated with (11b) if we prepose the VP complement following *has* in (12), and move it to the relevant position in front of the overall IP – as in (13) below (where ___ marks the position out of which the bracketed preposed verb phrase moves, and *t* is the trace of *he*):

(13)   [*t* Compromised himself], *he* certainly *has* ___

Since the subject of the preposed bracketed VP is the trace *t* of the moved (third person masculine singular) subject *he*, the subject trace inside the bracketed VP can only bind (i.e. serve as the antecedent of) the third person masculine singular reflexive *himself*; hence, replacing *himself* by the third person plural reflexive *themselves* in (13) leads to ungrammaticality.

We can construct essentially parallel arguments in support of the claim that apparently subjectless VPs contain a trace subject in spec-VP in relation to structures such as the following (where *t* denotes a trace of the italicized moved subject, and where ___ denotes the position out of which the preposed verb phrase moves):

(14)   (a) *They* probably will [*t* become **millionaires**/***a millionaire**]
       (b) [*t* Become **millionaires**/***a millionaire**], *they* probably will ___

(15)   (a) *John* certainly has [*t* damaged **his**/***my own** credibility]
       (b) [*t* Damaged **his**/***my** own credibility], *John* certainly has ___

(16)   (a) *You* definitely mustn't [*t* lose **your**/***his** cool]
       (b) [*t* Lose **your**/***his** cool], *you* definitely mustn't ___

(17)   (a) *We*/***I** never would [*t* hurt **each other**]
       (b) [*t* Hurt **each other**], *we*/***I** never would ___

(18) (a) *They/*He* really shouldn't [*t* live **together**]
      (b) [*t* Live **together**], *they/*he* really shouldn't ___

If we posit a trace subject occupying the specifier position within the bracketed VP, we can account for the fact that the predicate nominal in (14) has to be in the plural form *millionaires*, since it agrees with the trace subject *t* in spec-VP (which is plural because it is the trace of the moved plural subject *they*). In much the same way, we can posit that *his* in (15) agrees with the trace of *John*, and that *your* in (16) agrees with the trace of *you*. Similarly, we can claim that *each other* (which requires a local plural antecedent) is bound by the trace of *we* in (17), and that *together* (which similarly requires a local plural antecedent) is bound by the trace of *they* in (18). The logic of the argumentation should be clear: in each case we have an expression which requires a local antecedent, and which will only have a local antecedent if we assume that subjects originate in spec-VP and thence raise to spec-IP, leaving behind a trace in spec-VP which can bind the expression requiring a local antecedent.

A rather different kind of argument relating to the syntax of quantified expressions can be formulated in relation to the syntax of quantifiers (cf. Sportiche 1988). In sentences such as (19) below:

(19) (a) **They** are *both* helping her
      (b) **We** can *all* work harder
      (c) **You** will *each* receive a present

the italicized quantifiers *both/all/each* are separated from the bold-printed subjects ***they/we/you*** which they quantify. In this use, they are referred to as *floating quantifiers* (or *stranded quantifiers*), for obvious reasons. How can we account for the fact that (for example) in (19a) *both* quantifies *they*, and yet the two clearly occupy different positions? The VP-internal subject hypothesis provides us with an answer. Let us suppose that the pronoun *they* in (19a) originates as the complement of *both* (in much the same way as *of them* seems to function as the complement of *both* in an expression such as *both of them*). Let's also assume that the relevant QP (quantifier phrase) *both they* (which has essentially the same interpretation as *both of them*) originates as the subject of the VP headed by *helping*, and that the pronoun *they* is subsequently raised up to become the subject of *are*, as in (20) below:

(20)

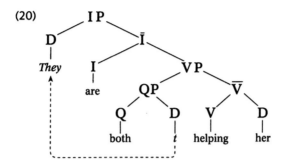

The quantifier *both* thereby ends up modifying the trace of the moved pronoun *they*. Movement of *they* leaves the quantifier *both* stranded within QP, separated from the pronoun *they* which it quantifies. The analysis in (20) correctly specifies that *both* superficially occupies an intermediate position between *are* and *helping* (the QP *both t* occupying spec-VP and so serving as the subject of *helping*).

Thus the assumption that subjects originate in spec-VP and raise to spec-IP provides us with an interesting account of how quantifiers come to be separated from the subject expressions which they quantify. A parallel separation argument can be formulated in relation to the syntax of *idioms*. We can define *idioms* as expressions (such as those italicized below) which have an idiosyncratic meaning that is not a purely componential function of the meaning of their individual parts:

(21) (a) Let's have a couple of drinks to *break the ice*
      (b) Be careful not to *upset the applecart*
      (c) The president must *bite the bullet*
      (d) We'll have to *grasp the nettle*
      (e) He'll *hit the roof* when you tell him

There seems to be a constraint that only a string of words which forms a unitary *constituent* can be an idiom. Thus, while we find idioms like those in (21) which are of the form *verb + complement* (but where the subject isn't part of the idiom), we don't find idioms of the form *subject + verb* where the verb has a complement which isn't part of the idiom: this is because in *subject + verb + complement* structures, the verb and its complement form a unitary constituent (a *V-bar*), whereas the subject and the verb do not (and only unitary constituents can be idioms).

In the light of the constraint that an idiom is a string of words which forms a unitary constituent with an idiosyncratic interpretation, consider now more restrictive idioms such as the following:

(22) (a) All hell broke loose

      (b) The shit hit the fan

      (c) The cat got his tongue

      (d) The chickens came home to roost

In idioms like those in (22), not only is the choice of verb and complement fixed, but so too is the choice of subject. In such idioms, we can't
replace the subject, verb or complement by near synonyms, so that sentences like (23) below are ungrammatical (on the intended idiomatic
interpretation):

(23) (a) *The whole inferno broke free

      (b) *Camel dung was sucked into the air conditioning

      (c) *A furry feline bit his lingual articulator

      (d) *The hens returned to nest

Hence, since the choice of all three constituents (subject, verb and
complement) in clauses like (22) is fixed, we might refer to such idioms
as *clausal* idioms.

    However, what is puzzling about clausal idioms like those in (22) is
that auxiliaries can freely be inserted between the subject and verb: cf.

(24) (a) All hell *will* break loose

      (b) All hell *has* broken loose

      (c) All hell *could have* broken loose

(25) (a) The shit *might* hit the fan

      (b) The shit *has* hit the fan

      (c) The shit *must have* hit the fan

If (as suggested earlier) only a string of words which form a *unitary
constituent* can constitute an idiom, how can we account for the fact
that (for example) the idiom *all hell . . . break loose* is not a unitary
constituent in any of the sentences in (24), since the subject *all hell* and
the predicate *break loose* are separated by the auxiliaries *will/has/could
have*? To put the question another way: how can we account for the fact
that although the choice of subject, verb and complement is fixed, the
choice of auxiliary is not?

    A *movement* analysis for the subjects of auxiliaries provides a
straightforward answer, if we suppose that clausal idioms like those in
(22) are *VP idioms* which require a fixed choice of head, complement
and specifier in the VP containing them. For instance, in the case of

(22a), the relevant VP idiom requires the specific word *break* as its head verb, the specific adjective *loose* as its complement, and the specific quantifier phrase *all hell* as its subject/specifier. We can then account for the fact that *all hell* surfaces in front of the auxiliary *will* in (24a) by positing that the QP *all hell* originates in spec-VP as the subject of the V-bar constituent *break loose*, and is then raised across the auxiliary *will* into spec-IP, where it becomes the subject of the I-bar constituent *will break loose* (by application of **raising**). Given these assumptions, (24a) will have the simplified derivation (26) below:

(26)

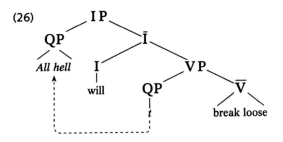

We can then say that (in the relevant idiom) *break loose* must be predicated of *all hell*, and that this condition will be met only if *all hell* originates in spec-VP as the subject of *break loose*. We can account for how the subject *all hell* comes to be separated from its predicate *break loose* by positing that subjects raise from spec-VP to spec-IP across an intervening auxiliary like *will*, so that the subject and predicate thereby come to be separated from each other.

Hitherto, the arguments which we have presented in support of the VP-internal subject hypothesis have been syntactic in nature. However, there is also strong semantic evidence in favour of the hypothesis, relating to **argument structure**. For those of you not familiar with this traditional term from predicate logic, I'll briefly outline some of the relevant concepts.

Traditional work in logic maintains that **propositions** (which can be thought of as the semantic counterpart of simple clauses) comprise a **predicate** and a set of **arguments**. Simplifying somewhat, we can say that a predicate is an expression denoting (for example) an activity or event, and an argument is an expression denoting a participant in the relevant activity or event. For example, in sentences such as the following:

(27) (a) [One of the prisoners] *died*
      (b) [A member of the audience] *yawned*
      (c) [Everybody] *laughed*

(28) (a) [The police] *arrested* [the suspects]
      (b) [John] *replied* [to her letter]
      (c) [The pen] *rolled* [under the bed]

the italicized verbs are predicates, and the bracketed expressions represent their arguments: each of the verbs in (27) has a single argument,
and so is said to function as a **one-place predicate** (in the use illustrated); each of the verbs in (28) has two arguments, and so is said to function as a **two-place** predicate. Using more familiar grammatical
terminology, we can say that the arguments of a verb are its subject and
complement. Since (according to the analysis we have assumed so far)
the complements of verbs are positioned inside V-bar whereas their
subjects are positioned outside V-bar (they originate in spec-VP and
typically raise to spec-IP), complements are said to be **internal arguments** and subjects **external arguments**. Thus, in a sentence such as
(28a) *The police arrested the suspects*, the DP *the suspects* is the complement and hence the internal argument of the predicate *arrested*, and
the DP *the police* is the subject and hence the external argument of
arrested. Using this terminology, we might say that the argument structure of the predicate *arrest* specifies that it is a two-place predicate
which takes a DP as its internal argument and another DP as its
external argument.

     Not all of the expressions which are associated with a verb function
as arguments of the verb; for example, in sentences like those in (29)
below:

(29) (a) [The police] *arrested* [the suspects] **on Saturday**
      (b) [The police] *arrested* [the suspects] **in Beverly Hills**
      (c) [The police] *arrested* [the suspects] **with minimum use of force**

it is clear that the bracketed DPs *the police* and *the suspects* are participants in the act of arrest, and so are arguments of the verb *arrested*.
However, there's no sense in which we can say that the bold-printed
prepositional phrases represent participants in the arrest. On the contrary, they simply serve to provide additional information about the
event; thus, *on Saturday* specifies the day on which the arrest took

place, *in Beverly Hills* specifies the place in which it took place, and *with minimum use of force* specifies the manner in which the arrest was effected (e.g. the suspects were forced to lie face down in the mud and kicked into submission). Expressions such as those bold-printed in (29) are **adjuncts**.

However, simply saying that a verb like *arrest* takes two DP arguments (one as its subject, the other as its complement) fails to account for the fact that the two arguments play very different semantic roles in relation to the act of arrest – i.e. it fails to account for the fact that the policeman is the person who performs the act (and hence gets to verbally and physically abuse the suspect), and that the suspect is the person who suffers the consequences of the act (viz. being handcuffed, thrown into the back of a windowless vehicle and beaten up). Hence, any adequate account of argument structure should provide a proper description of the *semantic role* which each argument plays with respect to its predicate.

In research over the past three decades – beginning with the pioneering work of Gruber (1965), Fillmore (1968) and Jackendoff (1972) – linguists have attempted to devise a universal typology of the semantic roles played by arguments in relation to their predicates. In (30) below are listed some of the terms traditionally used to describe a range of different roles, and for each such role an informal gloss is given, together with an illustrative example (in which the italicized expression has the semantic role specified):

(30)   THEME (or PATIENT) = entity undergoing the effect of some action
       (*Mary* fell over)
       AGENT/CAUSER = Instigator of some action
       (*John* killed Harry)
       EXPERIENCER = entity experiencing some psychological state
       (*John* felt happy)
       RECIPIENT/POSSESSOR = entity receiving/possessing some entity
       (John got *Mary* a present)
       GOAL = entity towards which something moves
       (John went *home*)

We can illustrate how the terminology in (30) might be used to describe the semantic roles fulfilled by arguments in terms of the following examples:

(31) (a) [The FBI] arrested [Larry Luckless]
       [AGENT]   [THEME]
    (b) [The suspect] received [a caution]
        [RECIPIENT]   [THEME]
    (c) [The audience] enjoyed [the play]
      [EXPERIENCER]   [THEME]
    (d) [The president] went [to Boston]
       [THEME]   [GOAL]

Given that – as we see from these examples – the THEME role is a central one, it has become customary over the past two decades to refer to the relevant semantic roles as **thematic roles**; and since the Greek letter θ (= *theta*) corresponds to *th* in English and the word *thematic* begins with *th*, it has also become standard practice to abbreviate the expression **thematic role** to **θ-role** (pronounced *theeta role* by some and *thayta role* by others). Using this terminology, we can say (for example) that in (31a) *the FBI* is the AGENT argument of the predicate *arrested*, and that *Larry Luckless* is the THEME/PATIENT argument of *arrested*.

The thematic role played by a given argument in relation to its predicate determines the range of expressions which can fulfil the relevant argument function, as we see from examples such as (32) below (from Lakoff, 1971, p. 332: ? and ! represent increasing degrees of anomaly):

(32) (a)   *My uncle* realizes that I'm a lousy cook
    (b) ? *My cat* realizes that I'm a lousy cook
    (c) ??*My goldfish* realizes that I'm a lousy cook
    (d) ?! *My pet amoeba* realizes that I'm a lousy cook
    (e) ! *My frying-pan* realizes that I'm a lousy cook

The nature of the relevant restrictions depends on the semantic properties of the predicate on the one hand and on the semantic (= thematic) role played by the argument on the other. As sentences such as (32) illustrate, the EXPERIENCER argument (i.e. subject) of a cognitive predicate like *realize* has to be an expression denoting a *rational* entity (i.e. an entity capable of rational thought – hence e.g. not an expression denoting a politician).

A central theoretical question which arises is how theta-roles are assigned to arguments. It seems clear that in V-bar constituents of the form verb + complement, the thematic role of the complement is determined by the semantic properties of the verb. As examples like (31a–d)

illustrate, the canonical (i.e. typical) θ-role associated with DP complements is that of THEME. However, the question of how subjects are
assigned theta-roles is more complex. Marantz (1984, pp. 23ff.) and
Chomsky (1986a, pp. 59–60) argue that although verbs directly assign
theta-roles to their internal arguments (i.e. complements), it is not the
verb but rather the whole V-bar constituent (i.e. *verb + complement*
string) which determines the theta-role assigned to its external argument (i.e. subject). The evidence they adduce in support of this
conclusion comes from sentences such as:

(33) (a) John threw a ball
      (b) John threw a fit

(34) (a) John broke the window
      (b) John broke his arm

Although the subject of the verb *threw* in both (33a) and (33b), *John*
plays a different thematic role in the two sentences – that of AGENT in
the case of *threw a ball*, but that of EXPERIENCER in *threw a fit*.
Likewise, although the subject of the verb *broke* in both (34a) and (34b),
John plays the role of AGENT in (34a) but that of EXPERIENCER on the
most natural (accidental) interpretation of (34b) (though if he deliberately broke his own arm to get out of taking a syntax exam, *John* would
have the role of AGENT). From examples such as these, Marantz and
Chomsky conclude that the thematic role of the subject is not determined by the verb alone, but rather is compositionally determined by
the whole verb + complement structure – i.e. by V-bar.

   In a nutshell, what is being claimed is that a verb assigns a theta-role
directly to its internal argument (i.e. complement), but only *indirectly*
(= compositionally, i.e. as a compositional function of the semantic
properties of the overall V-bar) to its external argument (= subject). To
use the relevant technical terminology, we might say that verbs **directly
θ-mark** their complements, but **indirectly θ-mark** their subjects.

   A related observation here is that auxiliaries seem to play no part
in determining the assignment of theta-roles to subjects. For example,
in sentences such as:

(35) (a) He *will* throw the ball/a fit
      (b) He *was* throwing the ball/a fit
      (c) He *had been* throwing the ball/a fit
      (d) He *might have been* throwing the ball/a fit

the thematic role of the subject *he* is determined purely by the choice of V-bar constituent (i.e. whether it is *throw the ball* or *throw a fit*), and is not affected in any way by the choice of auxiliary. Clearly, any explanatory theory of **θ-marking** (i.e. θ-role assignment) should offer us a principled account of how thematic roles are assigned, and why some constituents (e.g. auxiliaries) play no part in this process.

One way of resolving the various puzzles surrounding θ-marking would be along the following lines. Since auxiliaries are functional categories and play no role in theta-marking, let us assume that theta-roles are assigned only by **lexical categories** (i.e. contentive categories), not by **functional categories**. More specifically, let's assume that θ-roles are assigned to arguments via the process of **merger with a lexical category**. Given these assumptions, a sentence such as (35a) *He will throw the ball* will be derived as follows.

The verb *throw* will be merged with the DP *the ball* (itself formed by merging *the* with *ball*) to form the V-bar *throw the ball*. As a corollary of this merger operation, the DP *the ball* is assigned the θ-role of THEME argument of *throw*. The V-bar *throw the ball* is in turn merged with the pronominal determiner *he*; as a corollary of the merger operation, the subject *he* is assigned the role of AGENT argument of *throw the ball*. Thus, the relevant VP will have the simplified structure (36) below (where arrows indicate the assignment of thematic roles):

(36)

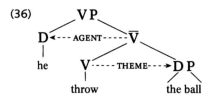

Subsequently, the VP in (36) is merged with an I constituent containing *will*, so forming the I-bar *will throw the ball*. The subject *he* then moves to spec-IP, as in (37) below:

(37)

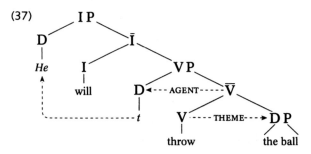

As noted earlier, the type of movement operation arrowed in (37) is traditionally known as **(subject-to-subject) raising**.

An important implication of our discussion here is that thematic considerations lend further support to the **VP-internal subject hypothesis**. The reason is that by positing that subjects originate internally within VP, we can arrive at a unitary and principled account of θ-marking, whereby *arguments are θ-marked by merger with a lexical (θ-assigning) category*, so that (for example) a complement is θ-marked by merger with a head V, and a subject is θ-marked by merger with a V-bar constituent. If subjects were directly generated in spec-IP, there would be no straightforward way of accounting for the fact that the thematic role of the subject is determined solely by V-bar, or for the fact that auxiliaries play no role in the θ-marking of subjects.

One final question which remains to be answered is this: if subjects originate in spec-VP, why do they subsequently raise to spec-IP e.g. in structures such as (37) above? One answer might be: to satisfy Rothstein's (1995) **predication principle**, which requires that syntactic predicates (i.e. constituents such as I-bar) should have subjects. Alternatively, we might look to **checking theory** to provide us with an answer. One checking account would be to suppose that INFL in English has strong specifier-features, and hence requires a subject in spec-IP to check its specifier-features: the subject would come to be in spec-IP as a result of a merger operation in structures like (5) (where the expletive subject *there* is merged with the I-bar *is someone knocking at the door*), but as the result of an (arrowed) movement operation in structures such as (7). One snag with this account is that if PRO remains in spec-VP in control structures such as (10) above, the account cannot be generalized to the kind of INFL constituent found in control structures. Another checking account would be to suppose that subjects carry a strong nominative case-feature which can only be checked if the subject raises to spec-IP (e.g. *they/he* in (20) and (37) above carry a strong nominative-case head-feature which is checked by raising the pronoun to spec-IP): if PRO does not raise to spec-IP, we might assume that null case is a weak case (hence not checked by movement of PRO to spec-IP); similarly, since the thematic subject *someone* in expletive structures like *There is someone knocking at the door* does not raise to spec-IP, we would have to assume that it too carries a weak case-feature (perhaps what Belletti 1988 calls partitive case). Numerous questions of detail and potential problems arise, but we shall not attempt to delve into these here. (For a technical discussion of expletive structures, see Authier 1991, Lasnik 1992, 1995, Chomsky 1995, Groat 1995, Rothstein 1995 and Vikner 1995.)

To summarize: we began this chapter by presenting a number of arguments (from facts relating e.g. to the syntax of expletive structures, *PRO*, floating quantifiers, idioms, etc.) that subjects originate in the specifier position within VP. (For additional supporting arguments from a variety of languages, see Kitagawa 1986, Speas 1986, Contreras 1987, Zagona 1987, Kuroda 1988, Sportiche 1988, Rosen 1990, Ernst 1991, Koopman and Sportiche 1991, Woolford 1991, Burton and Grimshaw 1992, Guilfoyle, Hung and Travis 1992, McNally 1992 and Huang 1993.) We noted that such an analysis would enable us to develop a principled theory of θ-**marking**, in which arguments are assigned a **θ-role** by merger with a lexical category: hence, the complement of a verb is θ-marked directly by the verb, and its subject is θ-marked by V-bar. We asked why subjects should raise from spec-VP to spec-IP, and briefly explored three possible answers. One is that (in consequence of Rothstein's **predication principle**) syntactic predicates like I-bar are required to have subjects: another is to suppose that INFL has strong specifier-features (except in control infinitives) and hence requires spec-IP to be filled; a third is to posit that subjects (other than PRO) carry strong case-features, and must raise to spec-IP to check these features.

Exercises

Exercise XIII

Discuss the derivation of the following sentences, paying particular attention to the syntax of subjects.

1a Both the men were watching him
 b The men were both watching him
2a They were both watching him
 b *Both they were watching him
3a Both of you were watching him
 b *You were both of watching him
4a There was someone watching him
 b Was there anyone watching him?
5a Someone was watching him

b Was anyone watching him?

6a The cat has got his tongue

b Has the cat got his tongue?

7a She said he had hurt himself

b *She said he had hurt herself

8a He may have helped her

b *He may've helped her

9a Who knows the answer?

b Who do you think knows the answer?

10a They wanna clinch the deal

b *Who do they wanna clinch the deal?

Helpful hints

Make the following set of assumptions about sentences 1, 2 and 3. Quantifiers like *all* or *both* have two different uses. They can function as the specifier of a DP headed by a determiner like *the* (though not of a personal pronoun like *them* because personal pronouns are normally unprojectable and so allow neither specifier nor complement). Quantifiers like *all/both* can also function as heads taking a complement, but are intransitive and so cannot directly check the case of their complement: this means that the complement must either be introduced by a *dummy* transitive preposition like *of*, or must move to a position where it can check its case. In relation to 4 and 5, note that words like *anyone* as used in such sentences are generally restricted to occurring in certain types of (e.g. interrogative or negative) clause – hence the ungrammaticality of *There was anyone watching him*. Expressions like *anyone* seem to have an inherent negative/interrogative polarity, and hence are referred to as *polarity items*. The traditional way of characterizing the restriction on polarity items is by saying that they must occur in a position where they are c-commanded by an appropriate (e.g. interrogative or negative) constituent. (Recall that in chapter 3 we gave the following informal characterization of **c-command** in terms of train networks: a node X c-commands another node Y if you can get from X to Y by taking a northbound train, getting off at the first stop, and then catching a southbound train on a different line.)

Model answer for 1

In the light of the suggestions in the *helpful hints*, we might assume that in 1a *both the men* is a DP in which *both* is the specifier of the D-bar *the men*, as in (i) below:

(i)
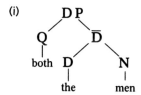

Given the VP-internal subject hypothesis, the DP *both the men* will originate in spec-VP as the subject of *watching*, and will then raise into spec-IP to become the subject of *were*, as in (ii) below:

(ii)
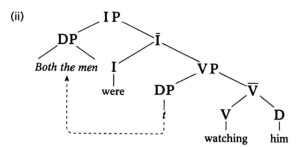

The DP *both the men* originates in spec-VP, where it receives its AGENT θ-role by merger with the V-bar *watching him*: it raises to spec-IP for reasons of **greed**, to check the strong nominative-case head-feature which it carries.

At first sight, it might seem plausible to derive 1b in essentially the same way, and to argue that *both the men* has the structure (i) and originates in spec-VP, with *the men* being preposed on its own, leaving the quantifier *both* stranded in spec-VP, as in (iii) below:

(iii)
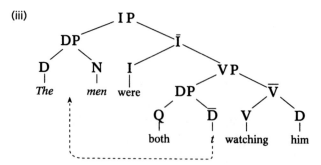

However, any such movement as that arrowed in (iii) would violate the **chain uniformity principle**, since the constituent at the head of the chain would be a maximal projection (viz. the DP *the men*), whereas the trace at the foot of the chain would be nonmaximal (since it is a D-bar which is nonmaximal because it projects into a larger DP containing *both*).

An alternative possibility is to suppose that in 1b, the phrase *both the men* which originates as the subject of *watching* has the structure (iv) below:

(iv)

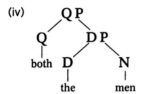

If we assume that *both* is intransitive, it follows that the DP *the men* occupies a caseless position in (iv), and so must move to a case position in order to check its case. It therefore moves into spec-IP (which is a nominative position), as in (v) below:

(v)

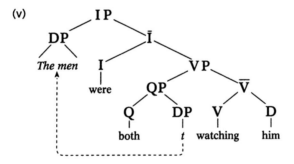

In this position, the DP *the men* can check its case and agreement properties against the specifier properties of *were* (which requires a plural or second person nominative subject). The resulting chain *the men . . . t* is uniform, since both the DP *the men* at the head of the chain and its trace *t* at the foot are maximal (DP) projections. Movement of the DP *the men* is motivated by **greed** – i.e. the need to move *the men* into a position where it can check its nominative case.

Exercise XIV
Discuss the derivation of the following Early Modern English (= EME) sentences (taken from various plays by Shakespeare):

1 Thee will I love   (Antipholus, *Comedy of Errors*, III.iv)

2 Welcome shall they be   (Duke, *All's Well That Ends Well*, III.i)

3 They'll none have her

          (= 'None of them will have her', Lafeu, *All's Well That Ends Well*, II.iii)

4 Answer made it none   (= 'It gave no answer', Horatio, *Hamlet*, I.ii)

5 Buy thou a rope!   (Antipholus, *Comedy of Errors*, IV.i)

6 Came you from the church?   (Tranio, *Taming of the Shrew*, III.ii)

7 What hast thou done?   (Oberon, *Midsummer Night's Dream*, II.ii)

8 What said she?   (Proteus, *Two Gentlemen of Verona*, I.i)

9 Who comes with him?   (Baptista, *Taming of the Shrew*, III.ii)

10 What visions have I seen!   (Titania, *Midsummer Night's Dream*, V.i)

Helpful hints

Sentence 1 illustrates a phenomenon sometimes called **topicalization**, whereby a constituent (in this case, *thee*) is made into the *topic* of the sentence by being moved to a more prominent position at the front of the sentence: assume that the topicalized constituent is moved into spec-CP. Example 5 illustrates a type of sentence traditionally called an **imperative** (used to issue a command): assume that the verb moves to C in EME imperatives. Example 10 illustrates a type of sentence called an **exclamative** (because it is used to exclaim surprise/delight): assume that exclamative clauses have a similar syntax to interrogative clauses in EME. If (as seems likely) interrogative clauses, topic clauses, imperative clauses and exclamative clauses are generally CPs in EME, we might suggest that *all* clauses are CPs in EME. What consequences would this have for sentences like 9, and for simple declarative sentences such as the following?

11 My master is grown quarrelsome   (Grumio, *Taming of the Shrew*, I.ii)

Model answer for 1

We might suppose that 1 is derived as follows. The verb *love* merges with its complement *thee* (thereby checking the objective case of *thee* and assigning *thee* the θ-role of THEME) to form the V-bar *love thee*; this in turn merges with (and assigns the θ-role EXPERIENCER to) the pronoun *I*, so forming the VP (i) below:

(i)

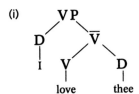

The VP in (i) then merges with the INFL constituent *will*, forming an I-bar; the subject *I* raises from spec-VP to spec-IP to check its strong nominative case (or perhaps to satisfy the strong specifier-features of INFL, or to satisfy the requirement that a syntactic predicate have a subject), so forming the IP (ii) below:

(ii)

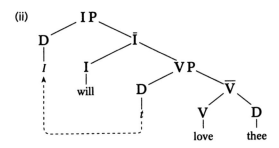

If we assume (as in the *helpful hints*) that topic clauses (and indeed perhaps all clauses) are CPs in EME, the IP in (ii) will then merge with a COMP node into which the auxiliary *will* moves, and the topicalized constituent *thee* will move into spec-CP as in (iii) below:

(iii)

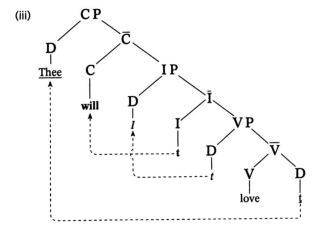

It may be that topic clauses in EME are CPs headed by a strong C (perhaps containing an abstract topic affix) which has a [Top] specifier-feature (indicating that it requires a topic constituent as its specifier). The requirement for the strong (affixal) COMP to be filled is satisfied by moving the auxiliary *will* from I to C. Since the pronoun *thee* is topicalized, we might assume that it also carries a [Top] head-feature; movement of *thee* to spec-CP will check (and erase) the [Top] specifier-feature of C.

❽ A movement

In the previous chapter, we looked at the syntax of *subjects*, arguing that these originate in a θ-marked specifier position within VP, and typically move into a case-marked specifier position within IP by application of **raising**. In this chapter, we turn to look at further instances of raising, and at an additional type of movement operation traditionally termed **passivization**. We go on to argue that raising and passivization are two different variants of the same **A movement** (= argument movement) operation, and we look at the syntax of A movement.

To get our discussion onto a concrete footing, consider the alternations illustrated below:

(1) (a) It **seems** [that *he* understands her]
    (b) *He* **seems** [to understand her]

(2) (a) It would **appear** [that *they* are lying]
    (b) *They* would **appear** [to be lying]

(3) (a) It **happened** [that *she* came across an old love-letter]
    (b) *She* **happened** [to come across an old love-letter]

(4) (a) It **turned out** [that *Mary* was right]
    (b) *Mary* **turned out** [to be right]

The bold-printed verbs in these examples have a *that*-clause complement in the (a) examples, and an infinitive complement in the (b) examples. But what is puzzling about sentences like (1–4) is that the italicized expression which functions as the subject of the bracketed complement clause in the (a) examples surfaces as the subject of the matrix clause (i.e. the clause containing the complement clause) in the (b) examples: for example, *he* is the subject of *understands* in (1a), but the subject of *seems* in (1b). Moreover, the bracketed infinitive complements in the (b) examples appear to have no subject.

So, sentences like (1–4) raise two related questions: 'How does the complement-clause subject in the (a) examples come to be the matrix-clause subject in the (b) examples, and how does the complement clause in the (b) examples end up seemingly subjectless?' A unitary answer to both questions is to suppose that the italicized nominal originates as the subject of the complement clause and is then raised up to become the matrix clause subject by application of (**subject-to-subject**) **raising**, leaving behind an empty category trace as the subject of the complement clause. In other words, *he* in a sentence like (1b) originates as the subject of *understands*, but is subsequently raised up to become the subject of *seems*. If this is so, an obvious question to ask is *how* the subject comes to be raised.

In this connection, consider the following set of sentences:

(5) (a)   The men do *all* seem to understand the situation
     (b) ? The men do seem *all* to understand the situation
     (c) ?? The men do seem to *all* understand the situation

Given that floating quantifiers modify the traces of moved subjects, the fact that the quantifier phrase headed by *all* in (5a–c) can serve as the subject of *understand the situation*, or *to understand the situation*, or *seem to understand the situation* suggests that the subject DP *the men* is raised in a successive cyclic fashion. In other words, in a sentence such as:

(6) The *men* do seem to understand the situation

the italicized DP *the men* originates as the subject of *understand*, then becomes the subject of *to*, then becomes the subject of *seem*, and finally becomes the subject of *do*. In case that was too fast for you, let's look at a slow-motion replay of what's going on here.

The verb *understand* merges with its DP complement *the situation* to form the V-bar *understand the situation*; this in turn merges with the DP *the men* to form the VP (7) below:

(7)

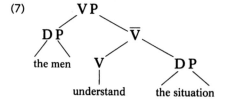

The VP (7) then merges with the infinitive particle *to* to form an I-bar; the DP *the men* is then raised to become the subject of this I-bar, as in (8) below:

(8)

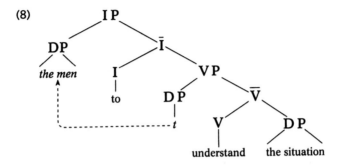

The resulting IP (8) in turn merges with the verb *seem* to form a V-bar; the DP *the men* raises to become the subject of this V-bar, as in (9) below:

(9)

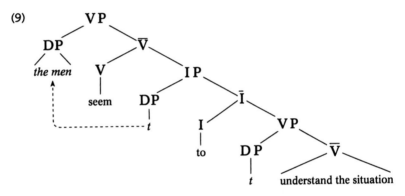

The VP thereby formed then merges with the auxiliary *do* to form an I-bar; the DP *the men* then raises to become the subject of this I-bar, as in (10) below:

(10)

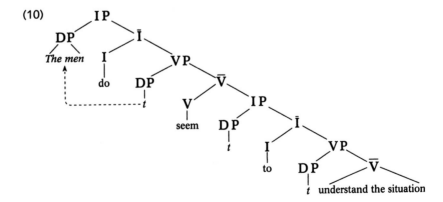

– and (10) is the structure associated with (6) *The men do seem to under-stand the situation*. What (10) claims is that the DP *the men* originates as the subject of *understand the situation*, then raises in a successive cyclic fashion to become first subject of *to understand the situation*, then sub-ject of *seem to understand the situation*, and finally subject of *do seem to understand the situation*. In each case, the movement operation which applies is (**subject-to-subject**) **raising**; assuming that each separate appli-cation of **raising** leaves behind a separate trace, there will be three (itali-cized) traces of the moved subject *the men* in (10) – one serving as the subject of *understand the situation*, another as the subject of *to under-stand the situation*, and the other as the subject of *seem to understand the situation*. If we further assume (as in the previous chapter) that floating quantifiers modify traces of moved subjects, we can account for sentences like those in (5) by supposing (in relation to (10) above) that *all* modifies the rightmost trace of *the men* in (5c) *The men do seem to **all** understand the situation*, the middle trace in (5b) *The men do seem **all** to understand the situation*, and the leftmost trace in (5a) *The men do **all** seem to under-stand the situation*. (What remains to be accounted for is why (5a) is bet-ter than (5b), and (5b) better than (5c); perhaps floating quantifiers become more awkward the further away they are from the expression they quantify; perhaps they are only fully grammatical as the specifier of the complement of a finite INFL; and perhaps the awkwardness of (5c) is in part attributable to violation of the traditional prohibition against *split infinitive* structures in which *to* is separated from its dependent verb – however, we shall not pursue these possibilities any further here.)

The conclusion which our discussion leads us to is that **raising verbs** like *seem* take an infinitive complement with a trace subject (since the subject of *seem* serves as the subject of the infinitive complement prior to being raised up to become the subject of *seem*). In this respect, **raising verbs** like *seem* clearly have a very different syntax from **control verbs** like *try* which take an infinitive complement with a *PRO* subject, as in (11) below:

(11)   *She* will try [to **PRO** help him]

where *PRO* has a controller (= *she*) in the *will try* clause. An important question to ask, therefore, is how we can tell whether a given verb which selects an apparently subjectless infinitive complement is a raising pred-icate or a control predicate, and how we can explain the differences between the two classes of predicate.

One difference between the two is that raising verbs like *seem* allow
a *dummy* subject like expletive *there*, whereas control verbs like *try* do
not: cf.

(12) (a) *There* **seemed/*tried** to be someone living there
      (b) *There* **seemed/*tried** to be no milk left in the fridge
      (c) *There* **seemed/*tried** to be little hope of finding them alive

The derivation of the *seem*-sentences in (12) seems straightforward:
there originates as the subject of *be*, and is then raised in a successive
cyclic fashion to become first the subject of *to*, then the subject *seem*,
and finally the subject of the abstract INFL constituent preceding *seem*.
More puzzling is the question of why a control verb like *try* doesn't
allow expletive *there* as its subject – e.g. why we can't have a structure
such as (13) below in which *there* is the controller of *PRO*:

(13) *There* tried to **PRO** be a strike

One reason is that *PRO* is a referential pronoun which takes its reference from its controller; hence, the controller of *PRO* must be a referential expression. But since expletive *there* is a nonreferential pronoun (as
we see from the fact that we can't question its reference – cf. *Where is*
someone living there?), it cannot serve as the controller of *PRO*, and
hence cannot serve as the subject of a control predicate like *try* which
selects an infinitive complement with a *PRO* subject. From this, it
follows that the subject of a control predicate like *try* must always be
a referential expression.

A second reason why structures like (13) are ill formed relates to
thematic considerations. It is a thematic property of the verb *try* that it
assigns the θ-role AGENT to its subject: hence, it requires as its subject
an expression denoting a rational being. Since *there* is a nonreferential
dummy pronoun, the requirement for *try* to have an AGENT subject is
clearly not met in sentences like (12/13) where *try* has expletive *there* as
its subject. Conversely, the fact that *seem* allows expletive *there* as its
subject in sentences like (12) suggests that it does not θ-mark its subject
(e.g. it does not require an AGENT or EXPERIENCER subject), and hence
allows a nonreferential subject like expletive *there*.

Our assumption that *try* θ-marks its subject whereas *seem* does not
accounts for a further difference between the two. By virtue of requiring
an agent subject, the verb *try* can only have as its subject an expression
denoting a a entity capable of rational thought, as we see from

examples such as the following (where ? and ! indicate increasing degrees of anomaly):

(14) (a)   *John* tried to understand the problem
      (b) ? *My goldfish* tried to escape
      (c) ?? *My pet amoeba* is trying to reproduce
      (d) ?! *Your kettle* is trying to boil over
      (e)   ! *Your theory* is trying to be foolproof

By contrast, the verb *seem* (by virtue of the fact that it doesn't θ-mark its subject) imposes no such restrictions on its choice of subject, as we can see by comparing (14) above with (15) below:

(15) (a) *John* seemed to understand the problem
      (b) *My goldfish* seems to have escaped
      (c) *My pet amoeba* seems to be reproducing
      (d) *Your kettle* seems to be boiling over
      (e) *Your theory* seems to be foolproof

We noted in the previous chapter that verbs which θ-mark their subjects impose restrictions on their choice of subject: hence, the fact that *try* constrains its choice of subject in (14) whereas *seem* imposes no restrictions on its choice of subject in (15) suggests that *try* θ-marks its subject whereas *seem* does not.

What our discussion here suggests is that the essential difference between control and raising predicates is that control predicates (like *try*) θ-mark their subjects, whereas raising predicates (like *seem*) do not. This core thematic difference between the two can be argued to determine why *seem* can function as a raising predicate but not as a control predicate, and conversely why *try* can function as a control predicate but not as a raising predicate. A crucial premise of the argumentation is that the way in which θ-roles are assigned to arguments is constrained by the following UG principle (called the **θ-criterion** because it is a criterion which a structure must meet in order to be well formed):

(16) θ-CRITERION
      Each argument bears one and only one θ-role, and each θ-role is
      assigned to one and only one argument.   (Chomsky 1981, p. 36)

We can illustrate how this constraint works in terms of contrasts such as the following:

(17)   (a) Percy Peabrain admires himself
     (b)*Percy Peabrain admires

In (17a), *Percy Peabrain* is the EXPERIENCER argument of *admire*, and *himself* the THEME argument; thus, each separate θ-role is associated with a separate argument expression (and conversely), so the θ-criterion is satisfied. But what goes wrong in (17b)? One possibility is that *Percy Peabrain* is assigned the role of EXPERIENCER argument of *admire*, but that the THEME role associated with *admire* is unassigned: however, this would violate the θ-criterion requirement that each θ-role associated with a predicate must be assigned to some argument. An alternative possibility is that both the EXPERIENCER and THEME roles of *admire* are assigned to *Percy Peabrain*, thereby wrongly predicting that (17b) can have the same interpretation as (17a): however, this is ruled out by the θ-criterion requirement that each argument can carry only a single θ-role.

Consider now the role of the θ-criterion in determining that verbs (like *try*) which θ-mark their subjects can serve as control (but not raising) predicates, whereas conversely verbs (like *seem*) which don't θ-mark their subjects can serve as raising (but not control) predicates. More concretely, consider how we derive sentence pairs such as the following:

(18)   (a) He does seem to enjoy syntax
     (b) He does try to enjoy syntax

If *seem* is a raising predicate, *he* will originate as the subject of *enjoy syntax* in (18a) and be assigned an appropriate θ-role (that of EXPERIENCER argument of *enjoy*). Subsequently, *he* will be raised up (in successive cyclic fashion) to become first the subject of *to enjoy syntax*, then the subject of *seem to enjoy syntax*, and finally the subject of *does seem to enjoy syntax* – as represented in simplified form in (19) below:

(19)   [IP *He* does [VP *t* seem [IP *t* to [VP *t* enjoy syntax]]]]

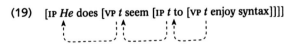

Give the assumption that auxiliaries, infinitival *to* and raising predicates like *seem* do not θ-mark their subjects, the only θ-role assigned to the pronoun *he* will be that of EXPERIENCER argument of *enjoy* (thereby satisfying the θ-criterion requirement that 'Each argument bears one and only one θ-role'). We might assume that *he* has to raise to become the subject of *does* for reasons of **greed** (i.e. to check its nominative case), and that it has to raise in a successive cyclic fashion in order to satisfy the **shortest movement principle**.

But now consider what would happen if we tried to use *seem* as a control predicate. The pronoun *he* would originate as the subject of *seem* (raising to become subject of *does*), and would serve as the controller of the *PRO* subject of *enjoy syntax*, as in (20) below:

(20)   [IP *He* does [VP *t* seem [IP to [VP *PRO* enjoy syntax]]]]

The complement clause subject PRO would be assigned the θ-role of EXPERIENCER argument of *enjoy syntax*. However, the pronoun *he* would be assigned no θ-role at all, since it originates as the subject of the raising verb *seem* and then raises to become the subject of *does* (and neither raising verbs nor auxiliaries θ-mark their subjects). Thus, a derivation such as (20) would violate the **θ-criterion** requirement that 'Each argument bears one and only one θ-role,' and hence crash at LF.

Consider now the syntax of (18b) *He does try to enjoy syntax*. If we suppose that *try* is a *control* predicate, the pronoun *he* will originate as the subject of *try* (subsequently raising to become subject of *does*) and will control the *PRO* subject of *enjoy syntax*, as in (21) below:

(21)   [IP *He* does [VP *t* try [IP to [VP *PRO* enjoy syntax]]]]

The null pronoun PRO will be assigned the θ-role of EXPERIENCER argument of *enjoy*, and the nominative pronoun *he* will be assigned the θ-role of AGENT argument of *try* (by virtue of originating as the subject of *try*). Since PRO and *he* are each assigned a θ-role of their own, the **θ-criterion** is satisfied. However, the picture is very different if we use *try* as a raising predicate, with *he* originating as the subject of *enjoy syntax* and then being raised up successive-cyclically to become subject of *to enjoy syntax*, *try to enjoy syntax* and *does try to enjoy syntax*, as in (22) below:

(22)   [IP *He* does [VP *t* try [IP *t* to [VP *t* enjoy syntax]]]]

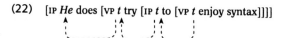

The problem here is that *he* ends up with two different θ-roles, viz. as EXPERIENCER argument of *enjoy* (at the stage of derivation where it is subject of *enjoy syntax*) and AGENT argument of *try* (at the point where it becomes subject of *try to enjoy syntax*). This leads to obvious violation of the **θ-criterion** requirement that 'Each argument bears one and only one θ-role.'

Having looked briefly at the syntax of *raising* predicates (and how they differ from *control* predicates), we now turn to look at the syntax of **passive predicates**. Traditional grammarians maintain that the bold-printed verbs in sentences such as the (a) examples below are in the **active voice**, whereas the italicized verbs in the corresponding (b) sentences are in the **passive voice**;

(23) (a) Hundreds of passers-by **saw** the attack
      (b) The attack was *seen* by hundreds of passers-by

(24) (a) Lex Luthor **stole** the cryptonite
      (b) The cryptonite was *stolen* by Lex Luthor

(25) (a) They **took** everything
      (b) Everything was *taken*

There are four main properties which differentiate passive sentences from their active counterparts – as the examples in (23–5) illustrate. One is that passive (though not active) sentences generally require the auxiliary *be*. Another is that the lexical verb in passive sentences is in the *n*-participle form (cf. *seen/stolen/taken*), known in this use as the *passive participle* form. A third is that passive sentences may (though need not) contain a *by*-phrase in which the complement of *by* seems to play essentially the same thematic role as the subject in the corresponding active sentence: for example, *hundreds of passers-by* in the active structure (23a) serves as the subject of *saw the attack*, whereas in the passive structure (23b) it serves as the complement of the preposition *by* (though in both cases seems to have the role of EXPERIENCER). The fourth difference is that the expression which serves as the *complement* of an active verb surfaces as the *subject* in the corresponding passive construction: for example, *the attack* is the complement of *saw* in the active structure (23a), but is the subject of *was seen by hundreds of passers-by* in the passive structure (23b). Here, we focus on the syntax of the superficial subjects of passive sentences (setting aside the derivation of *by*-phrases).

Evidence that passive subjects do indeed play the same thematic role as active complements comes from the fact that the two are subject to the same restrictions on the choice of expression which can fulfil the relevant argument function, as we see from sentences such as the following (where ?, ?! and ! mark increasing degrees of pragmatic anomaly):

(26) (a) *The students/?the camels/?!The flowers//!The ideas* were arrested
      (b) They arrested *the students/?the camels/?!the flowers//!the ideas*

How can we account for this fact? If we assume that principles of UG correlate thematic structure with syntactic structure in a *uniform* fashion, then it follows that two arguments which fulfil the same thematic function with respect to a given type of predicate must occupy the same underlying position in the syntax. The assumption that there is a uniform mapping between thematic structure and syntactic structure is embodied in the **uniform theta assignment hypothesis/UTAH** argued for at length in Baker 1988. If we adopt UTAH, it follows that passive subjects must originate in the same position as active complements. Since the passive subject *the students* in (26a) *The students were arrested* bears that THEME/PATIENT role which is normally assigned to the complement of *arrest* (so that the students are the ones taken away for questioning), a natural suggestion to make is that *the students* originates as the complement of the verb *arrested*. But if this is so, how does *the students* come to be subject of the auxiliary *were*?

The answer we shall suggest here is that the DP *the students* is raised in a successive cyclic fashion to become first the subject of the passive participle *arrested* and then the subject of the auxiliary *were* – as in (27) below:

(27)

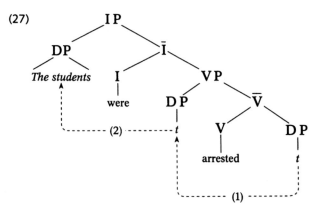

Thus, *the students* originates as the complement of *arrested*, then undergoes **passivization** (i.e. movement from being complement of the passive participle *arrested* to becoming its subject), and finally undergoes

raising (i.e. movement from being subject of *arrested* to becoming
subject of *were*).

Some evidence in support of the assumption that *the students*
becomes the subject of the passive participle *arrested* before becoming
subject of the auxiliary *were* comes from facts relating to floating quantifiers in sentences such as:

(28)   The students were *all* arrested

If we assume (as in the previous chapter) that a floating quantifier modifies the trace of a moved subject, we can say that the quantifier *all* in
(28) modifies the trace in spec-VP of the moved DP *the students* in (27).

Additional evidence in support of the claim that passivized arguments first become the subject of the passive participle before moving
on to become the subject of the passive auxiliary comes from expletive
structures such as:

(29)   There were *several students* arrested

The quantifier phrase *several students* in (29) originates as the complement of the verb *arrested*. But where does it end up? Since it is positioned immediately in front of the passive participle *arrested*, it seems
likely that it moves into (and remains in) spec-VP, and hence serves as
the subject of *arrested*; this would mean that (29) has the (simplified)
derivation (30) below:

(30)

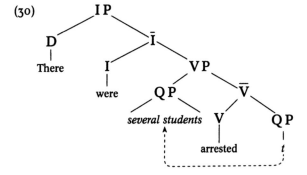

We might suppose that the person/number features of *several students*
are attracted to *were*, so that *were* agrees with *several students*.

Thus far, the simple instances of passivization which we have
looked at have involved movement from complement to subject position. However, in passive structures such as (31) below:

(31) (a) *He* is thought [to admire her]
    (b) *Several prisoners* are believed [to have escaped]
    (c) *They* were alleged [to have lied under oath]
    (d) *He* is rumoured [to be writing a new syntax book]
    (e) *Rock around the Clock* is considered [to be a classic]

passivization seems to have the effect of raising the italicized expression out of subject position in the bracketed complement clause into subject position within the main clause. In other words, passivization in structures such as (31) appears to involve movement from one subject position to another. What lends empirical support to the claim that structures like (31) involve passivization of the subject of an infinitive complement is the fact that subject expressions which are part of VP idioms can be passivized in such structures – as we see from the grammaticality of examples such as (32) below:

(32) (a) *The jig* is thought to *be up*
    (b) *All hell* is believed to have *broken loose*
    (c) *The chips* were said to *be down*
    (d) *The fur* was alleged to be *flying*

Let's try and work out what's going on here, by looking at how (31a) *He is thought to admire her* is derived.

    The passivized pronoun *he* originates as the subject of *admire her*. Some empirical evidence in support of this claim comes from the fact that the restrictions imposed on the choice of subject in (31a) above mirror those found in a simple sentence such as *He admires her*, as we see from (33) below:

(33) (a) *He/?His goldfish/?!His piano/!His theory* is thought to admire her
    (b) *He/?His goldfish/?!His piano/!His theory* admires her

Thus, it seems reasonable to suppose that the pronoun *he* in (33a) will originate as the subject of *admire her* and will then be raised up (in a successive cyclic fashion) to become first the subject of *to admire her*, then the subject of *thought to admire her*, and finally the subject of *is thought to admire her*. This being so, (33a) will be derived in the manner indicated in (34) below:

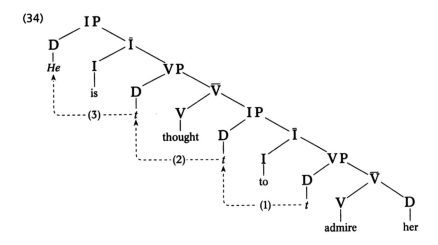

Step (1) in the derivation involves raising *he* to become the subject of the IP headed by infinitival *to*; step (2) involves passivizing *he*, i.e. moving it into a position where it becomes the subject of the VP headed by the passive participle *thought*; step (3) involves raising *he* to become the subject of the IP headed by the auxiliary *is*.

Although in describing the travels of the subject in (34), we used the terms **raising** and **passivization** as if they denoted different processes, closer reflection suggests that there is no meaningful distinction between the two. In relation to our earlier discussion of structures such as (27) above, we implicitly thought of raising as movement from one subject position to another, and passivization as movement from complement to subject position. But the fact that passivization in structures such as (34) involves subject-to-subject movement undermines this distinction. In reality, passivization and raising are different manifestations of a single argument-movement operation (conventionally termed **A movement**) which has the effect of moving a constituent from one argument position into another (more specifically, from a subject or complement position into a subject position). Extending this terminology in a conventional way, we might say that operations which move maximal projections into a nonsubject position are instances of **Ā movement** (where the bar here is a negation operator, so that A-bar movement is movement to a nonsubject position): so, for example, **operator movement** is one type of A-bar movement operation, since it moves wh-operators into spec-CP (and spec-CP is not a subject position).

Since the ultimate goal of any theory is to *explain* the phenomena which fall within its domain, an important question for us to ask is *why* arguments should undergo A movement in the way that they do (e.g. why *he* should move from being the subject of *admire* to becoming the subject of *is* in (34) above). The most principled answer which we can give to this question is that the syntax of A movement is entirely determined by principles of UG. Let's look at some of the principles which are involved.

Consider first the question of why A movement should involve movement from a *lower* to a *higher* position in structures such as (8–10), (27), (30) and (34). This follows from principles of **trace theory** which require that a moved constituent leaves behind a trace which must be bound by its antecedent, and from the **c-command condition on binding** (outlined in chapter 3) which requires a bound constituent to be c-commanded by its binder (i.e. its antecedent). This latter condition is satisfied e.g. in (34) by virtue of the fact that the trace subject of *admire* is c-commanded and bound by the trace subject of *to*, which in turn is c-commanded/bound by the trace subject of *thought*, which in turn is c-commanded/bound by the *he* subject of *is*.

Now let's look at the question of why A movement should involve movement to a higher *specifier* position, never to a higher complement position (e.g. the DP *the students* in (27) moves first to become subject and specifier of *arrested* and then to become subject/specifier of *were*). The answer is that within the theory assumed here, a complement position can only be created by *merger* with a head (not by *movement*), whereas a specifier position can be created either by *merger* or by *movement*.

A third aspect of the syntax of A movement which we need to explain is why it should apply in a successive cyclic fashion: e.g. why should *he* in (34) first become subject of *to admire her* and then subject of *thought to admire her* before finally becoming subject of *is thought to admire her*? Again, the answer comes from principles of UG: for example, the **shortest movement principle** requires that each application of A movement should move the relevant constituent into the *next-highest subject position* in its containing structure. Alternatively, it may be that

Rothstein's (1995) **predication principle** (requiring syntactic predicates
to have a subject) will ensure successive cyclicity, if we assume that
V-bar and I-bar are syntactic predicates (and hence require a subject at
some stage of derivation).

   A further principle which constrains the operation of A movement is
the **θ-criterion** (16). This plays an important role not only in the syntax
of raising (as we saw earlier), but also in the syntax of passivization. In
this connection, consider how we account for why the complement of a
passive verb can be passivized, but not the complement of an active verb
– e.g. why *the jewels* can become the subject of the passive sentence
(35a) below, but not the subject of its active counterpart (35b):

(35) (a) *The jewels* were stolen
      (b)* *The jewels* stole (intended as synonymous with (35a))

The derivation of (35b) on its intended interpretation would be as follows. The DP *the jewels* originates as the complement of the verb *stole*,
and is then raised in successive cyclic fashion to become first the subject
of *stole*, and then the subject of the abstract INFL constituent heading
IP, as in (36) below:

(36)

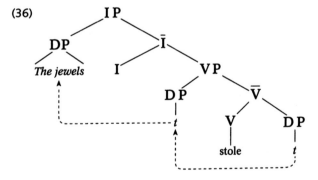

Why is the resulting sentence (35b) ungrammatical on the intended
interpretation (35a)? The answer should be obvious enough. The verb
steal is a two-place predicate which (in active uses) requires an AGENT
subject and a THEME complement. By virtue of originating as the complement of *stole*, the DP *the jewels* is assigned the θ-role of THEME argument of *stole*; but by virtue of moving into spec-VP and becoming the
subject of *stole*, *the jewels* is also assigned the θ-role of AGENT argument
of *stole*. However, since the θ-criterion specifies that no argument can
carry more than one θ-role, the resulting derivation is correctly ruled

out as ungrammatical. In other words, the θ-criterion correctly predicts that active verbs don't allow passivization.

But now consider the derivation of the corresponding passive sentence (35a) *The jewels were stolen*. If we assume that the DP *the jewels* originates as the THEME complement of *stolen* and is then raised up successive-cyclically to become first the subject of the passive participle *stolen* and then the subject of the auxiliary *were*, (35a) will have the derivation (37) below:

(37)

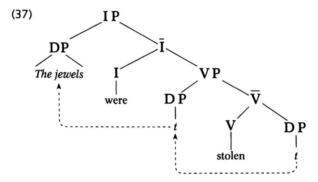

At first sight, it might seem as if the derivation (37) violates the θ-criterion, by virtue of the fact that the DP *the jewels* goes from being THEME complement of *stolen* to becoming AGENT subject of *stolen* (before eventually becoming subject of *were*). However, let us suppose (following Chomsky 1981, pp. 124–7) that passive participles θ-mark their complements but not their subjects: to use a traditional metaphor, we might say that the passive participle suffix +*n* **absorbs** the subject θ-role, thereby **dethematizing** the passive subject position (i.e. removing the ability of the passive participle to θ-mark its subject). If passive participles don't θ-mark their subjects, it follows that the θ-criterion will not prevent the DP *the jewels* from moving through spec-VP into spec-IP as in (37) above: the only θ-role which *the jewels* receives is that of THEME argument of *stolen*. (For a discussion of the thematic properties of passive verbs, see Roberts 1986, and Baker, Johnson and Roberts 1989.)

Thus, we see that passivization is made possible by the fact that passive participles do not θ-mark their subjects. However, an important question for us to ask is why it isn't just possible but rather *necessary* for a passivized argument to move. One answer is provided by the principle of **greed** – i.e. by the need for constituents to selfishly satisfy their own morphological requirements. We might suppose that (pro)nominal arguments have intrinsic case properties (e.g. *he* is nominative and *him* objective) which have to be *checked* in the course of a derivation (and this will only be possible if e.g. a nominative pronoun occupies a nominative position at some stage in the course of a derivation). Let us make the traditional assumption that passive participles are inherently *intransitive*; if this is so, then we can provide a straightforward account of why transitive verbs allow objective complements when used actively, but not passively – cf. contrasts such as:

(38)   (a) They saw *him*
       (b)* It was seen *him*

The objective case carried by *him* can be checked when *him* is used as the complement of the active verb *saw* (since this is transitive), but not when used as the complement of the passive participle *seen* (since passive participles are intransitive). To use our earlier **absorption** metaphor, we might say that the passive participle +*n* inflection on *seen* absorbs the ability of a transitive verb like *see* to check objective case, and thereby **detransitivizes** the verb. Since the case-features carried by *him* cannot be checked in (38b), the resulting derivation crashes, so that such *impersonal passive* structures are ungrammatical in English.

But now suppose that in place of the objective pronoun *him*, we use the nominative pronoun *he*. We cannot use *he* as the complement of a passive participle like *seen*, as we see from the fact that impersonal passives such as (39) below are ungrammatical:

(39)   *It was seen *he*

The reason why (39) is ungrammatical is that a nominative pronoun cannot check its case if used as the complement of a passive participle like *seen*. But now suppose that *he* undergoes passivization, becoming first the subject of *seen*, and then the subject of *was* – as in (40) below:

(40)

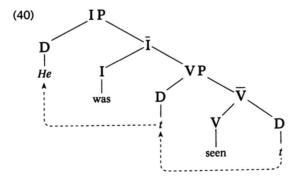

Since (as a result of two applications of A movement) *he* comes to occupy a nominative position (as the subject and specifier of the finite auxiliary *was*) in (40), its nominative case can be checked. The resulting sentence is therefore fully grammatical.

On this account, **greed** triggers passivization (i.e. the requirement for *he* to move into a position where it can check its nominative case-feature). One consequence of the greed analysis is that a constituent will move no further than it needs to in order to satisfy its morphological requirements. In this connection, consider how we account for contrasts such as the following:

(41) (a) He is said [to have lied to Parliament]
      (b)*He is said [has lied to Parliament]

How come we can passivize the subject of an infinitive clause like that bracketed in (41a), but not the subject of a finite clause like that bracketed in (41b)? **Greed** provides us with the answer. If the subject does not passivize but remains *in situ* within the bracketed clause, the result will be:

(42) (a)*It is said [*he* to have lied to Parliament]
      (b) It is said [*he* has lied to Parliament]

The pronoun *he* cannot remain *in situ* in (42a), since if it does it will be unable to check its nominative case-feature; hence, morphological (case-checking) requirements force it to passivize, and move into the nominative position it occupies in (41a). But the converse is the case in (42b): here *he* already occupies a nominative position (as subject of the finite auxiliary *has*), so that its nominative case-feature can be checked (and erased) *in situ*; hence, *he* in (42b) need not (and therefore, by the **economy principle**, *cannot*) move into another nominative position, so accounting for the ungrammaticality of passivization in (41b).

To summarize: we began this chapter by suggesting that a handful of nonauxiliary verbs (like *seem*) resemble auxiliaries in that they do not θ-mark their subjects; in consequence, such verbs (traditionally known as **raising predicates**) allow the subject of an embedded complement to be raised up to become the subject of the raising verb. We contrasted **raising** predicates with *control* predicates, noting that control predicates θ-mark their subjects and take a complement clause with a PRO subject which is θ-marked by the predicate in the complement. We went on to examine the syntax of passivized arguments, claiming that (in simple cases) they originate as complements of passive participles, and are raised up (in a successive cyclic fashion) to become first the subject of the passive participle, and then the subject of the passive auxiliary *be*. We argued that passive participles have two distinctive characteristics which differentiate them from the corresponding active verb forms – namely that they do not θ-mark their subjects and do not check the case of their complements. We noted that in infinitival passives such as *He is thought to admire her*, the passive subject *he* originates as the subject of the verb *admire* in the infinitive complement, and is raised up (by successive movement operations) to become first subject of *to*, then subject of *thought* and finally subject of *is*. We argued that raising and passivization are two different manifestations of a single **A movement** operation whereby an argument moves from a subject or complement position into a higher subject position. We suggested that the operation of **A movement** is constrained by a number of UG principles, including the **c-command condition on binding**, the **shortest movement principle**, the θ-**criterion** and the **principle of greed**.

Exercises

Exercise XV

Say whether the italicized verbs as used in the type of construction illustrated in the examples below function as **raising** and/or **control** predicates, and discuss the derivation of each sentence, giving arguments in support of your answer.

1 Power *tends* to corrupt people
2 John has *decided* to quit his job
3 We *came* to understand her point of view
4 You *have* to listen to me
5 They *failed* to achieve their objectives
6 You *appear* to have misunderstood me
7 He *refused* to sign the petition
8 He's *beginning* to irritate me
9 They *attempted* to pervert the course of justice
10 I *happened* to be passing your house
11 He is *going* to quit his job

12   He *stands* to lose a fortune

13   Dork *promises* to be a good student

14   He *needs* to have a shave

15   They *managed* to open the door

16   We *intend* to look into it

17   The weather is *threatening* to ruin our holiday

18   We are *hoping* to get a visa

19   She has *chosen* to ignore him

20   They are *planning* to visit their family

Model answer for 1

There are a number of reasons for suggesting that *tend* functions as a raising predicate when it takes an infinitive complement. For one thing, it allows a nonthematic subject like expletive *there*: cf.

(i)   *There* tends to be a lot of confusion about syntax

It also seems to impose no restrictions on its choice of subject: cf.

(ii)   (a)   *Larry Loudmouth* tends to exaggerate
       (b)   *My goldfish* tends to eat too much
       (c)   *My pet amoeba* tends to reproduce in the evenings
       (d)   *My kettle* tends to boil over
       (e)   *My theory* tends to confuse people

The fact that *tend* can have a nonreferential subject like expletive *there* and imposes no restrictions on the type of referential subject it allows is consistent with the assumption that it does not θ-mark its subject, and hence can function as a raising predicate (for the reasons set out in the text in relation to *seem*).

A further piece of evidence (not noted in the text) in support of the same conclusion comes from the fact that *tend* can have an idiomatic subject: cf.

(iii)   (a)   *All hell* tends to break loose
        (b)   *The shit* tends to hit the fan
        (c)   *The chickens* tend to come home to roost

Given that *all hell* can serve only as the subject of *break loose* in the relevant idiom, it is clear that we could not analyse *tend* as a control predicate in (iii) (a) and claim that *all hell* originates as the subject of *tends* and PRO as the subject of *break loose*, since this would violate the requirement that *all hell* can occur only as the subject of *break loose* (in the relevant idiom). By contrast, if *tend* is a raising predicate, we can claim that *all hell* originates as the subject of *break loose* and then raises up in a successive cyclic fashion to become first subject of *to break loose*, then subject of *tends to break loose*, and finally subject of the abstract INFL constituent preceding *tends*.

Given the assumption that *tend* is a raising predicate, sentence I will have the simplified derivation (iv) below:

(iv) [IP *Power* INFL [VP *t* [V tends] [IP *t* [I to] [VP *t* [V corrupt] people]]]]

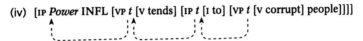

That is, *power* will originate as the subject of *corrupt people*, and will then be raised (by successive arrowed applications of **A movement**) first to become the subject of *to corrupt people*, then to become subject of *tends to corrupt people* and finally to become the subject of the abstract INFL constituent which heads the overall IP. The relevant derivation satisfies the θ-**criterion** by virtue of the fact that *power* is assigned only a single θ-role (by the V-bar *corrupt people*); it also satisfies the **shortest movement principle** because movement applies in a successive cyclic fashion; and it satisfies the principle of **greed** in that the subject moves only the minimal distance required in order to get into a position (as the specifier of the INFL constituent in the main clause) where it can check its nominative case (the *present-tense* head-features and *third person nominative singular* specifier-features of *tends* are attracted to the main-clause INFL).

Exercise XVI

Discuss the derivation of the following sentences:

1 She may get arrested
2 They don't seem to understand syntax
3 We would all like to be consulted
4 The prisoners were thought to be planning to escape from jail
5 The defendants both seem to want to plead guilty
6 What was he alleged to have done?
7 Nobody was intended (*for) to get hurt

8 Who is believed to have attempted to bribe the judge?

9 He is thought to have tried to get arrested

10 Justice must be seen to be done

Helpful hints

Assume that *have* in 6/8/9 and *be* in 10 occupy the head V position of
VP (since the head I position of IP is filled by *to/must*) and that *have/be*
in this use take a VP complement of their own.

Model answer for 1

The pronoun *she* here is the PATIENT argument of *arrested* (i.e. represents the person taken away for questioning), and so originates as the
complement of *arrested*. It is then raised in successive cyclic fashion to
become first subject of *arrested*, then subject of *get arrested*, and finally
subject of *may get arrested* as in (i) below:

(i)

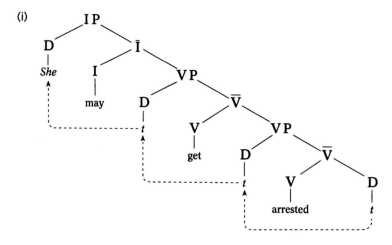

The derivation in (i) satisfies the **c-command condition on binding** by
virtue of the fact that the rightmost trace is c-commanded (and bound)
by the middle trace, which in turn is c-commanded (and bound) by the
leftmost trace, which itself is c-commanded (and bound) by the moved
pronoun *she*. The derivation (i) also satisfies the **shortest movement
principle** by virtue of the fact that each movement of *she* takes it into
the next-highest subject position in the structure. The **principle of greed**
is also satisfied, since *she* moves from (and through) a series of positions
in which it can't check its nominative case, into its ultimate position as
subject of *may* (where it can check its case against the *nominative*

specifier-feature of *may*). Since the resulting sentence ɪ is grammatical, it follows that the derivation (i) must also satisfy the θ-**criterion**. This means that neither *arrested* nor *get* nor *may* θ-marks its subject: *arrested* because it is a passive participle (and passive participles have dethematized subjects), *get* because it is a raising predicate in this use (and raising predicates don't θ-mark their subjects) and *may* because it is an auxiliary (and functional categories aren't θ-markers). Thus, the only θ-role which *she* is assigned is that of PATIENT argument of *arrested* (thereby satisfying the θ-criterion requirement that each argument is assigned one and only one θ-role).

⑨ VP shells

In this chapter, we turn to consider the internal constituent structure
of verb phrases. We shall argue that VPs have a complex structure, comprising an inner **VP** and an outer **vp** shell, and that some (e.g. AGENT)
arguments originate within the outer vp shell, while other (e.g. THEME)
arguments originate within the inner VP.

Thus far, the verb phrase structures we have looked at have generally contained verbs with a single complement. Such verbs can easily be
accommodated within the binary-branching framework adopted here,
since all we need say is that a verb merges with its complement to form
a (binary-branching) V-bar constituent. However, a particular problem
for the binary-branching framework adopted here is posed by three-
place predicates like those italicized in (1) below which have two
[bracketed] complements:

(1) (a) We *rolled* [the ball] [down the hill]
    (b) He *filled* [the bath] [with water]
    (c) He *broke* [the vase] [into pieces]

If we make the conventional assumption that complements are sisters to
heads, it follows that the V-bar constituent headed by *rolled* in (1a) will
have the structure (2) below:

(2)

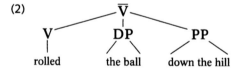

However, a structure such as (2) is problematic within the framework
adopted here. After all, it is a *ternary-branching* structure ($\bar{V}$ branches
out into the three separate constituents, namely the V *rolled*, the DP *the
ball* and the PP *down the hill*), and this poses an obvious problem within
a framework which assumes that the merger operation which forms
phrases is an inherently binary operation which can only combine constituents in a *pairwise* fashion. Moreover, a ternary-branching structure
such as (2) would wrongly predict that the string following the verb *rolled*
does not form a constituent, and so cannot be coordinated with another
similar string (given the traditional assumption that only constituents
can be conjoined); yet this prediction is falsified by sentences such as:

(3) He rolled *the ball down the hill* and **the acorn up the mountain**

How can we overcome these problems?

One way would be to suppose that the string *the ball down the hill* in (3) is a clausal constituent of some kind, in which *the ball* functions as the subject of the clause, and *down the hill* functions as the complement of the clause. Such an analysis is by no means implausible, since many three-place predicates like *roll* can also be used as two-place predicates in which the DP which immediately follows the verb in the three-place structure functions as the subject in the two-place structure – as we see from sentence pairs such as the following:

(4) (a) We **rolled** *the ball* down the hill
     (b) *The ball* **rolled** down the hill

(5) (a) He **filled** *the bath* with water
     (b) *The bath* **filled** with water

(6) (a) He **broke** *the vase* into pieces
     (b) *The vase* **broke** into pieces

(7) (a) They **withdrew** *the troops* from the occupied territories
     (b) *The troops* **withdrew** from the occupied territories

(8) (a) They **moved** *the headquarters* to Brooklyn
     (b) *The headquarters* **moved** to Brooklyn

(9) (a) They **closed** *the store* down
     (b) *The store* **closed** down

(Verbs which can be used in this way, either as three-place or as two-place predicates, are sometimes referred to as **ergative predicates**.) Moreover, the italicized DP seems to play the same thematic role with respect to the bold-printed verb in each pair of examples: for example, *the ball* is the THEME argument of *roll* (i.e. the entity which undergoes a rolling motion) both in (4a) *We rolled the ball down the hill* and in (4b) *The ball rolled down the hill*. Evidence in support of the claim that *the ball* plays the same semantic role in both sentences comes from the fact that the italicized argument is subject to the same restrictions on the choice of expression which can fulfil the relevant argument function in each type of sentence: cf.

(10) (a) *The ball/the rock/!the theory/!sincerity* rolled down the hill
      (b) John rolled *the ball/the rock/!the theory/!sincerity* down the hill

If we assume that principles of UG correlate thematic structure with syntactic structure in a *uniform* fashion (in accordance with Baker's 1988 **uniform theta-assignment hypothesis/UTAH**) then it follows that two arguments which fulfil the same thematic function with respect to a given predicate must occupy the same underlying position in the syntax.

An analysis within the spirit of UTAH would be to assume that since *the ball* is clearly the subject of *roll* in (4b) *The ball rolled down the hill*, then it must also be the case that *the ball* originates as the subject of *roll* in (4a) *We rolled the ball down the hill*. But if this is so, how come *the ball* is positioned *after* the verb *rolled* in (4a), when subjects are normally positioned *before* their verbs? A natural answer to this question within the framework we are adopting here is to suppose that the verb *moves* from its original (postsubject) position after *the ball* into a higher verb position to the left of *the ball*. More specifically, adapting ideas put forward by Larson (1988, 1990), Hale and Keyser (1991, 1993, 1994) and Chomsky (1995), let's suppose that the (b) examples in sentences like (4–9) are simple VPs, but that the (a) examples are complex double-VP structures which comprise an outer VP **shell** with an inner VP core embedded within it.

More concretely, let's make the following assumptions. In (4b) *The ball rolled down the hill*, the V *rolled* is merged with its PP complement *down the hill* to form the V-bar *rolled down the hill*; this is then merged with the DP *the ball* to form a VP with the structure (11) below:

(11)

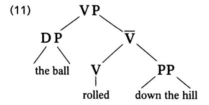

In the case of (4b), the resulting VP will then be merged with a null INFL constituent to form an I-bar *INFL the ball rolled down the hill*; the subject *the ball* will then be raised to spec-IP (by **A movement**), as in (12) below:

(12)

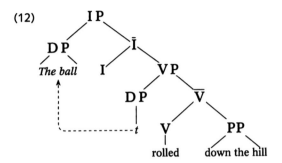

But what of (4a) *We rolled the ball down the hill*? Let's suppose that
once the VP structure (11) has been formed, it is then merged with an
abstract causative **light verb** ø – i.e. a null verb with much the same
causative interpretation as a verb like *make* (so that *We rolled the ball
down the hill* has a similar interpretation to *We made the ball roll down
the hill*). Let's also suppose that this causative light verb is affixal in
nature (and so a strong head), and that the verb *rolled* raises to adjoin
to it (producing a structure which can be paraphrased literally as 'We
made + roll the ball down the hill'). The resulting V-bar structure is then
merged with the subject *we* (which is assigned the θ-role of AGENT by
the causative light verb), to form the complex vp (13) below (lower-case
letters are used to denote the light verb and its projections):

(13)

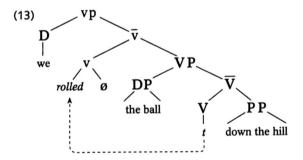

Subsequently, the vp in (13) merges with an abstract INFL to form I-bar,
and the subject *we* raises into spec-IP to check its nominative case, as in
(14) below:

(14)

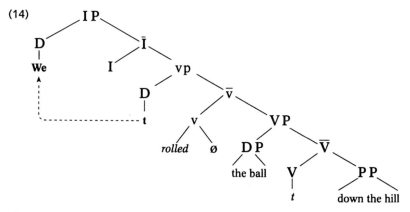

If we assume that the agentive light verb ø is transitive, it can check the objective case carried by the DP *the ball*.

The VP shell analysis in (14) provides a straightforward account for an otherwise puzzling aspect of the syntax of sentences like (4a) – namely the fact that adverbs like *gently* can be positioned either before *rolled* or after *the ball*, as we see from:

(15) (a) We *gently* rolled the ball down the hill
     (b) We rolled the ball *gently* down the hill

Let us make the traditional assumption that so-called *VP adverbs* like *gently* merge with intermediate verbal projections like V-bar and v-bar. Let's also assume that such adverbs are **adjuncts** which have the property that they when they merge with a given category, they form an expanded category of the same type (so that an adverb merged with V-bar forms an expanded V-bar, and an adverb merged with v-bar forms an expanded v-bar). Given these assumptions and the light verb analysis in (14), we could then propose the following derivations for (15a–b).

In (15a), the verb *rolled* merges with the PP *down the hill* to form the V-bar *rolled down the hill*, and this V-bar in turn merges with the DP *the ball* to form the VP *the ball rolled down the hill*, as in (11) above. This VP then merges with a causative light verb ø to which the verb *rolled* adjoins, forming the v-bar *rolled the ball down the hill*. The resulting v-bar merges with the adverb *gently* to form the expanded v-bar *gently rolled the ball down the hill*; and this v-bar in turn merges with the subject *we* to form the vp *we gently rolled the ball down the hill*. The vp thereby formed merges with an abstract INFL constituent, forming an I-bar; the subject *we* raises to spec-IP forming the IP (15a) *We gently rolled the ball down the hill*. Thus (15a) has the derivation (16) below:

(16)

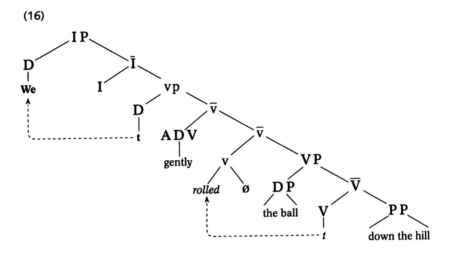

Now consider how (15b) *We rolled the ball gently down the hill* is derived. As before, the verb *roll* merges with the PP *down the hill*, forming the V-bar *rolled down the hill*. The adverb *gently* then merges with this V-bar to form the expanded V-bar *gently rolled down the hill*. This V-bar in turn merges with the DP *the ball* to form the VP *the ball gently rolled down the hill*. The resulting VP is merged with a causative light verb ø to which the verb *rolled* adjoins, so forming the v-bar *rolled the ball gently down the hill*. This v-bar is then merged with the subject *we* to form the vp *we rolled the ball gently down the hill*. The vp thereby formed merges with an abstract INFL constituent, forming an I-bar; the subject *we* raises to spec-IP forming the IP (15b) *We rolled the ball gently down the hill*, which has the derivation (17) below:

(17)

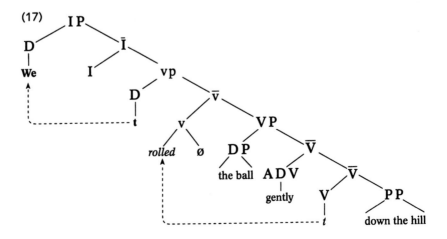

The different positions occupied by the adverb *gently* in (16) and (17) reflect a subtle meaning difference between (15a) and (15b): (15a) means that the action which initiated the rolling motion was gentle, whereas (15b) means that the rolling motion itself was gentle.

A light verb analysis such as that sketched above also offers us an interesting account of adverb position in sentences like:

(18) (a) He had *deliberately* rolled the ball *gently* down the hill
      (b)*He had *gently* rolled the ball *deliberately* down the hill

It seems reasonable to suppose that *deliberately* (by virtue of its meaning) can only be an adjunct to a projection of an *agentive* verb (i.e. a verb whose subject has the thematic role of AGENT). If we suppose (as earlier) that the light verb ø is a causative verb with an agentive subject, the contrast in (18) can be accounted for straightforwardly: in (18a) *deliberately* is contained within a vp headed by the agentive causative light verb ø; but in (18b) it is contained with a VP headed by the nonagentive verb *roll* (*roll* is a nonagentive verb because its subject has the θ-role THEME, not AGENT). We can then say that adverbs like *deliberately* are strictly vp adverbs.

This in turn might lead us to expect to find a corresponding class of VP adverbs. In this connection, consider the following contrasts (adapted from Bowers 1993, p. 609):

(19) (a) Mary jumped the horse *perfectly* over the last fence
      (b)*Mary *perfectly* jumped the horse over the last fence

Given the assumptions made here, the derivation of (19a) would be parallel to that in (17), while the derivation of (19b) would be parallel to that in (16). If we assume that *perfectly* (in the relevant use) can function only as a VP adverb, the contrast between (19a) and (19b) can be accounted for straightforwardly: in (19a), *perfectly* is merged with a V-bar (consistent with its status as a VP adverb), whereas in (21b) it is merged with a v-bar (in violation of the requirement that it can only serve as a VP adverb).

As we have seen, the VP shell analysis outlined here provides an interesting solution to the problems posed by three-place predicates which appear to take two complements. However, the problems posed by verbs which take two complements arise not only with transitive verbs (like those in (4–9) above) which have intransitive counterparts, but also with verbs such as those in (20) below (the complements of the verbs are bracketed):

(20) (a) They loaded [the truck] [with hay]
      (b) He gave [no explanation] [to his friends]
      (c) They took [everything] [from her]
      (d) Nobody can blame [you] [for the accident]
      (e) He assured [her] [of his good intentions]

Verbs like those in (20) cannot be used intransitively, as we see from
the ungrammaticality of sentences such as (21) below:

(21) (a) *The truck loaded with hay
      (b) *No explanation gave to his friends
      (c) *Everything took from her
      (d) *You can blame for the accident
      (e) *She assured of his good intentions

However, it is interesting to note that in structures like (20) too we find
that VP adverbs can be positioned either before the verb or between its
two complements: cf.

(22) (a) They *carefully* loaded the truck with hay
      (b) They loaded the truck *carefully* with hay

This suggests that (in spite of the fact that the relevant verbs have no
intransitive counterpart) a VP shell analysis is appropriate for structures
like (20) too. This would mean (for example) that a sentence such as
(20a) would have the derivation (23) below:

(23)

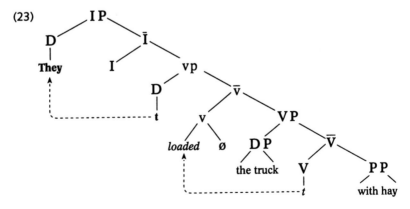

We could then say that the adverb *carefully* adjoins to v-bar in (22a), and
to V-bar in (22b). If we suppose that verbs like *load* are essentially affixal
in nature (and so must adjoin to the agentive light verb ø) we can
account for the ungrammaticality of intransitive structures such as (21a)

The truck loaded with hay. Alternatively, we might suppose that verbs like *load* are inherently transitive, and so must be used in a structure like (23) where they can check objective case. (In (23), *loaded* checks the objective case of *the truck*.)

The *VP shell* analysis outlined above can be extended from predicates which have a prepositional argument to so-called **resultative** predicates which have an adjectival argument – i.e. to structures such as those below:

(24) (a) The acid turned the *litmus-paper* red
        (b) They painted *the house* pink

In (24a), the verb *turned* would originate in the head V position of VP, with the DP *the litmus-paper* as its subject and the adjective *red* as its complement (precisely as in *The litmus-paper turned red*): *turned* would then raise to adjoin to a strong causative light verb ø heading vp; the subject of this light verb (the DP *the acid*) would in turn raise from spec-vp to spec-IP, as shown informally in (25) below:

(25) [_{IP} **The acid** [_I] [_{vp} t [_v *turned*+ø] [_{VP} the litmus-paper [_V t] red]]]

(For very different analyses of resultative structures like (24), see Carrier and Randall 1992 and Keyser and Roeper 1992.)

We can extend the *VP shell* analysis still further, to take in *double-object* structures such as:

(26) (a) They got [the teacher] [a present]
        (b) Could you pass [me] [the salt]?
        (c) I showed [her] [my credentials]

For example, we could suggest that (26a) is derived as in (27) below:

(27)
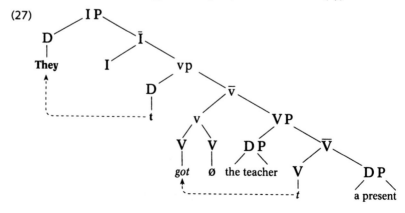

That is, *got* originates as the head V of VP (with *the teacher* as its subject and *a present* as its complement, much as in *The teacher got a present*), and then raises up to adjoin to the strong causative light verb ø heading vp; the subject *they* would in turn originate in spec-vp (assigned the role of AGENT by the causative light verb ø) and would then raise to spec-IP to check its strong nominative case-feature. (For a range of alternative analyses of the *double-object* construction, see Larson 1988, 1990, Johnson 1991, Bowers 1993 and Pesetsky 1995.)

The light verb analysis outlined above also provides us with an interesting solution to the problems posed by so-called **object-control predicates**. In this connection, consider the syntax of the infinitive structure in (28) below:

(28)   What decided you to take syntax?

In this use, *decide* seems to function as a three-place predicate, taking *what* as its subject, *you* as its object and the IP *to take syntax* as a further complement. If we suppose that the infinitive complement *to take syntax* has a PRO subject, (28) will have the simplified structure (29) below (where the three arguments of *decided* are bracketed):

(29)   [What] decided [you] [to PRO take syntax]?

Since PRO here is controlled by the object *you*, the verb *decide* (in this use) functions as an **object-control predicate**.

There are a number of reasons for thinking that the verb *decide* in sentences like (28) is indeed a three-place object-control predicate, and that *you* is the object of *decided* (rather than the subject of *to take syntax*). Thus, for some speakers, (28) can be paraphrased (albeit clumsily) as:

(30)   What decided *you* [that **you** should take syntax]?

where the first *you* corresponds to the object *you* in (29), and the second *you* corresponds to PRO in (29). Moreover, the verb *decide* imposes restrictions on the choice of expression following it (which must be a rational entity – not an irrational entity like *the exam*):

(31)   *What decided *the exam* to be difficult?

Furthermore, the expression following *decide* cannot be an expletive pronoun such as *there*:

(32)   *What decided *there* to be an election?

The obvious conclusion to draw from facts such as these is that the (pro)nominal following *decide* is an (object) argument of *decide* in sentences such as (28), and serves as the controller of a PRO subject in the following *to*-infinitive.

However, this means that *decide* has two complements in structures such as (28) – the pronoun *you* and the infinitive *to take syntax*. If we make the traditional assumption that complements are sisters to the verb which θ-marks them, this would seem to lead us to the conclusion that the V-bar headed by *decided* in (28) has the structure (33) below:

(33)

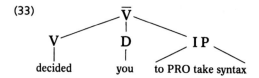

However, a ternary-branching structure such as (33) is incompatible with the core assumption made here that the merger operation by which phrases are formed is intrinsically binary. One way of overcoming this problem is to suppose that (28) has a structure akin to that of:

(34) What made you decide to take syntax?

but differing from (34) in that in place of the overt causative verb *made* is an abstract causative light verb ø, with the verb *decide* raising to adjoin to the light verb as in (35) below:

(35)

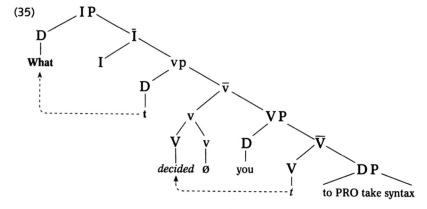

The light verb analysis in (35) offers two main advantages over the traditional analysis in (33). Firstly, (35) is consistent with the view that the merger operation by which phrases are formed is binary; and secondly,

(35) enables us to attain a more unitary theory of control under which the controller of PRO is always a *subject*, never an *object* (since PRO in (35) is controlled by *you*, and *you* is the subject of the VP which was originally headed by the verb *decided*). This second result is a welcome one, since the verb *decide* clearly functions as a subject-control verb in structures such as:

(36) He decided to PRO take syntax

where the PRO subject of *take syntax* is controlled by the *he* subject of *decided*. (See Bowers 1993 for a similar analysis of so-called object-control verbs; and see Larson 1991 for an analysis of the control verb *promise*.)

Thus far, we have considered how we deal with the complements of three-place transitive predicates. But what about the complements of two-place transitives – i.e. transitive verbs used with a single complement, as in:

(37) He read the book

Chomsky (1995) proposes a light verb analysis of simple transitive structures like (37) under which (37) would (prior to merger with INFL) be derived as in (38) below:

(38)

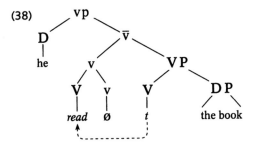

That is, *read* would originate as the head V of VP, and would then be raised to adjoin to a null agentive light verb ø which has a *performative* sense, so that (38) can be loosely paraphrased as *He performed the action of book-reading.* (An alternative account of transitive complements as VP-specifiers is offered in Stroik 1990 and Bowers 1993.)

Chomsky's light verb analysis of two-place transitive predicates might be extended in an interesting way to handle the syntax of a class of verbs which are known as **unergative predicates**. These are verbs like those italicized in (39) below which have agentive subjects, but which appear to have no complement:

(39) (a) They are *lunching*   (b) Let's *party!*
     (c) Don't *fuss!*   (d) Why not *guess?*
     (e) He was *lying*   (f) He *overdosed*
     (g) He was *fishing*   (h) We were *golfing*

Such verbs pose obvious problems for our assumption that subjects originate in spec-VP and merge with a V-bar which is itself formed by merger
of a verb with its complement: the reason should be obvious – namely
that such verbs appear to have no complements. However, it is interesting to note that unergative verbs like those in (39) have close paraphrases
involving an overt light verb (i.e. a verb such as *have/make* etc. which
has little semantic content) and a nominal complement: cf.

(40) (a) They are *having lunch*   (b) Let's have a *party!*
     (c) Don't *make a fuss!*   (d) Why not *make a guess?*
     (e) He was *telling lies*   (f) He *took an overdose*
     (g) He was *catching fish*   (h) We were *playing golf*

This suggests an obvious way of overcoming the problem posed by
unergative verbs – namely to suppose (following Baker 1988 and Hale
and Keyser 1993) that unergative verbs are formed by incorporation of a
complement into an abstract agentive light verb. This would mean (for
example) that the verb *lunch* in (39a) is an implicitly transitive verb,
formed by merging the noun *lunch* with a null verb as in (41a) below,
and then adjoining the noun to the null verb as in (41b):

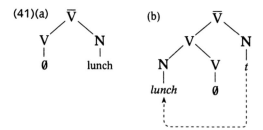

The resulting V-bar in (41b) would then be merged with (and would
θ-mark) a subject (e.g. a pronominal determiner like *they*), and the
resulting VP would be combined with an agentive light verb and then
with INFL to project into IP (as in (39a), where the verb *lunching*
occurs in the +*ing* form because it is the complement of the progressive
auxiliary *are*). On this view, unergative predicates are not intransitive at
all – rather, they are implicitly transitive.

We end our discussion in this chapter by looking at the syntax of a special class of verbs which have become known in recent work as **unaccusative predicates**. In this connection, consider the syntax of the italicized arguments in unaccusative structures such as the following:

(42) (a) There arose *an unfortunate misunderstanding*
     (b) There came *a cry of anguish* from inside the house
     (c) There appeared *a ghostly face* at the window
     (d) There could have occurred *a diplomatic incident*
     (e) In front of the house, there stands a statue of *General Ghouly*

In some respects, the italicized arguments seem to behave like complements – for example, they occupy the postverbal position canonically associated with complements. However, in other ways, they seem to behave like subjects: for instance, the italicized argument agrees with the verb preceding it, as we see (for example) from the fact that *stands* in (42e) is a singular form which agrees with the singular nominal *a statue of General Ghouly*, so that we require the plural form *stand* if we are unfortunate enough to have *several statues of General Ghouly*. Moreover, the postverbal argument carries the *nominative* case associated with subjects, not the objective/accusative case associated with complements. This is clearer in languages where nouns carry overt case-marking (cf. Vikner 1995), but is also suggested by (somewhat archaic) structures such as:

(43) There (but for the grace of God) go *I*

(It should be noted, however, that Belletti 1988 suggests that unaccusative subjects carry *partitive* case.)

Only certain types of verb seem to allow postverbal subjects, as we see from the fact that structures such as those in (44) below are ungrammatical:

(44) (a) *When the British Rail snail arrived five hours late, there *complained* many passengers
     (b) *In the dentist's surgery, there *groaned* a toothless patient
     (c) *Every time General Wynott Nukem goes past, there *salutes* a guard at the gate
     (d) *There *waved* Wee Willie Widget at the window
     (e) *There has *apologized* Major Muddle for his minor indiscretions

We might refer to verbs like those in (42) which can have postverbal subjects as **unaccusative verbs**. By contrast, verbs with AGENT subjects but no overt object like those in (44) are known as **unergative verbs** (as noted earlier).

In addition to the contrast illustrated in (42/44) above, there are a number of other important syntactic differences between unaccusative verbs and other types of verb (e.g. unergative verbs or transitive verbs). For example, Alison Henry (1995) notes that in one dialect of Belfast English (which she refers to as *dialect A*) unaccusative verbs can be used with (italicized) postverbal subjects in imperative structures like (45) below:

(45) (a) Be going *you* out of the door when he arrives!
      (b) Leave *you* now!
      (c) Arrive *you* before 6 o'clock!

By contrast, other (unergative or transitive) verbs don't allow postverbal imperative subjects, so that imperatives such as (46) below are ungrammatical in the relevant dialect:

(46) (a) *Read *you* that book!
      (b) *Eat *you* up!
      (c) *Always laugh *you* at his jokes!

Additional evidence for positing that unaccusative verbs are syntactically distinct from other verbs comes from *auxiliary selection* facts in relation to earlier stages of English when there were two perfective auxiliaries, *have* and *be*, each taking a complement headed by a specific kind of verb. The sentences in (47) below (taken from various plays by Shakespeare) give examples of verbs which could be used with the perfective auxiliary *be* in Early Modern English:

(47) (a) Mistress Page is *come* with me   (Mrs Ford, *Merry Wives of Windsor*, V.v)
      (b) Is the duke *gone*? Then is your cause *gone* too

                                                    (Duke, *Measure for Measure*, V.i)
      (c) How chance thou art *returned* so soon?   (Antipholus, *Comedy of Errors*, I.ii)
      (d) She is *fallen* into a pit of ink   (Leonato, *Much Ado About Nothing*, IV.i)
      (e) You shall hear I am *run* away   (Countess, *All's Well That Ends Well*, III.ii)

We find a similar contrast with the counterparts of perfective *have/be* in a number of other languages – e.g. Italian and French (cf. Burzio 1986), Sardinian (cf. Jones 1994), German and Dutch (cf. Haegeman 1994) and Danish (cf. Spencer 1991).

A further difference between unaccusative predicates and others relates to the adjectival use of their perfective participle forms. As the examples below indicate, perfective participle (+*n*/+*d*) forms of unaccusative verbs can be used adjectivally (to modify a noun), e.g. in sentences such as:

(48)   (a) The train *arrived* at platform 4 is the 8.28 for London Euston
      (b) They arrested a business man recently *returned* from Thailand
      (c) Several facts recently *come* to light point to his guilt
      (d) A number of objects *gone* from the church were found in his room
      (e) OJ is something of a *fallen* hero

By contrast, participle forms of transitive or unergative verbs cannot be used in the same way, as we see from the ungrammaticality of examples like (49) below:

(49)   (a) *The man *committed* suicide was a neighbour of mine
      (b) *The thief *stolen* the jewels was never captured
      (c) *The man *overdosed* was Joe Doe
      (d) *The *yawned* student eventually fell asleep in class

In this respect, unaccusative verbs resemble passive participles, which can also be used adjectivally (cf. *a **changed** man, a **battered** wife, a woman **arrested** for shoplifting*, etc.). Additional syntactic differences between unaccusative verbs and others have been reported for other languages (cf. Burzio 1986 on *ne*-cliticization in Italian, and Contreras 1986 on bare nominals in Spanish).

We thus have a considerable body of empirical evidence that unaccusative subjects behave differently from subjects of other (e.g. unergative or transitive) verbs. Why should this be? A traditional answer (cf. Burzio 1986) is that the subjects of unaccusative verbs do not originate as the subjects of their associated verbs at all, but rather as their *complements*, and that unaccusative structures with postverbal arguments involve leaving the relevant argument *in situ* in VP-complement position (e.g. in unaccusative expletive structures such as (42), and in Belfast English unaccusative imperatives such as (45) above). However, analysing unaccusative arguments as complements poses obvious

problems in relation to two-place unaccusative predicates – i.e. unaccusative verbs which take two arguments. In this connection, consider
unaccusative imperative structures such as the following in (dialect A
of) Belfast English:

(50) (a) Go you to school!
      (b) Run youse to the telephone!
      (c) Walk you into the garden!

If (as suggested in Henry 1995) postverbal arguments of unaccusative
predicates are *in situ* complements, this means that each of the verbs in
(50) must have two complements. But since complements are defined
configurationally as sisters of a head, this means (for example) that if
both *you* and *to school* are complements of the verb *go* in (50a), they
must be sisters of *go*, and hence the VP headed by *go* must have the
(simplified) structure (51) below:

(51)

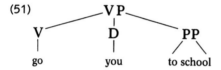

However, a ternary-branching structure such as (51) is obviously incompatible with a framework such as that used here which assumes that the
merger operation by which phrases are formed is inherently binary.
    Since analysing unaccusative subjects as underlying complements
proves problematic, let's consider whether they might instead be
analysed as subjects. On this view, we might suppose that the inner
VP *core* of a Belfast English unaccusative imperative structure such
as (50a) *Go you to school!* is not (51) above, but rather (52) below:

(52)

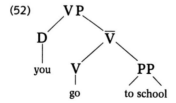

But the obvious problem posed by a structure like (52) is that it provides
us with no way of accounting for the fact that unaccusative subjects sur-
face postverbally in structures such as (42) and (45) above. How can we
overcome this problem? One suggestion might be the following. Let us

suppose that unaccusative VPs like (52) (i.e. VPs headed by an unaccusative verb) are embedded as the complement of an outer vp shell headed by a strong v, and that the unaccusative verb raises to v in the manner indicated by the arrow in (53) below:

(53)

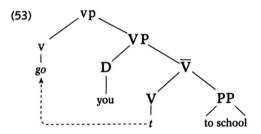

(It may be that *v* is strong because it contains an affixal eventive light verb – i.e. a light verb denoting an event – which has much the same sense as *happen*.) If we assume (as Alison Henry argues) that subjects remain *in situ* in imperatives in dialect A of Belfast English, the postverbal position of unaccusative subjects in sentences such as (50) can be accounted for straightforwardly. And the *vp shell* analysis is consistent with the assumption that the merger operation by which phrases are formed is intrinsically binary.

Moreover, the *vp shell* analysis in (53) enables us to provide an interesting account of the position of VP adverbs like *quickly* in unaccusative imperatives (in dialect A of Belfast English) such as:

(54) Go you quickly to school!

If we suppose that VP adverbs like *quickly* are adjuncts which merge with an intermediate verbal projection (i.e. a single-bar projection comprising a verb and its complement), we can say that *quickly* in (54) is adjoined to the V-bar *go to school* in (52). What remains to be accounted for (in relation to the syntax of imperative subjects in dialect A of Belfast English) is the fact that subjects of transitive and unergative verbs occur in *preverbal* (not postverbal) position: cf.

(55) (a) You read that book!   (b) *Read you that book!
      (c) You protest!   (d) *Protest you!

Why should this be? If we assume (following Chomsky 1995) that transitive verbs originate as the head of a VP complement of an agentive light verb ø, imperatives such as (55a) will contain a vp derived as in (56) below:

(56)

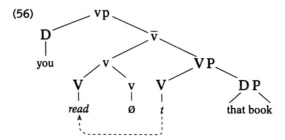

The AGENT subject *you* will originate in spec-vp, as the subject of the agentive light verb ø. Even after the verb *read* adjoins to the light verb ø, the subject *you* will still be preverbal. We can extend the light verb analysis from transitive verbs like *read* to unergative verbs like *protest*, if we assume (as earlier) that such verbs are formed by incorporation of a noun into the verb (so that *protest* is analysed as having a similar structure to *make [a] protest*), and if we assume that unergative subjects (like transitive subjects) originate as specifiers of an agentive light verb.

Given these assumptions, we could then say that the difference between unaccusative subjects and transitive/unergative subjects is that unaccusative subjects originate in spec-VP (as the subject of a lexical verb), whereas transitive/unergative subjects originate in spec-vp (as the subject of an agentive light verb). If we assume that verb phrases canonically contain an outer vp shell headed by a strong v (e.g. a light verb) and an inner VP core headed by a lexical verb, and that lexical verbs always raise from V to v, the postverbal position of unaccusative subjects can be accounted for by positing that the subject remains *in situ* in such structures.

The light verb analysis sketched here also offers us a way of accounting for the fact that in Early Modern English, the perfective auxiliary used with unaccusative verbs was *be* (as we see from the examples in (47) above), whereas that used with transitive and unergative verbs was *have*. We could account for this by positing that the perfective auxiliary *have* in EME selected a vp complement headed by an agentive light verb with a thematic subject, whereas the perfective auxiliary *be* in EME selected a complement headed by an eventive light verb which lacked a thematic subject. The distinction has been lost in Modern English, with perfective *have* being used with either type of vp complement (though sentences such as *They are gone* are a last vestige of the earlier use of *be* as a perfective auxiliary).

One final detail of our analysis of unaccusatives which needs to be clarified is how we account for the fact that unaccusative subjects can occur not only postverbally in structures like (57) below, but also preverbally: cf.

(57) (a) There came *a cry of anguish* from inside the house
      (b) *A cry of anguish* came from inside the house

In (57a), we might suppose that *a cry of anguish* is in spec-VP, that *came* originates in V and raises to v, and that *there* originates in the nonthematic spec-vp position, and from there raises to spec-IP, as in (58) below:

(58)

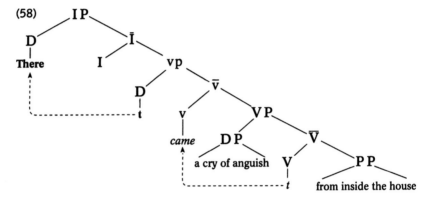

But in (57b), the need for the sentence to have a subject is satisfied not by the use of expletive *there* but rather by raising the subject *a cry of anguish* from spec-VP through spec-vp into spec-IP, as in (59) below:

(59)

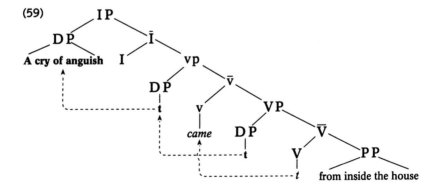

Thus, the subject *a cry of anguish* remains *in situ* in expletive structures such as (58), but raises to spec-IP in structures such as (59).

To summarize: we began this chapter by looking at the syntax of ergative verbs, noting that many of these have a dual transitive/intransitive use (e.g. *roll* in *They rolled the ball down the hill* and *The ball rolled down the hill*). We suggested that the transitive use might involve a complex verb phrase structure comprising an outer **vp** shell headed by an agentive light verb ø (with a causative sense) and an inner **VP** headed by the verb *roll*, with the verb *roll* raising to adjoin to the light verb ø. We suggested that such an analysis could be extended to other transitive verbs which take two complements (e.g. *load* in sentences like *They loaded the truck with hay*). We noted Chomsky's suggestion that simple transitive structures (like *He read the book*) may also involve a vp headed by a null performative light verb ø which has an AGENT subject. We further suggested that unergative verbs which have AGENT subjects but appear to have no complement might be analysed as having a complement incorporated into a null verb, so that e.g. in a sentence such as *What time shall we lunch?*, the verb *lunch* has much the same structure as *have lunch*, save that in place of *have* is a covert light verb into which the noun *lunch* is incorporated. We went on to look at the syntax of unaccusative verbs (like *come, go, occur*, etc.), arguing that the subject of such verbs originates in spec-VP, and that the unaccusative verb originates as the head V of VP but raises up to the head v position of vp (because v is strong, perhaps containing an affixal eventive verb), so giving rise to the *verb + subject* order found (for example) in Belfast English imperatives like *Go you to school!*

Exercises

Exercise XVII

Discuss the syntax of the following sentences, giving arguments in support of your analysis (sentence 9 is from Shakespeare, and sentence 10 from dialect A of Belfast English):

1   He had reduced his speed to 30 mph
2   She woke him up
3   They kept the food warm
4   It made him angry
5   He put his feet on the table
6   She reminded him to close the windows
7   The customers were complaining

8 A face appeared at the window

9 My master is grown quarrelsome (Grumio, *Taming of the Shrew*, I.ii)

10 Run youse to the telephone!

Model answer for 1

Since the verb *reduce* can be used not only as a transitive verb in sentences such as 1 above, but also as an intransitive verb in sentences such as (i) below:

(i) His speed reduced to 30 mph

we might suppose that *reduce* is an ergative predicate, and hence has much the same syntax as the verb *roll* discussed in the text. This would mean that 1 is derived as follows. The verb *reduced* merges with its PP complement *to 30 mph* to form the V-bar *reduced to 30 mph*; this V-bar in turn merges with the DP *his speed* to form the VP (ii) below:

(ii)

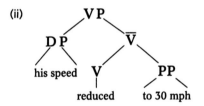

Subsequently the VP in (ii) merges with an abstract causative light verb ø (to which the verb *reduced* adjoins), and the resulting v-bar *reduced+ø his speed to 30 mph* merges with the subject *he* to form the vp (iii) below:

(iii)

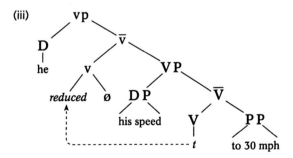

The vp in (iii) is then merged with an INFL constituent containing *had*, and the subject *he* raises to spec-IP to check its nominative case, as in (iv) below:

(iv)

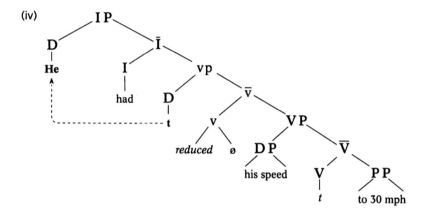

Evidence in support of the light verb analysis in (iv) comes from the two positions which can be occupied by the adverb *gradually* in:

(v) (a) He had *gradually* reduced his speed to 30 mph
    (b) He had reduced his speed *gradually* to 30 mph

Given the analysis in (iv), we can account for the dual position of *gradually* by supposing that *gradually* is an adjunct which merges with v-bar in (v) (a), and with V-bar in (v) (b) (cf. our discussion of structures (16) and (17) in the main text).

Exercise XVIII

Melissa Bowerman (1995) reports the following errors produced by children in the way they use verbs (the initials represent the children's names, and the figures indicate their age in years;months: informal glosses in adult English are provided where appropriate):

1 She came it over there (C 3;4 = 'brought it over there')
2 Singing goes it faster (C 5;0 = 'makes it go faster')
3 Let's stay this open (C 2;4 = 'keep this open')
4 Salt clings it together (C 12;3 = 'makes it cling')
5 Will you climb me up there? (E 3;3 = 'help me climb')
6 That will water my eyes (E 3;9 = 'make my eyes water')
7 Can I glow him? (E 4;3 = 'make him glow')

8 I meant to be it like this (C 5:5 = 'have it be')

9 I want to watch you this book (C 4;3 = 'show you')

10 Bert knocked down (C 2;11 = 'fell down')

11 It blowed up (C 2;3 = 'The beach ball inflated')

12 It stirs around (E 3:11 = 'The ice tea swirls around')

Discuss the derivation of the relevant sentences, and the nature of the errors made by the children.

Model answer for 1

One way in which we might analyse 1 is as follows. Let us suppose that the verb *came* initially projects into the VP (i) below (with *it* serving as the subject of *came*, and *over there* as its complement):

(i)

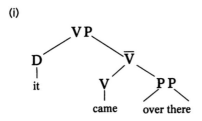

Let's further assume that the VP in (i) is merged with a strong (affixal) causative light verb ø (whose AGENT subject is *she*), and that *came* raises to adjoin to ø as in (ii) below:

(ii)

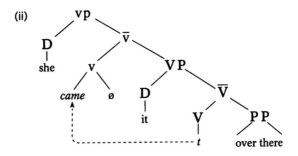

Subsequently, the subject *she* raises to spec-IP in order to check its nominative case, as in (iii) below:

(iii)

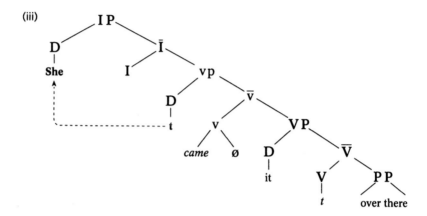

However, since the corresponding sentence *She came it over there* is ungrammatical in adult English (instead, we say *She brought it over there*), an important question to ask is what is wrong with sentences like 1 in adult English?

One answer might be to suppose that *come* is a nonaffixal verb, and hence cannot be adjoined to the causative light verb ø: conversely, we might say that its causative counterpart *bring* (which cannot be used intransitively, cf. **It brought over there*) is intrinsically affixal, and hence must be bound to the causative light verb ø (so that *bring* can only be used causatively, not intransitively). An alternative possibility would be to suppose that *bring* is inherently transitive (and so can only occur in a structure such as (iii) where it can check the case of an objective argument like *it*), whereas *come* is inherently intransitive (and so cannot occur in a structure like (iii), since if it did the objective case carried by *it* would remain unchecked). On the first view, the child's error lies in not having learned which verbs are (and which aren't) affixal in nature; on the second, it lies in not having identified which verbs are transitive, and which intransitive.

⑩ Agreement projections

In this chapter, we take a closer look at the internal structure of clauses, examining the range of projections which they contain. We shall argue that clauses have a much more richly articulated constituent structure than we have hitherto supposed, and that they contain subject and object **agreement phrases**.

Let's begin our discussion of clause structure by looking at the syntax of the adverb *probably* and the quantifier *all* in the following sentence:

(1) They have *probably* **all** given up smoking

At first sight, (1) seems relatively unproblematic. After all, we might suppose that *all* is a floating quantifier stranded in spec-vp (by movement of *they* into spec-IP), and *probably* is an adverb adjoined to vp, so that (1) has the simplified derivation (2) below:

(2)

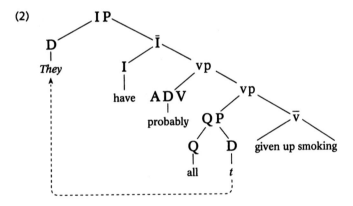

Of course, the analysis in (2) requires us to posit that adverbs like *probably* are adjuncts to maximal projections rather than (as assumed in the previous chapter) to intermediate projections. However, there are theoretical reasons for supposing that this is a plausible assumption.

The relevant considerations relate to the traditional assumption that languages contain movement rules which **adjoin** one constituent to another (for obvious reasons, the relevant type of movement operation is referred to as **adjunction**). For example, a traditional way of handling the relation between sentence pairs such as (3a–b) below:

(3) (a) He *does not* understand syntax
    (b) He *doesn't* understand syntax

is to suppose that the word *not* (in the guise of its contracted form *n't*) **adjoins** to the auxiliary *does*, so forming *doesn't* (which behaves like a single word e.g. in respect of undergoing inversion in sentences like *Doesn't he understand syntax?*). Similarly, one way of describing what happens when the italicized phrase *such behaviour* is preposed (in order to emphasize it in some way) in a sentence pair such as:

(4) (a) You must know that we cannot tolerate *such behaviour*
     (b) You must know that *such behaviour* we cannot tolerate

is to say that the DP *such behaviour* **adjoins** to the IP headed by *cannot* (cf. Grimshaw 1993). We might then conclude (as Chomsky does in his *Barriers* monograph, 1986b) that the only type of adjunction operations which can result from movement are adjunction of one head to another or of one maximal projection to another. It would therefore seem natural to suppose that the same is true of the merger operations which attach adverbial adjuncts to the expressions they modify: and this in turn would rule out the possibility of merging an adverb with an intermediate projection, but would allow for structures like (2) in which *probably* (which is itself a maximal projection in (2) above) is an adjunct to the maximal projection vp.

However, the analysis in (2) proves to be descriptively inadequate for a number of reasons. For one thing, it assumes that adverbs like *probably* can serve as vp adjuncts. Yet if this were so, we'd expect that *probably* could be positioned before or after another vp adjunct like *completely*, given the traditional assumption that adjuncts of the same kind can be freely ordered with respect to one another. However, this is not so, as we see from sentences such as:

(5) (a) They have *probably* **completely** given up smoking
     (b)*They have **completely** *probably* given up smoking

The fact that *probably* must be positioned to the left of the vp adverb *completely* suggests that it is a different kind of adverb altogether. In traditional terms, *probably* is an IP adverb – i.e. an adverb which merges with an IP to form an extended IP. But, of course, if *probably* is not a vp adverb, the analysis in (2) cannot be right.

The problems are compounded when we come to consider how to deal with sentences such as:

(6) They *probably* **all** have given up smoking

It is less than obvious how we might deal with sentences like (6) if we make the traditional assumption that finite auxiliaries like *have* are generated in INFL, and that floating quantifiers are stranded in subject QPs: after all, how can *they* and (the QP containing) *all* both be subjects of the same auxiliary *have*?

Given the conventional assumption that each auxiliary permits only one subject, the answer is that they can't. So, an alternative possibility which we might pursue is that there are in fact two different auxiliary positions between CP and vp, with *they* serving as the subject of one of them, and the QP containing the stranded quantifier *all* as the subject of the other. Since auxiliaries like *have/be* typically inflect for **tense** and **agreement**, one suggestion which has been made (cf. Pollock 1989, Belletti 1990 and Chomsky 1993) is to suppose that (rather than containing a single INFL head) finite clauses contain separate **tense** and **agreement** heads, each of which projects into a separate phrasal projection – tense into a **tense phrase** and agreement into an **agreement phrase**. Let us also suppose (following Belletti and Chomsky) that the agreement head occupies a higher position than the tense head, and that auxiliaries are generated in the tense position and from there can move into the separate agreement position, and that nominative subjects raise from spec-vp to the specifier position in the agreement phrase, to check their case features. Since the agreement relation in question involves subjects, it has become conventional in the linguistic literature to denote the relevant subject agreement head as **AgrS** (and its subject agreement phrase projection as **AgrSP**); the tense head is conventionally abbreviated to **T** (and its tense phrase projection to **TP**). If we go down this road, our earlier **INFL** head will in effect be split into two different heads – a **T** head and an **AgrS** head: hence, for obvious reasons, this analysis has become known as the **split INFL hypothesis**.

Within the *split INFL* framework, a sentence such as (1) *They have probably all given up smoking* might be derived as follows. The QP *all they* originates in spec-vp (as the subject of *given up smoking*), and from there raises up into spec-TP, as in (7) below; the adverb *probably* adjoins to TP, so deriving:

(7)

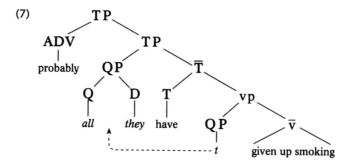

TP is then merged with an AgrS (= subject agreement) head which projects into AgrSP (= subject agreement phrase); the pronoun *they* raises
to spec-AgrSP (= into the specifier position within the subject agreement phrase) to check its nominative case, and the auxiliary *have* raises
from T to AgrS (thereby enabling it to check its agreement properties)
as in (8) below:

(8)

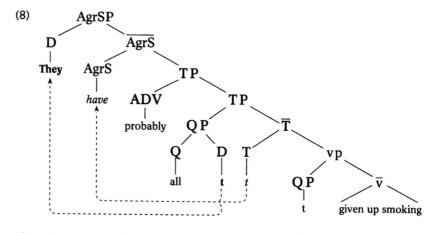

Since there are two functional projections above vp in (8) (AgrSP and
TP), it follows that there are two different subject positions outside VP,
one of which (= spec-AgrSP) houses the subject pronoun *they*, and the
other of which (= spec-TP) houses the QP containing the stranded
quantifier *all*.

We might propose to derive (6) *They probably all have given up
smoking* in essentially the same way, except that the auxiliary *have*
remains in the head T position of TP, and does not move to AgrS. If this
is so, (6) will have the (simplified) derivation (9) below (where the right-
hand trace is left behind by movement of the QP *all they* from spec-vp to
spec-TP):

(9)

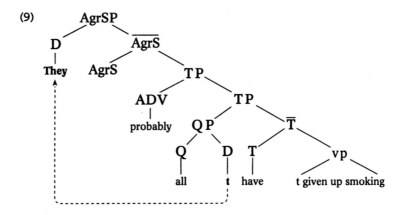

The fact that the auxiliary *have* is positioned after the TP adverb *proba-bly* in (9) but before it in (8) would suggest that *have* occupies the head T position in TP in (9), and moves from there to occupy the head AgrS position of AgrSP in (8) (as argued by Koizumi 1995, p. 41). We might fol-low Bošković (1995, p. 22) in supposing that finite auxiliaries in English can have either strong or weak agreement-features, and raise to AgrS when they have strong agreement-features, but remain in T when they have weak agreement-features. If we assume that AgrS has strong specifier-features in English, it follows that subjects will always raise to spec-AgrSP.

A different kind of argument in favour of the split IP hypothesis can be formulated in relation to a phenomenon sometimes referred to as **scrambling**. As the Shakespearean examples below illustrate, in Early Modern English the complement of a verb could be *scrambled* – i.e. moved out of its underlying position as a complement of the verb into some position higher up in the clause (in the examples below, the scrambled constituent is italicized):

(10) (a) *Thy physic* I will try   (King, *All's Well That Ends Well*, II.i)

      (b) She may *more suitors* have   (Tranio, *The Taming of the Shrew*, I.ii)

      (c) The king *your mote* did see   (Boyet, *Love's Labour's Lost*, IV.i)

Scrambling is traditionally analysed as involving adjunction of the moved constituent to a maximal projection higher up in the structure. Sentences such as (10a) and (10b) can be dealt with straightforwardly within the traditional IP analysis of clauses if we assume that *thy physic* is adjoined to the left of the IP headed by *will* in (10a), and that *more suitors* is adjoined to the left of the VP headed by *have* in (10b). But this leaves us with the question of where *your mote* is positioned in (10c). Under the traditional IP analysis, there is no obvious answer to this question: if we assume that maximal projections can only adjoin to other maximal projections (as suggested above), we can't say that *your mote* in (10c) is adjoined to an I-bar headed by *did*, since I-bar is an intermediate projection, not a maximal projection. However, the *split IP* analysis provides us with an alternative analysis. If we suppose that *did* in (10c) occupies the head T position of TP, we can then say that the scrambled complement *your mote* is adjoined to TP, while the subject *the king* occupies spec-AgrSP. More specifically, we might suggest that (10c) is derived as in (11) below:

(11)
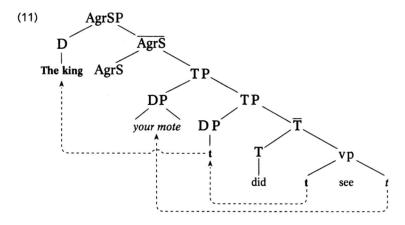

Of course, given the assumption that scrambling in (11) involves adjunction of the scrambled DP *your mote* to TP, we might propose to analyse (10b) in a parallel fashion, with the auxiliary *may* moving from T to AgrS (hence preceding the scrambled phrase *more suitors* which adjoins to TP).

Alison Henry (1995) presents an interesting argument from the syntax of Belfast English (BE) in support of the *split INFL* (AgrSP/TP) analysis of clause structure. She notes that in BE, we find sentences such as (12) below in which a singular verb form is used with a plural objective subject:

(12) (a) **Themuns** *is* annoying youse (themuns = 'them ones')
      (b) **Usuns** *was* late (usuns = 'us ones')
      (c) **Us students** *doesn't* have much money
      (d) **Me and you** *is* supposed to help ourselves
      (e) **Him and me** *goes* there every week

She argues that the +s inflection on verb forms like *is/was/has/does/ goes* in BE structures like (12) marks present tense (as indeed is the case in many other varieties of English – e.g. in south-western British English, where we find paradigms such as *I/we/you/he/she/they **hates** syntax*), and that consequently there is no morphological marking of agreement in structures like (12). She notes that absence of agreement-marking correlates with the assignment of objective case to the subject of the verb. (Where a nominative subject is used, the verb must obligatorily agree with the subject, as in *They are/*is working hard.*) She also notes that agreementless finite verb forms like those in (12) cannot undergo auxiliary inversion – as we see from the ungrammaticality of such questions as:

(13) (a) **Is* themuns annoying youse?
         (b) **Is* us students entitled to free condoms?
         (c) **Is* you and me supposed to help ourselves?

(By contrast, sentences with nominative subjects and agreement-inflected verbs do indeed allow inversion – cf. *Are they going to the disco?*) How can we account for the fact that agreementless finite verbs and auxiliaries have objective subjects and don't allow inversion?

Henry argues that the absence of agreement-marking in finite clauses like (12) means that AgrS in such clauses has weak head-features, and so does not allow movement of an auxiliary from T to AgrS. She conjectures that (again in consequence of the absence of subject agreement) AgrS also has weak specifier features, and so does not trigger raising of the subject to spec-AgrSP. Accordingly, agreementless finite auxiliaries remain in T, and their subjects raise only as far as spec-TP, where they check objective case by default (i.e. because the subject needs to be case-checked but is unable to raise to spec-AgrSP to check nominative case, the subject checks objective case in spec-TP as a last resort). On this view, a sentence such as (12a) *Themuns is annoying youse* will contain the TP (14) below (*t* is the trace left behind by movement of the subject *themuns* from spec-vp to spec-TP):

(14)

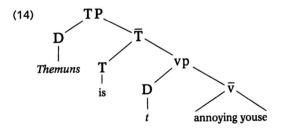

Consider now why the interrogative counterpart (13a) **Is themuns annoying youse?* is ungrammatical. If we suppose that questions are CP/AgrSP/TP structures and involve movement of an auxiliary into the head C position of CP, there are two ways in which we might seek to move the auxiliary *is* from T to C. One is in two short steps, moving *is* first into AgrS (as in movement (1) below) and then into C (as in movement (2) below); the other is in a single step, moving *is* directly from T to C (as in movement 3 below: *Op* is the abstract yes–no question operator which we posited in chapter 6):

(15)

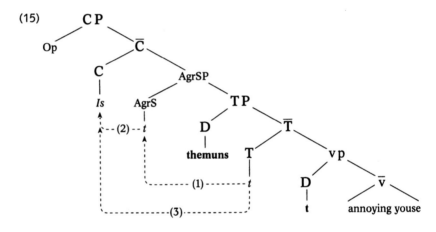

(The bold-printed trace **t** is the trace of the subject *themuns*, which moves from spec-vp to spec-TP.) However, the successive cyclic (1+2) derivation in (15) is ruled out by virtue of the fact that AgrS is weak in agreementless finite clauses, so step (1) of the derivation violates the principle of **greed** (which allows movement only as a way of checking strong features). Moreover, direct movement of *is* from T to C (as in (3)) will violate the **head movement constraint** (or the **shortest movement principle**), because *is* does not move into the next-highest head position (which would be AgrS), but rather into the next-highest-but-one head (i.e. C). Since we cannot derive (13a) either by a single long movement of *is* from T to C, or by two successive short movements of *is* from T to AgrS to C, our grammar correctly specifies that sentences such as (13a) are ungrammatical. But note that a central pillar of the argumentation is the assumption that all finite clauses contain an AgrSP projection in addition to (and *on top of*) a TP projection.

Just as recent work has argued in favour of splitting IP into two different projections (a subject agreement phrase and a tense phrase), so too it has been argued that the verb phrase should similarly be split into a number of different projections including one headed by an **object agreement** constituent (designated as **AgrO**). Although there are a number of variants of this proposal in the relevant literature, the one which we shall outline here assumes that the object agreement phrase (= **AgrOP**) is positioned between the two different verbal projections **vp** and **VP**: for obvious reasons, this has come to be known as the **split VP hypothesis** (cf. Bobaljik 1995, Carnie 1995, Harley 1995 and Koizumi 1995). The core assumption underlying the analysis is that just as nominative DPs raise to spec-AgrSP in order to check their nominative case and subject agreement-features under spec–head agreement with AgrS, so too objective DPs raise to spec-AgrOP in order to check their objective case-feature and (in languages in which verbs inflect for agreement with their objects) their object-agreement features under spec–head agreement with AgrO. From a theoretical perspective, the obvious advantage that such an analysis offers is that it enables us to provide a unified account of case- and agreement-checking, in which all case- and agreement-features are checked under a spec–head relation between a functional head and its specifier. Let's look at some of the evidence in support of such an analysis.

One argument that objective DPs move in order to check their case comes from systematic differences between the position of CP complements and DP complements, illustrated by the examples below:

(16) (a) He reported to the police *that there had been a robbery*
      (b) He reported **the robbery** to the police

(17) (a) He admitted to her *that he was guilty*
      (b) He admitted **his guilt** to her

(18) (a) He announced *to the press* that he was retiring
      (b) He announced **his retirement** to the press

It seems reasonable to suppose that *that*-clause complements don't carry objective case. After all, they can't occur as the complements of transitive prepositions like those bold-printed in the examples below:

(19) (a) *I was sure **of** *that she'd come*
      (b) *Concern was expressed **about** *that he had lied*
      (c) *There isn't time **for** *that we have a meal*

If *that*-clause complements don't carry case, we can assume that they don't move for case-checking purposes, but rather remain *in situ*. This being so, consider how we account for the clause-final position of the *that*-clause in a sentence such as (16a) *He reported to the police that there had been a robbery*.

Given the VP shell analysis outlined in the previous chapter, (16a) can be derived as follows. The verb *reported* merges with its THEME argument (the CP *that there had been a robbery*) to form a V-bar; the resulting V-bar *reported that there had been a robbery* merges with its RECIPIENT argument (the PP *to the police*) to form the VP (20) below:

(20)

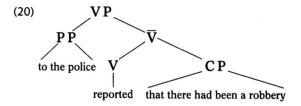

The VP in (20) then merges with a performative light verb ø whose AGENT subject is *he*, and the verb *reported* adjoins to the light verb, as below:

(21)

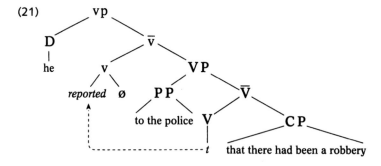

Subsequently, the subject *he* raises through spec-TP to spec-AgrSP to check its nominative case. A crucial assumption underlying the derivation in (21) is that the CP *that there had been a robbery* remains *in situ* throughout.

If we adopt the **uniform theta-assignment hypothesis**, it follows that the DP complement *the robbery* in (16b) *He reported the robbery to the police* must originate in the same position as the CP complement *that there had been a robbery* in (20), since the relevant DP and CP constituents play the same thematic role as THEME argument of *reported*.

But since the DP *the robbery* ends up in a position between the verb *reported* and the PP *to the police*, it must subsequently move to some higher position between the vp containing the verb *reported* in (21) and the VP containing the PP *to the police*. By hypothesis, the higher position which *the robbery* moves to is the specifier position within an AgrOP projection positioned between vp and VP. If this is so, (16b) will have the following derivation.

The verb *reported* merges with its DP complement *the robbery* to form a V-bar; the resulting V-bar *reported the robbery* then merges with the PP *to the police* to form the VP in (22) below:

(22)

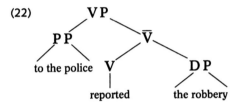

The resulting VP merges with an AgrO constituent to form an AgrO-bar projection, with the verb *reported* raising to AgrO; the DP *the robbery* raises to become the specifier of AgrO-bar, so forming the AgrOP (23) below:

(23)

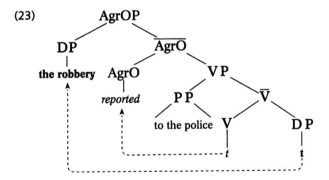

Since the DP *the robbery* and the AgrO constituent containing the transitive verb *reported* are in a spec–head relation in (23), the objective case-feature carried by each can be checked against that of the other, and erased. Subsequently, the AgrOP constituent in (23) merges with a performative light verb ø (whose AGENT subject is *he*) and the verb *reported* adjoins to this light verb as in (24) below:

(24)

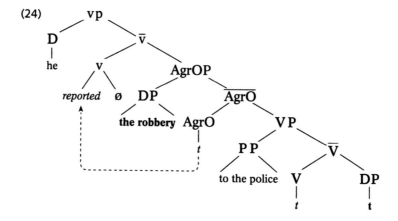

Lastly, the subject *he* raises through spec-TP to spec-AgrSP to check its nominative case.

An analysis along the lines sketched out above has both empirical and theoretical merits. From an empirical point of view, its main merit is that it accounts for why DP objects are postverbal, whereas CP complements are clause-final – i.e. it accounts for the word-order contrasts illustrated in (16–18) above. On the analysis presented here, this follows from the fact that DP complements carry objective case and hence have to raise to spec-AgrOP for case-checking; by contrast, CP complements are caseless and so need not (and therefore, by the **economy principle** cannot) raise to spec-AgrOP. (We might also assume that the **economy principle** determines that clauses which have no DP object do not contain an AgrOP projection at all – as indeed we tacitly assumed earlier in relation to the derivation sketched out in (21) above.)

From a theoretical point of view, the main merit of the AgrOP analysis in (24) is that it enables us to arrive at a more unitary theory of checking. Until now, we had assumed that two different types of relation were involved in checking, viz. a relation between a head and its specifier, or a relation between a head and its complement. This led to obvious asymmetries, in that (for example) checking the case of a nominative D(P) involved a specifier–head relation, whereas checking the case of an objective D(P) involved a head–complement relation (or, in ECM structures, a relation between a matrix head and a complement specifier). But suppose we now eliminate the possibility that head–complement relations are involved in checking, and argue instead that a head can only check its features against those of its specifier. If we further suppose that nominative and objective D(P)s in English carry strong case-features, it follows that the only way in which an objective D(P) can check its case-feature is by raising into a position in which it can enter into a spec–head relation with a transitive verb: the required spec–head configuration will obviously come about if the object raises to spec-AgrOP and the transitive verb raises to AgrO.

We can formulate a different kind of argument in support of the claim that DP objects move to spec-AgrOP for case-checking purposes in relation to the position of *adverbs*. In this connection, consider how we account for the following contrasts:

(25) (a) He plays chess well
      (b) * He plays well chess
      (c) * He well plays chess

If we make the traditional assumption that *well* is a VP adverb, and if we further assume (as we did in relation to our discussion of *probably* in (7) and (8) above) that adverbs merge with maximal projections, (25a) will be derived as follows. The verb *plays* originates in the head V of VP, and merges with its complement *chess* (which is a DP headed by a null determiner Ø) to form the VP *plays chess*; the adverb *well* merges with this VP, so deriving the extended VP in (26) below:

(26)

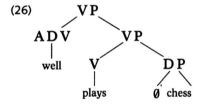

The VP in (26) is then merged with an AgrO morpheme (which projects into AgrOP); the verb *play* raises to AgrO, and the DP Ø *chess* raises to spec-AgrOP as in (27) below:

(27)

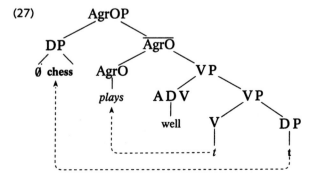

The objective case-feature carried by the DP Ø *chess* (cf. *He plays lots of games, and plays **them** well*) is checked at this point, since the DP Ø *chess* is in a spec–head relation with the transitive verb *plays* (by virtue of the fact that *plays* is in AgrO, and Ø *chess* is in spec-AgrOP).

The AgrOP constituent in (27) is then merged with a performative light verb ø whose subject is *he*; the verb *plays* adjoins to the light verb, as below:

(28)

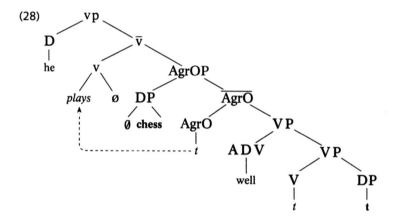

The pronoun *he* then raises through spec-TP to spec-AgrSP, so deriving (25a) *He plays chess well*. The assumption that both verbs and objective DPs raise across VP adverbs correctly predicts that sentences like (25b–c) are ungrammatical.

An analysis along the lines sketched out above accounts for the fact that verbs in English are immediately adjacent to their objects (as illustrated in (25) above) and cannot be separated from them by intervening adverbials. On this account, the only way in which a transitive verb could be separated from its object would be for an adverb to be adjoined to AgrOP. But if we make the traditional assumption that adverbs modify projections whose heads have specific semantic content, it follows that we can have adverbs adjoined to projections of V, v or T (since V contains a lexical verb with its own semantic properties, v contains an abstract light verb which has a specific – e.g. causative or performative – sense, and T has temporal properties), but that we can't adjoin adverbs to projections of agreement heads, since these have a purely formal function (viz. that of checking case/agreement properties).

The AgrOP analysis also turns out to provide us with a solution to a puzzling problem which arises in relation to how we analyse ECM (= *exceptional case-marking*) structures such as the following, involving a bracketed infinitive complement with an objective subject:

(29) (a) The DA **proved** [the witness *conclusively* to have lied]

(adapted from Bowers 1993, p. 632)

   (b) I **suspect** [him *strongly* to be a liar]   (Authier 1991, p. 729)

   (c) I've **believed** [Gary *for a long time now* to be a fool]

(Kayne 1984, p. 114)

   (d) I have **found** [Bob *recently* to be morose]   (Postal 1974, p. 146)

In sentences such as these, the italicized adverbial/prepositional expression is positioned *inside* the bracketed infinitive complement, and yet is construed as modifying a (bold-printed) verb which lies *outside* the bracketed complement clause. How can we account for this seeming paradox? To make our discussion more concrete, let's consider how we might derive (29a).

If we assume that an adverb such as *conclusively* is a VP adverb and that *proved* originates in the head V position of VP, the obvious problem we are left with is accounting for how both the verb *proved* and the DP *the witness* end up in front of the adverb *conclusively*. One answer might be the following. Let's suppose that the verb *proved* merges with the infinitive phrase *the witness to have lied* to form the VP *proved the witness to have lied*, and that the adverb *conclusively* merges with this VP to form the expanded VP (30) below. (Here infinitive phrases are labelled as IPs, though they are arguably AgrSPs with essentially the same internal structure as finite clauses.)

(30)

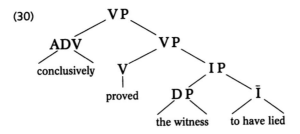

Let's further suppose that the VP in (30) then merges with an AgrO constituent, that the verb *proved* moves into AgrO and that the DP *the witness* raises to spec-AgrOP, as in (31) below:

(31)

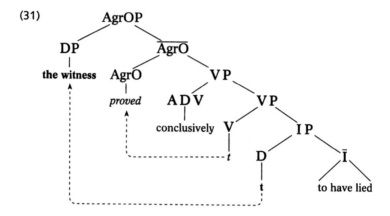

The objective case-features carried by *the witness* (cf. *The DA proved him conclusively to have lied*) and by the transitive verb *proved* are checked at this point, via a spec–head relation between the verb *proved* in AgrO and its specifier *the witness* in spec-AgrOP.

The AgrOP in (31) is then merged with an abstract light verb ø whose AGENT subject/specifier is the nominative DP *the DA*: because ø is a strong (affixal) head, the verb *proved* raises to adjoin to it, as in (32) below. (The subject *the DA* subsequently raises from spec-vp to spec-TP and spec-AgrSP, but we do not show these later stages of derivation here.)

(32)

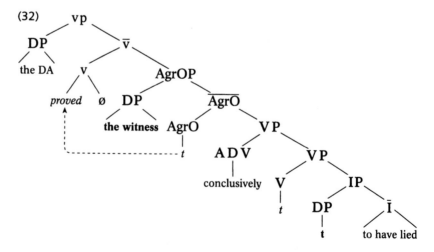

As a result of movement of the DP *the witness* to spec-AgrOP and of the verb *proved* to the head v position of vp, both end up positioned in front of the adverb *conclusively* – precisely as we find in (29a). Thus, in effect what happens in ECM structures is that the subject of the infinitive raises up to become the object of the matrix verb (as suggested in an earlier framework by Postal 1974).

Bošković (1995, p. 176) argues that an AgrOP analysis provides a straightforward account of the syntax of floating quantifiers in ECM structures such as (24) below:

(33) The DA proved the defendants *all* to be lying

We can derive (33) as follows. Let's assume that (at some point in the derivation), the verb *proved* is merged with an infinitive phrase (= IP) complement whose subject is the QP *all the defendants*, as in (34) below:

(34)

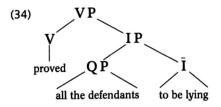

The VP in (34) is then merged with AgrO, the verb *believe* adjoins to AgrO and the DP *the defendants* moves to spec-AgrOP as in (35) below, stranding the quantifier *all* in spec-IP:

(35)

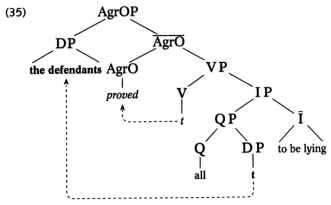

The objective case carried by *the defendants* (cf. *The DA proved **them** all to be lying*) is checked at this point; case-checking involves a spec–head relation between the transitive verb *proved* in AgrO and the objective DP *the defendants* in spec-AgrOP.

The V *proved* then adjoins to the strong light verb ø heading vp, deriving:

(36)

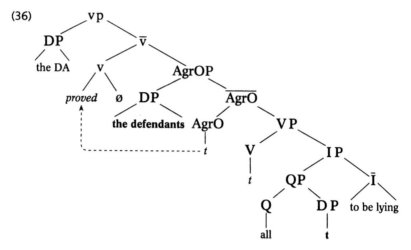

The subject *the DA* then raises through spec-TP into spec-AgrSP, so deriving (33) *The DA proved the defendants all to be lying*. Thus, facts from floating quantifiers lend further support to the claim that the objective infinitive subject in an ECM structure raises overtly to spec-AgrOP.

So far, we have argued that nominative DPs raise to spec-AgrSP in order to check their nominative-case head-feature, and similarly that objective DPs raise to spec-AgrOP in order to check their objective-case head-feature. An interesting extension of this analysis might be to suppose that *all* DPs in English have to check their case by moving to the specifier position within an AgrP projection of some kind. As we shall see, this unifying assumption has far-reaching consequences for how we analyse the syntax of a range of structures. For example, it means that in *double-object* structures such as *give someone something*, not only direct objects (like *something*) but also indirect objects (like *someone*) must move to a higher specifier position within an agreement phrase in order to check their case.

To see what this means in practice, consider how we might derive related sentence-pairs such as the following:

(37) (a) The crew handed back the passengers their passports
     (b) The crew handed the passengers back their passports
     (c) The crew handed the passengers their passports back

Let's suppose that at an intermediate stage of derivation, *handed back* is a complex verb (perhaps formed by merging *handed* with *back*, or by movement of *back* from some lower position to adjoin to *handed*) which projects into the VP (38) below:

(38)

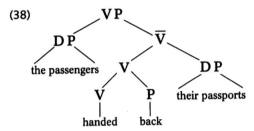

The direct object DP *their passports* in (38) has the θ-role THEME, and the indirect object DP *the passengers* has the θ-role of RECIPIENT. Let us suppose that the case carried by *internal arguments* such as these is determined by their thematic function, and that *dative* is the case canonically associated with RECIPIENT DPs and *objective* the case canonically associated with THEME DPs. In languages like Romanian which have a relatively rich nominal morphology, dative and objective DPs are morphologically distinct; but in languages like English which have an impoverished nominal morphology, the two have the same morphological form (e.g. *them* is an objective pronoun in *I gave them to Mary* and a dative pronoun in *I gave them a present*).

The VP in (38) merges with AgrO, and the complex verb *handed back* moves to AgrO and the objective DP *their passports* raises to spec-AgrOP as in (39) below (simplified by not showing the precise internal structure of AgrO; it is likely that the V *handed back* adjoins to AgrO, but this is a technical detail which we ignore here):

(39)

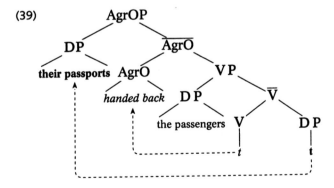

The objective case of the DP *their passports* in spec-AgrOP can then be checked under a spec–head relation with the transitive verb *handed (back)* in AgrO.

Let's suppose that the AgrOP in (39) is then merged with an indirect object agreement constituent (here symbolized as **AgrIO**); the complex verb *handed back* moves to AgrIO, and the dative DP *the passengers* raises to spec-AgrIOP as in (40) below:

(40)

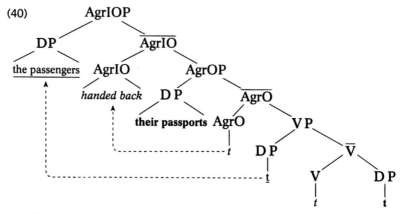

The dative case carried by the DP *the passengers* in spec-AgrIOP is then checked under a spec-head relation with the ditransitive (i.e. double-object) verb *handed (back)* which is in AgrIO.

Finally, let's suppose that the complex verb *handed back* raises to adjoin to the strong affixal light verb ø which heads vp (and whose AGENT subject is the nominative DP the *crew*), so forming the vp (41) below:

(41)

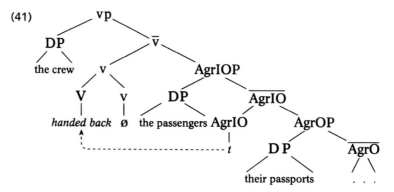

The DP *the crew* then raises through spec-TP into spec-AgrSP to check its nominative case, so deriving (37a) *The crew handed back the passengers their passports*.

Now consider how we derive (37b) *The crew handed the passengers back their passports*. Let's suppose that the derivation proceeds essentially as for (37a), until we reach the stage of derivation represented in (40) above. The AgrIOP in (40) is then merged with the abstract light verb ø: this light verb is a verbal affix, and so must be attached to a verb. But there are two possible candidate verbs here: either the whole

complex verb *handed back* or the simple verb *handed* on its own. In
(37a), the whole complex verb *handed back* adjoins to ø; but let's suppose that in (37b), only the simple verb *handed* adjoins to ø, as in (42)
below:

(42)

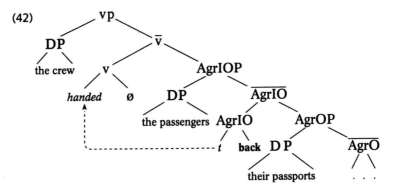

What has happened in (42) is that the simple verb *handed* has **excorpo-**
rated out of (i.e. detached itself from) the complex verb *handed back*,
leaving the particle *back* stranded in AgrIO between the indirect object
the passengers and the direct object *their passports*. Raising the DP *the*
crew through spec-TP to spec-AgrSP will then derive (37b) *The crew*
handed the passengers back their passports. (On *excorporation*, see
Roberts 1991.)

Finally, consider how we derive (37c) *The crew handed the passen-*
gers their passports back. Let's assume that the derivation proceeds as
for (37a) until we reach the stage represented in (39) above. At that
point, the verb *handed* excorporates out of AgrO and moves to AgrIO
on its own (stranding *back* in AgrO), and the indirect object *the passen-*
gers raises to spec-AgrIOP to check its case, as in (43) below:

(43)

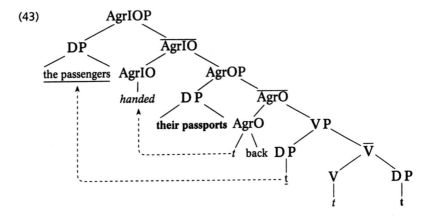

Subsequently, the verb *handed* adjoins to the strong light verb ø as in (44) below:

(44)

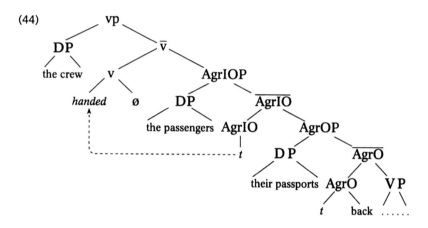

The DP *the crew* then raises through spec-TP to spec-AgrSP, thereby deriving (37c) *The crew handed the passengers their passports back.*

So, we see that the assumption that indirect object DPs raise to spec-AgrIOP in order to check their dative case (taken together with the assumption that when the verb in a *verb + particle* complex raises, the particle can either be pied-piped along with the verb or stranded) provides us with a principled account of the syntax of double-object particle structures such as (37a–c) above. From a theoretical standpoint, the assumption that dative DPs raise to spec-AgrIOP to check their case offers the obvious advantage of providing us with a unitary account of case-checking under which all DPs check their case by raising to the specifier position within an appropriate agreement phrase (nominative DPs raising to spec-AgrSP, objectives to spec-AgrOP and datives to spec-AgrIOP).

To summarize: in this chapter, we have argued that clauses contain three different types of agreement phrase. We began by outlining the **split INFL hypothesis**, arguing that we need to posit the existence of separate tense phrase (TP) and subject agreement phrase (AgrSP) projections in order to account for the fact that adverbs like *probably* and floating quantifiers like *all* can be positioned either before or after a finite auxiliary. We also saw that the split INFL analysis would provide a straightforward account of **scrambling** in Early Modern English, and would enable us to say that in sentences like *The king your mote did see,* the DP *your mote* has adjoined to TP, while the subject *the king* is in spec-AgrSP. In addition, we noted Alison Henry's arguments that the *split INFL* analysis enables us to provide an insightful description of the syntax of the case and agreement properties of subjects and auxiliaries in Belfast English, under which nominative subjects are in spec-AgrSP, and any auxiliary which checks the agreement properties of the subject is in AgrS (and so can move to C in questions), whereas objective subjects are in spec-TP and any associated auxiliary is in T, and (by virtue of lacking agreement properties) can't move through AgrS to C in questions.

We then went on to outline the **split VP hypothesis**, under which clauses headed by transitive verbs contain an object agreement phrase (AgrOP) positioned between vp and VP: a direct object DP raises to spec-AgrOP and its associated verb to AgrO in order to check objective case (the verb subsequently raising still further to v). We noted that such an analysis would provide a principled account of why object DPs occupy a different position from object CPs (e.g. in sentences such as *He reported to the police that there had been a robbery* and *He reported the robbery to the police*), and why DP objects are positioned in front of VP adverbs (e.g. in sentences such as *He plays chess well*). We further argued that the *split VP* analysis provides an interesting account of two otherwise puzzling aspects of the syntax of ECM structures, namely the position of the adverb *conclusively* in sentences such as *The DA proved the witness conclusively to have lied*, and the position of the quantifier *all* in sentences like *The DA proved the defendants all to be lying*.

We subsequently suggested that indirect object DPs carry dative case, and check their case by raising to the specifier position within an indirect object agreement projection (AgrIOP) which is positioned immediately above AgrOP (with the verb raising first to AgrO, then to AgrIO and finally to v). We saw that such an analysis would allow us to claim that in sentences such as *The crew handed the passengers back their passports*, the particle *back* has been stranded in AgrIO. More generally, we concluded that an analysis in which a nominative DP checks its case by raising to spec-AgrS, an objective DP by raising to spec-AgrOP, and a dative DP by raising to spec-AgrIOP would enable us to maintain the position that case-checking in English canonically involves a spec–head relation between a functional (agreement) head and its specifier.

It need scarcely be pointed out that the analyses we have presented in this chapter are not fully worked out (and doubtlessly flawed) in a number of respects. The reason is simple: the ideas explored in this chapter (inspired by Chomsky's **minimalist program** in the 1990s) are part of an ongoing research programme which is leading different researchers in different directions. Many important questions of detail and principle remain unresolved for the present. For example, there is disagreement on whether *all* objective DPs (or *some*, or *none*) in English check their case by raising overtly to spec-AgrOP. Koizumi (1995) maintains that all objective DPs check their case in this way; Bošković (1995) maintains that while it is plausible to analyse objective subjects in ECM structures as raising to spec-AgrOP in English, it is not plausible to extend the raising-to-spec-AgrOP analysis to other direct (or indirect) object DPs. Bobaljik (1995) goes even further and rejects the claim that any objective DPs raise to spec-AgrOP in English, prefer-ring to maintain that objective case-checking canonically involves a head–complement relation (much as we assumed in chapter 3). And Chomsky (1995) questions the need for positing any agreement projec-tions in any languages, suggesting that only constituents with intrinsic semantic content can serve as heads projecting into phrases. While it might seem ironic that linguists can't agree about the syntax of agree-ment, it should be emphasized that work in this domain is only in its infancy: and the first step in understanding any problem is to identify the nature of the problem, to outline possible solutions and to be aware of the hidden costs associated with such solutions. While it is true that there is a wide range of alternative analyses of particular structures (e.g. double-object constructions) found in the contemporary linguistic liter-ature, it is equally true that a considerable amount of the relevant research work presupposes some variant of the richly articulated AgrSP/TP/vp/AgrIOP/AgrOP/VP clause structure that we have argued for in this chapter and the last – and in particular, assumes the existence of subject agreement and object agreement projections (and perhaps also indirect object agreement projections); and indeed, some work goes still further and posits the existence of **aspect phrase**, **voice phrase** and **modal phrase** projections as well (cf. e.g. Ouhalla 1991 and Cinque 1995). Moreover, even work which questions the empirical and theoreti-cal motivation for positing agreement phrases presupposes familiarity with work on the syntax of AgrP projections. So, for both AgrOphiles and AgrOphobes alike, the syntax of agreement remains at the very heart of contemporary debates about the nature of syntactic structure.

Exercises

Exercise XIX

Discuss the syntax of the following sentences:

1a She complained bitterly that he let her down

  b She bitterly complained that he let her down

  c *She complained that he let her down bitterly

2a He recommended to her that she should try the restaurant

  b He recommended the restaurant to her

  c *He recommended that she should try the restaurant to her

3a She warmly congratulated the winner

  b *She congratulated warmly the winner

  c She congratulated the winner warmly

4a He taught the students French audiovisually

  b *He taught the students audiovisually French

  c *He audiovisually taught the students French

5a They definitely have proved that he is innocent

  b They have definitely proved that he is innocent

  c *They have proved definitely that he is innocent

6a They will probably subsequently claim that he was cheating

  b They probably will claim subsequently that he was cheating

  c *They will subsequently probably claim that he was cheating

7a They all have done the assignment

  b They have all done the assignment

  c *They have done all the assignment

8a The CIA handed the tapes over secretly to the FBI

  b The CIA handed over the tapes secretly to the FBI

  c *The CIA secretly handed the tapes to the FBI over

Model answer for 1

If we suppose that *bitterly* can modify a verbal projection and so serve as a VP/vp adverb, we might derive 1a as follows. The verb *complained* merges with its CP complement *that he let her down* to form the VP *complained that he let her down*. This in turn merges with the adverb *bitterly* to form the extended VP (i) below:

(i)

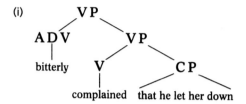

The VP in (i) then merges with a light verb ø (whose AGENT subject is *she*), and the verb *complained* adjoins to ø thereby deriving:

(ii)

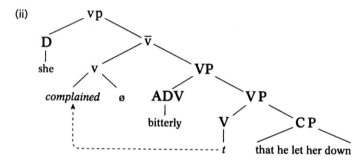

The subject *she* then raises through spec-TP into spec-AgrSP, so deriving ɪa *She complained bitterly that he let her down*.

By contrast, ɪb is derived by merging the verb *complained* with the CP *that he let her down* to form the VP (iii) below:

(iii)

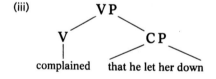

This in turn is merged with the light verb ø (to which *complained* adjoins), forming a vp to which the adverb *bitterly* adjoins, as in (iv) below:

(iv)

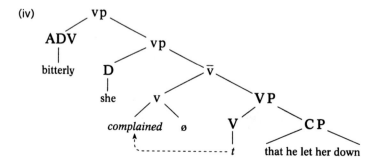

The subject *she* then raises through spec-TP into spec-AgrSP, so deriving
1b *She bitterly complained that he let her down*.

If we assume that adverbial modifiers are adjoined to the left of the
constituents they modify (just as adjectival modifiers typically precede
the nouns they modify), it follows that the only two positions which
bitterly can occupy are VP-initial position as in (i) above, or vp-initial
position as in (iv) above. We could then attribute the ungrammaticality
of sentences such as 1c to the fact that 1c requires us to generate the
adverb *bitterly* in VP-final or vp-final position.

Exercise XX

Discuss the syntax of the following complement-clause structures
(the Belfast English examples in 8 are from Henry 1995, p. 85):

1a   He admitted openly to her that he had stolen the money

 b *He admitted that he had stolen the money openly to her

2a   She found out that he was cheating on her

 b *She found that he was cheating on her out

3a   She wanted them desperately to start a family

 b *She wanted desperately them to start a family

4a   The DA made the witness out convincingly to have lied

 b *The DA made convincingly the witness out to have lied

5a   He made them all out to have lied

 b   He made them out all to have lied

6a   The KGB made the prisoners forcibly sign confessions

 b   I wouldn't let my children ever drive my car

7a   We proved Smith conclusively to the authorities to be the thief

 b *We proved conclusively Smith to the authorities to be the thief

8a   I wanted Jimmy for to come with me (Belfast English)

 b *I wanted for Jimmy to come with me (Belfast English)

(The adverb *desperately* is intended to be construed as modifying a
projection of *wanted* in 3; *convincingly* as modifying *made* (*out*) in 4;
forcibly as modifying *made* in 6a; and *ever* as modifying *let* in 6b. The
relevant adverbs in some cases could also be construed as modifying
some other constituent, but ignore alternative interpretations for the
purposes of this exercise.)

Model answer for 1

We might suppose that the verb *admitted* in 1a merges with its CP complement *that he had stolen the money* to form the V-bar *admitted that he had stolen the money*, and that this V-bar merges with the PP *to her* to form the VP *to her admitted that he had stolen the money*. Adjoining the adverb *openly* to the resulting VP will form the extended VP (i) below:

(i)

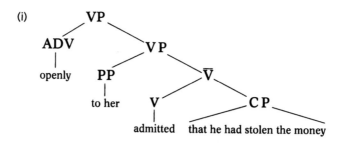

The VP in (i) is then merged with a light verb ø (with an AGENT subject *he*) to which the verb *admitted* adjoins, as in (ii) below:

(ii)

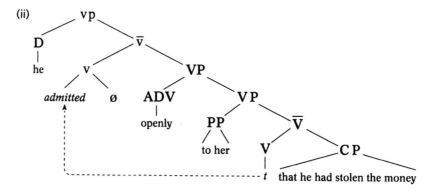

Subsequently, the subject *he* raises through spec-TP into spec-AgrSP to check its nominative case.

A crucial assumption underlying this analysis is that the CP *that he had stolen the money* remains *in situ* and doesn't raise to any higher position. In this respect, the CP *that he had stolen the money* in 1a behaves very differently from the DP *the theft* in (iii) below:

(iii)   He admitted *the theft* openly to her

How come the DP complement *the theft* in (iii) is positioned in front of *to her* when the CP complement *that he had stolen the money* in (ii) is positioned after *to her*? A plausible answer is that the DP *the money* carries objective case, and hence needs to raise to spec-AgrOP to check its case, as in (iv) below:

(iv)

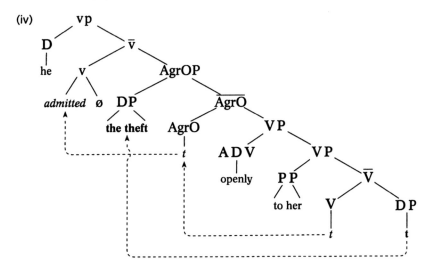

(Subsequently, *he* raises through spec-TP into spec-AgrSP to check its case.) This in turn raises the question of why the CP *that he had stolen the money* can't raise to spec-AgrOP in the same way (thereby generating the structure associated with the ungrammatical 1b *He admitted that he had stolen the money openly to her*. The answer suggested in the text is that *that*-clauses differ from DPs in that DPs can carry objective case, whereas *that*-clauses can't – as is illustrated by the fact that a DP like *the facts* can serve as the object of a transitive preposition like *about*, whereas a CP like *that he had stolen the money* can't: cf.

(v) (a) I wasn't sure about *the facts*
　　(b)*I wasn't sure about *that he had stolen the money*

If we assume that the *that*-clause in 1 has no case to check, it follows that it will remain *in situ* in VP-complement position as in (ii), and will not raise to spec-AgrOP (across *openly to her*), since any such movement would violate the principle of **greed** (which allows movement only as a way of checking strong features). Moreover, **economy** considerations mean that there cannot be an AgrOP projection in (ii), since there is no objective case to check (hence AgrOP would be a superfluous projection).

Glossary and list of abbreviations

(The abbreviation *ch.* is used for *chapter*, and bold-printed terms within glosses cross-refer to related entries elsewhere in the glossary.)

A See **adjective**.

A-bar movement An *A-bar movement* operation is one which moves a maximal projection into an *A-bar position* (i.e. a non-argument position, or more specifically, a position which can be occupied by expressions which are not arguments). So, **operator movement, scrambling** and the kind of **adjunction** operation whereby *this kind of behaviour* is adjoined to the clause containing it in a sentence such as *This kind of behaviour we cannot tolerate* are all specific types of A-bar movement operation.

Absorption A passive participle is said to *absorb* the theta-role which a verb would otherwise assign to its subject (thereby dethematizing the subject) and to absorb the objective case which a transitive verb would otherwise assign to its object (thereby detransitivizing the verb, so that passive participles are intransitive). See ch. 8.

Accusative See **case**.

Active A contrast is traditionally drawn between sentence pairs such as (i) and (ii) below:

(i) The thieves stole the jewels
(ii) The jewels were stolen by the thieves

Example (i) is said to be an *active* clause (or sentence), and (ii) to be its *passive* counterpart; similarly, the verb *stole* is said to be an *active* verb (or a verb in the *active voice*) in (i), whereas the verb *stolen* is said to be a *passive* verb (or a verb in the *passive voice* – more specifically, a *passive participle*) in (ii); likewise, the auxiliary *were* in (ii) is said to be a *passive auxiliary*.

Adjacency condition A condition requiring that two expressions must be immediately adjacent (i.e. one must immediately follow the other) in order for some operation to apply. For example, *to* can only contract onto *want* (forming *wanna*) if the two are immediately adjacent.

Adjective A category of word which often denotes states (e.g. *happy, sad*), which typically has an adverb counterpart in +*ly* (cf. *sad/sadly*), which typically has comparative/superlative forms in +*er/*+*est* (cf. *sadder/saddest*), which can often take the prefix +*un* (cf. *unhappy*), and which can often form a noun by the addition of +*ness* (cf. *sadness*). See ch. 2.

Adjoin See **adjunction**.

Adjunct One way in which this term is used is to denote an optional constituent typically used to specify e.g. the time, location or manner in which an event takes place (e.g. *in the pub* is an adjunct in a sentence such as *We had a drink in the pub*). Another way in which it is used is to denote a constituent which has been *adjoined* to another to form an extended constituent (see **adjunction**).

Adjunction A process by which one word is adjoined (= attached) to another to form a compound word, or one phrase is adjoined to another phrase to form an even larger phrase. For example, we might say that in a sentence such as *He shouldn't go, not* (in the guise of its contracted form *n't*) has been adjoined to the auxiliary *should* to form the negative auxiliary *shouldn't*. Likewise, in a sentence such as *You know that such behaviour we cannot tolerate*, we might argue that *such behaviour* has been adjoined to the *we*-clause. See ch. 10.

ADV/Adverb A category of word which typically indicates manner (e.g. *wait patiently*) or degree (e.g. *exceedingly patient*). In English, most (but not all) adverbs end in +*ly* (cf. *quickly* – but also *almost*). See ch. 2.

Affix A grammatical morpheme which cannot stand on its own as an independent word, but which must be attached to an item of an appropriate kind. An affix which attaches to the beginning of a word (e.g. *un*+ in *unhappy*) is called a *prefix*: an affix which attaches to the end of a word (e.g. +*s* in *chases*) is called a *suffix*.

AGENT A term used to describe the semantic (= thematic) role which a particular type of **argument** plays in a given sentence. It typically denotes a person who deliberately causes some state of affairs to come about – hence e.g. *John* plays the thematic role of an AGENT in a sentence such as *John smashed the bottle*. The terms ACTOR and CAUSER are sometimes used in a similar sense. See ch. 7.

Agreement Two words (or expressions) are said to *agree* in respect of some grammatical feature(s) if they have the same value for the relevant feature(s): so, in a sentence such as *He smokes*, the verb *smokes* is said to agree with its subject *he* because both are third person singular expressions. See also **AgrS, AgrO, AgrIO**.

AgrIO/$\overline{AgrIO}$/AgrIO-bar/AgrIOP *AgrIO* is an indirect object agreement constituent which has an intermediate projection into $\overline{AgrIO}$/*AgrIO-bar*, and a maximal projection into *AgrIOP*, an indirect object agreement phrase. See ch. 10.

AgrO/$\overline{AgrO}$/AgrO-bar/AgrOP *AgrO* is an object-agreement constituent which has an intermediate projection into $\overline{AgrO}$/*AgrO-bar*, and a maximal projection into *AgrOP*, an object agreement phrase. See ch. 10.

AgrS/$\overline{AgrS}$/AgrS-bar/AgrSP *AgrS* is a subject-agreement constituent which has an intermediate projection into $\overline{AgrS}$/*AgrS-bar*, and a maximal projection into *AgrSP*, a subject agreement phrase: See ch. 10.

Algorithm A term borrowed from mathematics to denote an explicit set of instructions which specify in precise detail the exact sequence of steps which you have to go through in order to perform some operation.

Altruism See **enlightened self-interest**.

Ambiguous An expression is *ambiguous* if it has more than one **interpretation**. For example, a sentence such as *He loves her more than you* is ambiguous by virtue of the fact that it has two interpretations, one paraphraseable as 'He loves her more than he loves you', the other as 'He loves her more than you love her.'

A movement Movement from one **A position** to another (typically, from a subject or complement position into another subject position). See ch. 8.

Anaphor An *anaphor* is an expression (like *himself*) which cannot have independent reference, but which must take its reference from an **antecedent** (i.e. expression which it refers to) within the same phrase or sentence. Hence, while we can say *John is deluding himself* (where *himself* refers back to

John), we cannot say **Himself is waiting*, since the anaphor *himself* here has no antecedent.

Antecedent An expression which is referred to by a pronoun or anaphor of some kind. For example, in *John cut himself shaving*, *John* is the antecedent of the **anaphor** *himself*, since *himself* refers back to *John*. In a sentence such as *He is someone whom we respect*, the antecedent of the pronoun *whom* is *someone*.

Antonym A term used to denote an expression which has the opposite meaning of another expression: e.g. *tall* is the antonym of *short* (and conversely) – hence *tall* and *short* are antonyms.

AP *Adjectival phrase* – i.e. a phrase headed by an adjective – e.g. *fond of chocolate, keen on sport, good at syntax*, etc.

A position A position which can be occupied by an **argument**, but not by a nonargument expression (e.g. not by an **adjunct**) – e.g. a **subject** position, or a position as the **complement** of a verb, adjective or noun. See ch. 8.

Argument This is a term borrowed by linguists from philosophy (more specifically, from predicate calculus) to describe the role played by particular types of expression in the semantic structure of sentences. In a sentence such as *John hit Fred*, the overall sentence is said to be a *proposition* (a term used to describe the semantic content of a clause), and to consist of the predicate *hit* and its two arguments *John* and *Fred*. The two *arguments* represent the two participants in the act of hitting, and the *predicate* is the expression (in this case the verb *hit*) which describes the activity in which they are engaged. By extension, in a sentence such as *John says he hates syntax* the predicate is the verb *says*, and its two arguments are *John* and the clause *he hates syntax*; the second argument *he hates syntax* is in turn a proposition whose predicate is *hates*, and whose two arguments are *he* and *syntax*. Since the complement of a verb is positioned internally within V-bar (in terms of the analysis in ch. 7) whereas the subject of a verb is positioned outside V-bar, complements are also referred to as *internal arguments*, and subjects as *external arguments*. Expressions which do not function as arguments are *nonarguments*. The *argument structure* of a predicate provides a description of the set of arguments associated with the predicate, and the **thematic role** which each fulfils in relation to the predicate (see ch. 7).

Aspect A term typically used to denote the duration of the activity described by a verb (e.g. whether the activity is ongoing or completed). In sentences such as:

(i)   He has taken the medicine
(ii) He is taking the medicine

the auxiliary *has* is said to be an auxiliary which marks *perfective aspect*, in that it marks the perfection (in the sense of 'completion' or 'termination') of the activity of taking the medicine; for analogous reasons, *taken* is said to be a perfective (participle) verb form in (i) (though is referred to in traditional grammars as a *past participle*). Similarly, *is* is said to be an auxiliary which marks *imperfective* or *progressive aspect* in (ii), because it relates to an activity which is not yet perfected (i.e. 'completed') and hence which is ongoing or in progress (for this reason, *is* in (ii) is also referred to as a *progressive* or *imperfective* auxiliary); in the same way, the verb *taking* in (ii) is said to be the *imperfective* or *progressive* (participle) form of the verb (though is known in traditional grammars as a *present participle*).

Attraction Movement of a set of features from one category position to another.

Attributive adjectives These are adjectives which are used to modify a following noun expression – e.g. *red* in *John has a red Ferrari*, where *red* attributes the property of being red to the noun *Ferrari*. Attributive adjectives contrast with *predicative adjectives*, which are adjectives used in structures such as *The house was red*, *They painted the house red*, etc. (where the property of being red is said to be predicated of the expression *the house*).

AUX/Auxiliary A term used to describe items such as *will/would/can/could/shall/should/may/might/must/ought* and some uses of *have/be/do/need/dare*. Such items differ from typical lexical verbs e.g. in that they undergo **inversion** (cf. *Can I help you?*). See ch. 2.

Auxiliary inversion See **inversion**.

Auxiliary selection This term relates to the type of verb which a given auxiliary selects as its complement: e.g. in many languages (the counterpart of) *be* when used as a perfective auxiliary selects only a complement headed by an **unaccusative** verb (like *come, go*, etc.), whereas (the counterpart of) *have* selects a complement headed by other types of verb. See ch. 9.

-bar An X-bar/$\overline{X}$ constituent is an intermediate projection of some head X – i.e. a projection which is larger than X but smaller than XP (see **projection**). In another use of the term (in which the -bar suffix has much the same function as the prefix *non-*), an A-bar/$\overline{A}$ position is a nonargument position (see **argument**).

Bare A *bare infinitive* clause is a clause which contains a verb in the infinitive form, but does not contain the infinitive particle *to* – e.g. the bracketed clause in *He won't let [me help him]*. A *bare noun* is a noun used without any determiner to modify it (e.g. *fish* in *Fish is smelly*).

Base form The *base form* of a verb is the simplest, uninflected form of the verb (the form under which the relevant verb would be listed in an English dictionary) – hence forms like *go/be/have/see/want/love* are the base forms of the relevant verbs.

Binary A term relating to a *two-valued* property or relation. For example, *number* is a binary property in English, in that we have a two-way contrast between singular forms like *cat* and plural forms like *cats*. It is widely assumed that parameters have binary settings, that features have binary values, and that all branching in syntactic structure is binary.

Binary-branching A tree diagram in which every nonterminal **node** (i.e. every node not at the very bottom of the tree) branches down into two other nodes is *binary-branching*.

Bind/Bound To say that one constituent *x* binds (or serves as the binder for) another constituent *y* (and conversely that *y* is bound by *x*) is to say that *x* determines the semantic (and grammatical) properties of *y*. For example, in *John wants to PRO leave*, *John* binds **PRO**.

Bracketing A technique for representing the categorial status of an expression, whereby the expression is enclosed in square brackets, and the lefthand bracket is labelled with an appropriate category symbol – e.g. [$_D$ the].

C/$\overline{C}$/C-bar/CP C represents the category of complementizer; $\overline{C}$/C-bar is an intermediate projection headed by C; and CP (complementizer phrase) is a maximal projection headed by C. See **complementizer** and **projection**.

Canonical A term used to mean 'usual', 'typical' or 'normal', as in 'The canonical word order in English is specifier + head + complement.'

Case The different *case* forms of a pronoun are the different forms which the pronoun has in different sentence positions. It is traditionally said that English has three cases – *nominative, objective/ accusative* and *genitive. Personal pronouns* typically inflect overtly for all three cases, whereas noun expressions inflect only for genitive case. The different case forms of typical pronouns and nouns are given below:

nominative	I	we	you	he	she	it	they	who		John
objective	me	us	you	him	her	it	them	who(m)	John
genitive	my	our	your	his	her	its	their	whose	John's

In chapter 10, we suggest that indirect **objects** in English (e.g. *him* in *I gave him some*) carry *dative case*, even though dative forms are not morphologically distinct from objective forms in English. Belletti (1988) suggests that in sentences like *There could have been an accident*, the expression *an accident* carries partitive case (Finnish has overt marking of partitive case forms). In Chomsky and Lasnik 1995, it is suggested that the null subject **PRO** found in (control) infinitive constructions carries **null case**. It is sometimes said that *of* in expressions like *loss of face* is a genitive case particle (since in languages with richer case morphology than English, *of face* would be translated by using the genitive form of the counterpart of the noun *face*).

Caseless A caseless constituent is one which has no case properties (i.e. which neither carries a case of its own nor checks the case of another constituent). A caseless position is a position in which no case can be checked (hence which cannot by occupied by a constituent carrying case).

Case particle See **case**.

Case position A position in which some case is checked.

Categorial constituent structure (A representation of) the way in which a phrase or sentence is built up out of a series of **constituents**, each of which belong to a specific **category**.

Category A term used to denote a set of expressions which share a common set of linguistic properties. In syntax, the term is used for expressions which share a common set of *grammatical* (i.e. morphological/syntactic) properties. For example, *boy* and *girl* belong to the (grammatical) category **noun** because they both inflect for plural number (cf. *boys/girls*),

and can both terminate a sentence such as *The police haven't yet found the missing ___*. See ch. 2.

Causative verb A verb which has much the same sense as 'cause'. For example, the verb *have* in sentences such as *He had them expelled* or *He had them review the case* could be said to be causative in sense (hence to be a causative verb).

C-command A structural relation between two constituents. To use a simple train-station metaphor, one node carrying the category label X c-commands another carrying the category label Y if you can get from X to Y by taking a northbound train from X, getting off at the first stop, and then taking a southbound train to Y (on a different line). The **c-command condition on binding** is a condition to the effect that a bound constituent (e.g. a reflexive **anaphor** like *himself* or the **trace** of a moved constituent) must be c-commanded by its **antecedent** (i.e. by the expression which binds it). This amounts to claiming that the antecedent must be higher up in the structure than the anaphor/trace which it binds.

Chain A set of one or more constituents comprising an expression and any traces associated with it.

Chain uniformity principle A principle of Universal Grammar requiring that a **movement chain** should be uniform in respect of its phrase structure status. See ch. 6.

Checked/Checker In a sentence such as *He has left*, the auxiliary *has* checks the nominative case-feature carried by *he*: accordingly, *has* is said to be the checker (for the relevant nominative case-feature) and *he* the checked.

Checking (theory) In Chomsky's *checking theory*, words carry grammatical features which have to be *checked* in the course of a derivation. For example, a nominative pronoun like *I* must have its nominative case checked, which means that it must occupy a nominative position (as the subject of the kind of constituent which allows a nominative subject, e.g. a finite auxiliary) at some point in the derivation. When a feature has been checked, it is erased if it is uninterpretable (i.e. if it is a purely formal feature with no semantic content). Any uninterpretable features which remain unchecked (and hence which have not been erased) at the level of logical form will cause the derivation to *crash* (i.e. to be ungrammatical).

Clause A clause is defined in traditional grammar as

an expression which contains a **subject** and a **predicate**, and which may contain other types of expression as well (e.g. a complement and an adjunct). In most cases, the predicate in a clause is a lexical (= nonauxiliary) verb, so that there will be as many different clauses in a sentence as there are different lexical verbs. For example, in a sentence such as *She may think that you are cheating on her*, there are two lexical verbs (*think* and *cheating*), and hence two clauses. The *cheating* clause is *that you are cheating on her*, and the *think* clause is *She may think that you are cheating on her*, so that the *cheating* clause is one of the **constituents** of the *think* clause. More specifically, the *cheating* clause is the **complement** of the *think* clause, and so is said to function as a **complement clause** in this type of sentence.

Clitic(ization) The term *clitic* denotes an item which resembles a word but which has the property that it must cliticize (i.e. attach itself) to another word. For example, we could say that the contracted negative particle *n't* is a clitic which attaches itself to a finite auxiliary verb, so giving rise to forms like *isn't, shouldn't, mightn't*, etc. Likewise, we might say that *'ve* is a clitic form of *have* which attaches itself to (for example) a pronoun ending in a vowel or diphthong, so giving rise to forms like *we've, you've, they've*, etc.

Cognition/Cognitive (Relating to) the study of human knowledge.

COMP See **complementizer**.

Comparative The comparative form of an adjective or adverb is the *+er* form used when comparing two individuals or properties: cf. *John is taller than Mary*, where *taller* is the comparative form of *tall*.

Competence A term used to represent fluent native speakers' knowledge of the grammar of their mother tongue(s). See ch. 1.

Complement This is a term used to denote a specific grammatical function (in the same way that the term **subject** denotes a specific grammatical function). A complement is an expression which combines with a **head** word to project the head into a larger structure of essentially the same kind. In *close the door, the door* is the complement of *close*; in *after dinner, dinner* is the complement of *after*; in *good at physics, at physics* is the complement of *good*; in *loss of face, of face* is the complement of *loss*. As these examples illustrate, complements typically follow their heads

in English. The choice of complement (and the morphological form of the complement) is determined by properties of the head: for example, an auxiliary such as *will* requires as its complement an expression headed by a verb in the infinitive form (cf. *He will go/*going/*gone home*). Moreover, complements bear a close semantic relation to their heads (e.g. in *kill him, him* is the complement of the verb *kill* and plays the **thematic role** of PATIENT argument of the verb *kill*). Thus, a complement has a close morphological, syntactic and semantic relation to its head. A *complement clause* is a clause which is used as the complement of some other word (typically as the complement of a verb, adjective or noun). Thus, in a sentence such as *He never expected that she would come*, the clause *that she would come* serves as the complement of the verb *expected*, and so is a complement clause. *Complement features* are features that specify the kind of complement which a given head can have (see ch. 3). On *complement selection*, see **selection**.

Complementizer This term is used in two ways. On the one hand, it denotes a particular category of clause-introducing word such as *that/if/for*, as used in sentences such as *I think that you should apologize, I doubt if she realizes, They're keen for you to show up*. On the other hand, it is also used to denote the presubject position in clauses ('the complementizer position') which is typically occupied by a complementizer like *that/if/for*, but which can also be occupied by an inverted auxiliary in sentences such as *Can you help?*, where *can* is taken to occupy the complementizer position in the clause. In general, I use the term *complementizer* to denote the relevant category, and the abbreviated terms *COMP* and *C* to denote the associated position. A *complementizer phrase* (CP) is a phrase/clause headed by a complementizer (or by an auxiliary or verb moved into COMP). See chs. 3 and 5.

Constituent A structural unit – i.e. an expression which is one of the components out of which a phrase or sentence is built up. For example, the various constituents of a prepositional phrase (= PP) such as *straight into touch* (e.g. as a reply to *Where did the ball go?*) are the preposition *into*, the noun *touch*, the adverb *straight*, and the intermediate projection (P-bar) *into touch*.

Constituent structure The constituent structure (or *phrase structure*, or *syntactic structure*) of an expression is (a representation of) the set of constituents which the expression contains. Constituent structure is usually represented in terms of a **labelled bracketing** or a **tree diagram**.

Constrained See **restrictive**.

Constraint A principle of Universal Grammar which prevents certain types of grammatical operation from applying to certain types of structure.

Content This term is generally used to refer to the *semantic content* (i.e. meaning) of an expression. However, it can also be used in a more general way to refer to other linguistic properties of an expression: e.g. the expression *phonetic content* is used to refer to the phonetic form of an expression: hence, we might say that **PRO** is a pronoun which has no/null *phonetic content* (meaning that it is a *silent* pronoun with no audible form).

Contentives/content words Words which have intrinsic descriptive content (as opposed to **functors**, i.e. words which serve essentially to mark particular grammatical functions). Nouns, verbs, adjectives and (most) prepositions are traditionally classified as contentives, while pronouns, auxiliaries, determiners, complementizers and **particles** of various kinds (e.g. infinitival *to*) are classified as **functors**. See ch. 2.

Contraction An informal term used to denote the process by which (in colloquial speech styles) a sequence of two words is reduced to one (with either or both of the words losing one or more of its component sounds). For example, *want to* can become *wanna* by contraction, and *I have* can become *I've*.

Control(ler)/Control predicate In an infinitive structure with a PRO subject like *John decided to PRO quit*, the **antecedent** of PRO (i.e. the expression which PRO refers back to, in this case *John*) is said to be the *controller* of PRO (or to *control* PRO), and conversely PRO is said to be controlled by its antecedent; the relevant kind of structure is called a *control* structure. Verbs like *try* which take a complement containing a PRO subject controlled by the subject of *try* are called *subject-control predicates*; verbs like *decided* (as used in sentences such as *What decided you to take syntax?*) which take an infinitive complement whose PRO subject is controlled by the object of the main verb (here, the *you* object of *decided*) are called *object-control predicates*. See chs. 4 and 9.

Converge A derivation *converges* at **LF** (logical form) if its LF-representation contains only features which are interpretable at LF (i.e. features with semantic content).

Coordination A process by which two similar expressions are joined together by *and/or* (e.g. *John* is coordinated with *Mary* in *I couldn't find John or Mary*).

Copula/Copular Verb A verb used to link a **subject** with a verbless **predicate**. The main copular verb in English is *be* (though verbs like *become, remain, stay*, etc. also have the same copular – i.e. linking – function). In sentences such as *They are lazy, They are fools* and *They are outside*, the verb *are* is said to be a copula in that it links the subject *they* to the adjective predicate *lazy*, or the noun predicate *fools*, or the prepositional predicate *outside*.

Count noun A noun which can be counted. Hence, a noun such as *chair* is a count noun since we can say *one chair, two chairs*, etc.; but a noun such as *furniture* is a *noncount noun* or *mass noun* since we cannot say **one furniture,* *two furnitures etc.

Covert A covert expression is one which has no phonetic content (i.e. which is *empty* of phonetic content and so is inaudible). For example, in a structure such as *He may try [to PRO escape from prison]*, the bracketed clause has a *covert* (= null = empty = silent) subject pronoun PRO. A *covert feature* (or *property*) is one which has no overt morphological realization: for example, we might say that an invariable noun like *sheep* has covert (singular/plural) number properties, since (unlike *cat/cats*) the word *sheep* doesn't add +s in the plural (cf. *one sheep/two sheep*).

CP Complementizer phrase (see **C/complementizer**).

Crash A derivation is said to *crash* if one or more features carried by one or more constituents is uninterpretable at the relevant level. For example, the derivation of a sentence like *Him might help* will crash at **LF** because the objective case-feature of the pronoun *him* remains unchecked (since finite auxiliaries like *might* don't allow objective subjects), and case-features are purely formal/grammatical features with no semantic content, and hence uninterpretable at the level of logical form. More generally, a derivation will crash if any purely formal features remain unchecked.

D/D̄/D-bar/DP D represents the category of *determiner;* D̄/D-bar is an intermediate projection headed by D; and DP ('determiner phrase') is a maximal projection headed by D. See **determiner, determiner phrase** and **projection**; see also ch. 4.

+d An affix used to form the past tense of a verb, so called because most regular verbs form their past tense by the addition of +(e)d in English (e.g. *showed*).

Dative See **case**.

Declarative A term used as a classification of the **illocutionary force** (i.e. semantic function) of a clause which is used to make a statement (e.g. *Syntax is fun*), as opposed to an **interrogative, exclamative** or **imperative** clause.

Default A default value/interpretation is one which obtains if all else fails (i.e. if other conditions are not satisfied). For example, if we say that clauses are interpreted as declarative by default we mean they are interpreted as declarative unless they contain (for example) an interrogative, exclamative or imperative constituent of some kind.

Derivation The derivation of a given structure is (a representation of) the set of (merger and movement) operations used to form the structure.

Derivational/Derivative Derivational morphology is the study of the processes by which one type of word can be formed from another: for example, by adding the derivational suffix +*ness* to the adjective *sad* we can form the noun *sadness*, so that +*ness* is a derivational suffix, and the word *sadness* is a derivative of the adjective *sad*. See ch. 2.

Descriptive adequacy A grammar of a particular language attains *descriptive adequacy* if it correctly specifies which strings of words do (and don't) form grammatical phrases and sentences in the language, and correctly describes the structure and interpretation of the relevant phrases and sentences. See ch. 1.

Descriptive content A noun like *car* could be said to have *descriptive content* in that you can draw a picture of a typical car, but not a pronoun like *they* (you can't draw a picture of *they*). See ch. 2.

DET/Determiner A word like *a/the/this/that* which is typically used to modify a noun, but which has no descriptive content of its own. Most determiners can be used either prenominally (i.e. in front of a noun that they modify) or pronominally (i.e. used on their own without a following noun) – cf. the two uses of *that* in *I don't like that idea/I don't like that*.

Determiner phrase/DP A phrase like *(such) a pity* which comprises a determiner *a*, a noun complement *pity* and an (optional) specifier *such*. In earlier work, a determiner + noun sequence would have been analysed as a **noun phrase** (= NP), with the determiner occupying the specifier position within NP.

Dethematize/Detransitivize See **absorption**.

Direct object See **object**.

Direct theta-marking See **theta-marking**.

Distribution(al) The *distribution* of an expression is the set of positions which it can occupy within an appropriate kind of phrase or sentence. Hence, a *distributional* property is a word-order property.

Ditransitive A ditransitive verb is one which takes both a direct and an indirect object – e.g. a verb like *tell* in a sentence such as *John told Mary nothing*, where *Mary* is the indirect object and *nothing* the direct object of *tell*. See **object** and **transitive**.

Do-support This refers to the requirement for the **dummy** auxiliary *do* to be used to form questions or negatives in sentences which would otherwise contain no auxiliary. Hence, an auxiliariless declarative sentence (= statement) such as *He hates syntax* has the negative counterpart *He doesn't hate syntax*, and the interrogative counterpart *Does he hate syntax?*

Double object construction See **object**.

DP See **determiner phrase**.

DP hypothesis The hypothesis that all **nominals** are D projections, so that e.g. *the president* is a DP headed by *the*, *politicians* (in a sentence like *Politicians lie*) is a DP headed by a null determiner, and a pronoun like *they* (e.g. in *They lie*) is a **pronominal** determiner. See ch. 4.

Dummy A type of word which has no intrinsic semantic content, but which is used simply to satisfy a structural requirement that a certain position in a structure be filled. For example, the auxiliary *do* in a sentence such as *Does he like pasta?* is said to be a dummy, satisfying the need for COMP to be filled in questions. Likewise, the first occurrence of the pronoun *there* in a sentence like *There is nobody there* is a dummy (i.e. contentless) pronoun, since it cannot have its **reference** questioned (cf. **Where is some-one there?*).

Early Modern English The type of English found in the early seventeenth century (at around the time Shakespeare wrote most of his plays, between 1590 and 1620). In the text, all examples of Early Modern English are taken from various plays by Shakespeare. It should perhaps be noted that some linguists have suggested that Shakespeare's English is rather conservative, and hence imitates a slightly earlier stage of English.

Echo question A type of sentence used to question something which someone else has just said (often in an air of incredulity), repeating all or most of what they have just said. For example, if I say *I've just met Nim Chimpsky* and you don't believe me (or don't know who I'm talking about), you could reply with an echo question such as *You've just met who?*

ECM See **exceptional case-marking**.

Economy principle A principle which requires that (all other things being equal) syntactic representations should contain as few constituents and syntactic derivations and involve as few grammatical operations as possible.

Ellipsis/Elliptical Ellipsis is a process by which an expression is omitted in order to avoid repetition. For example, in a sentence such as *I will do it if you will do it*, we can *ellipse* (i.e. omit) the second occurrence of *do it* to avoid repetition, and hence say *I will do it if you will*: the resulting sentence is an *elliptical* structure (i.e. a structure from which something has been omitted).

Embedded clause An *embedded clause* is a clause which is positioned internally within some other phrase or clause. For example, in a sentence such as *He may suspect that I hid them*, the *hid*-clause (= *that I hid them*) is embedded within the *suspect* clause.

EME See **Early Modern English**.

Empirical evidence Evidence based on observed linguistic phenomena. In syntax, the term *empirical evidence* usually means 'evidence based on grammaticality judgments by native speakers'. For example, the fact that sentences like **Himself likes you* are judged ungrammatical by native speakers of Standard English provides us with empirical evidence that **anaphors** like *himself* can't be used

without an appropriate **antecedent** (i.e. an expression which they refer back to).

Empty category A category which is **covert** (i.e. which is silent or null and hence has no overt phonetic form). Empty categories include **traces**, the null pronouns **PRO** and **pro**, the null generic/partitive determiner *Ø*, etc. See ch. 4.

Enlightened self-interest A principle of grammar suggested by Lasnik (1995) to the effect that constituents move in order to satisfy the morphological requirements of other constituents (e.g. auxiliaries undergo inversion in questions like *Can you help me?* because **COMP** contains a **Q** affix which needs a head to attach to). See ch. 6.

Entry A **lexical entry** is an entry for a particular word in a dictionary (and hence by extension refers to the set of information about the word given in the relevant dictionary entry).

Ergative This term originally applied to languages like Basque in which the complement of a transitive verb and the subject of an intransitive verb are assigned the same case. However, by extension, it has come to be used to denote verbs like *break* which occur both in structures like *Someone broke the window* and in structures like *The window broke*, where *the window* seems to play the same **thematic role** in both types of sentences, in spite of being the complement of *broke* in one sentence and the subject of *broke* in the other. See ch. 9.

Exceptional case-marking/ECM Objective subjects of infinitive clauses (e.g. *him* in *I believe [him to be innocent]*) are said to carry exceptional objective case (for the simple reason that the case of the objective subject is checked by the preceding verb *believe*, and it is exceptional for the case of the subject of one clause to be checked by the verb in a higher clause). Verbs (like *believe*) which take an infinitive complement with an objective subject are said to be *ECM verbs*. See chs. 4 and 10.

Exclamative A type of structure used to exclaim surprise, delight, annoyance, etc. In English syntax, the term is restricted largely to clauses beginning with wh-exclamative words like *What!* or *How!* – e.g. *What a fool I was! How blind I was!*

Excorporate A head which is adjoined to another head is said to *excorporate* out of the relevant structure if it becomes detached from the head to which it was adjoined, and moves elsewhere on its own.

Existential An *existential* sentence is one which relates to the existence of some entity. For example, a sentence such as *Is there any coffee left?* questions the existence of coffee. The word *any* here is similarly said to be an *existential quantifier* (as is *some* in a sentence like *There is some coffee in the pot*).

EXPERIENCER A term used in the analysis of semantic/thematic roles to denote the entity which experiences some emotional or cognitive state – e.g. *John* in *John felt unhappy*. See ch. 7.

Experiential verb A verb (like *feel*) which has an **EXPERIENCER** as its subject.

Explanatory adequacy A linguistic theory meets the criterion of *explanatory adequacy* if it explains why grammars have the properties that they do, and how children come to acquire grammars in such a short period of time. See ch. 1.

Expletive A dummy constituent with no inherent semantic content such as the pronoun *there* in sentences like *There is almost no truth whatever in the rumour* (which is nonreferential and so cannot be questioned by *where?*).

Extended projection In a 1991 paper, Jane Grimshaw suggested that IP and CP are extended projections of V, and that DP and PP are extended projections of N. See ch. 4.

External argument Subject (see **argument**).

Extraction An operation by which one constituent is moved out of another. For example, in a structure such as *Who do you think [he saw ___]?* the pronoun *who* has been extracted out of the position marked ___ in the bracketed clause, and moved to the front of the overall sentence. The *extraction site* for a moved constituent is the position out of which it is extracted/moved (marked by ___ in the example above).

Feature A device used to describe a particular linguistic property (e.g. we might use a feature such as [Nom] to denote the nominative **case**-feature carried by a pronoun such as *he*). By convention, features are normally enclosed in square brackets, and semantic features written in capital letters. The *head-features* of an item describe its intrinsic grammatical properties; the *complement-features* of an item determine the range of complements which it allows; the *specifier features* of an item determine the range of specifiers which it allows (see ch. 3). See also **strong features** and **weak features**.

Feminine This term is used in discussion of grammatical **gender** to denote pronouns like *she/her/hers* which refer to female entities.

Finite The term *finite verb/clause* denotes an auxiliary or nonauxiliary verb, or clause which can have a subject with nominative **case** like *I/we/he/she/they*. Thus, if we compare the two bracketed clauses in:

(i)   What if [people annoy her]?
(ii) Don't let [people annoy her]

We find that the bracketed clause and the verb *annoy* in (i) are finite because in place of the subject *people* we can have a nominative pronoun like *they*; by contrast, the bracketed clause and the verb *annoy* are nonfinite in (ii) because *people* cannot be replaced by a nominative pronoun like *they* (only by an objective pronoun like *them*): cf.

(iii) What if [*they* annoy her]?
(iv)*Don't let [*they* annoy her]

By contrast, a verb or clause which has a subject with objective or null case is *nonfinite*; hence the bracketed clauses and bold-printed verbs are nonfinite in the examples below:

(v)   Don't let [*them* **annoy** you]
(vi) You should try [to *PRO* **stay** calm]

In general, finite verbs carry tense/agreement properties, whereas nonfinite verbs are tenseless and agreementless forms (i.e. forms which do not overtly inflect for tense/agreement – e.g. infinitive forms like *be*, and *+ing/+n* participle forms like *being/been* are nonfinite).

First person See **person**.

Floating quantifier A **quantifier** which does not immediately precede the expression which it quantifies. For example, in a sentence such as *The students have* **all** *passed their exams*, all quantifies (but is not positioned in front of) *the students*, so that *all* is a *floating* (or *stranded*) quantifier here. See ch. 7.

Foot The foot of a (movement) **chain** is the rightmost constituent in the chain.

Formal In an expression such as *formal speech style*, the word *formal* denotes a very careful and stylized form of speech (as opposed to the kind of informal colloquial speech style used in a casual conversation in a bar): in an expression such as *formal features*, the word *formal* means 'grammatical' (i.e. **morphosyntactic**); in an expression such as *the formal* *properties of grammars*, the word *formal* means 'mathematical'.

Fronting An informal term to denote a movement operation by which a word or phrase is moved to the front of some phrase or clause.

Full interpretation The *principle of full interpretation* specifies that the representation of an expression must contain all and only those features which are relevant to determining its interpretation at the relevant level: e.g. the **LF-representation** for a given expression must contain all and only those semantic features which determine linguistic aspects of the meaning of the expression, and its **PF-representation** must contain all and only those phonetic features which determine its pronunciation.

Function word/Functional category/Functor A word which has no **descriptive content** and which serves an essentially grammatical function is said to be a *function word* or *functor*. (By contrast, a word which has descriptive content is a **content word** or **contentive**.) A *functional category* is a category like **INFL, COMP, D, T, AgrS**, etc. whose members are functors (i.e. items with an essentially grammatical function) – and, by extension, a category which is a projection of a functional head (e.g. I-bar, IP, C-bar, CP, D-bar, DP, T-bar, TP, $\overline{\text{AgrS}}$, AgrSP, etc.). See ch. 2.

Gapping A form of **ellipsis** in which a head word is omitted from one (or more) parallel structures, to avoid repetition. For example, the italicized second occurrence of *bought* can be *gapped* (i.e. omitted) in a sentence such as *John bought an apple and Mary bought a pear*, giving *John bought an apple, and Mary a pear*.

Gender A grammatical property whereby words are divided into different grammatical classes on the basis of inflectional properties which play a role in processes such as **agreement** or **anaphora**. In French, for example, nouns are intrinsically masculine or feminine in gender (e.g. *pommier* 'apple tree' is masculine, but *pomme* 'apple' is feminine), and determiners inflect for gender (as well as number), so that *un* 'a' is the masculine form of the determiner corresponding to English 'a', and *une* is its feminine form. Determiners in French have to agree in gender (and **number**) with the nouns they modify, hence we say *un pommier* 'an apple tree', but *une pomme* 'an apple'. In English, nouns no longer have inherent gender properties, and adjectives/determiners don't

inflect for gender either. Only personal pronouns like *he/she/it* carry gender properties in Modern English, and these are traditionally said to carry masculine/feminine/neuter gender respectively (though the term *inanimate* is sometimes used in place of *neuter*).

Generate To say that a grammar *generates* a given type of structure is to say that it specifies how to form the relevant structure.

Generic To say that an expression like *eggs* in a sentence such as *Eggs are fattening* has a generic interpretation is to say that it is interpreted as meaning 'eggs in general'.

Genitive See **case**.

Gerund This refers to a particular use of *+ing* verb forms in which they can be used as subjects, or as complements of verbs or prepositions, and in which they can have a genitive subject like *my*. Thus *writing* is a gerund (verb form) in a sentence such as *She was annoyed at [my writing to her mother]*, since the bracketed gerund structure is used as the complement of the preposition *at*, and has a genitive subject *my*.

Gradable Words are gradable if they denote a concept or property which can exist in varying degrees. For example, *tall* is a gradable word since we can say (for example) *fairly/very/extremely tall*; by contrast, *dead* is an *ungradable* word, since it denotes an absolute property (hence we don't say !*very dead*).

Grammar The study of how words, phrases and sentences are formed. A *grammar* of a language is a description of how words, phrases and sentences are formed in the relevant language.

Grammatical A phrase or sentence is *grammatical* if it contains no morphological error (i.e. no error relating to the morphological form of any word) or syntactic error (i.e. no error relating to the position occupied by any of the words or phrases).

Greed A principle of grammar (proposed by Chomsky 1995) which specifies that constituents move only in order to satisfy their own morphological requirements.

Head This term has two main uses. The *head* (constituent) of a phrase is the key word which determines the properties of the phrase. So, in a phrase such as *fond of fast food*, the head of the phrase is the adjective *fond*, and consequently the phrase is an adjectival phrase (and hence can occupy typical positions occupied by adjectival expressions – e.g. as the complement of *is* in *He is fond of fast food*). In many cases, the term *head* is more or less equivalent to the term *word* (e.g. in sentences such as 'An objective pronoun can be used as the complement of a transitive *head*'). In a different use of the same word, the *head* of a movement chain is the leftmost constituent in the chain. On *head-features*, see **feature**.

Head-first/-last language A *head-first language* is one in which heads are canonically (i.e. normally) positioned before their complements; a *head-last language* is one in which heads are canonically positioned after their complements. See ch. 1.

Head movement Movement of a word from one head position to another. See ch. 5.

For particular examples of head movement, see also **I movement** and **V movement**.

Head movement constraint A constraint (proposed by Travis 1984) which amounts to the requirement that a moved head can only move into the head position in the next-highest phrase immediately containing it (in any single movement operation).

Head (position) parameter The **parameter** which determines whether a language positions heads before or after their complements. See ch. 1.

Homophonous Two different expressions are homophonous if they have the same phonetic form (e.g. *we've* and *weave*).

Host An expression to which a **clitic** attaches. For example, if we say that *n't* cliticizes onto *could* in forms like *couldn't*, we can also say that *could* is the host onto which *n't* cliticizes.

I/Ī/I-bar/IP I represents the category of INFL/inflection; Ī/I-bar is an intermediate projection headed by I; and IP (inflection phrase) is a maximal projection headed by I. See **INFL** and **projection**.

Identify To say that an inflection serves to *identify* an empty category is to say that the inflection determines the **interpretation** of the empty category. For example, we might say that the second person singular inflection +*st* identifies the implicit null subject **pro** as second person singular in a Shakespearean sentence such as *Hast **pro** any more of this?* (Trinculo, *The Tempest*, II.ii). See ch. 5.

Idiom A string of words which has an idiosyncratic

meaning (e.g. *hit the roof* in the sense of 'get angry'). See ch. 7.

I language Language viewed as a computational system internalized within the brain. See ch. 1.

Illocutionary force The *illocutionary force* of a sentence (or clause) describes the kind of speech act which it is used to perform (e.g. a sentence is **declarative** in force if used to make a statement, **interrogative** in force if used to ask a question, **imperative** in force if used to issue an order, **exclamative** in force if used to exclaim surprise, etc.). See Grice 1975.

Immediate constituent The immediate constituents of a given phrase XP are those constituents which are contained within XP, but not within any other phrase which is itself contained within XP. In practice, the immediate constituents of XP are the head X of XP, the complement of X, the specifier of X, and any adjunct attached to a projection of X.

I(-to-C) movement Movement of a verb out of the head I position in **IP** into the head **C** position in **CP**. See ch. 5, and **inversion**.

Imperative A term used to classify a type of sentence used to issue an order (e.g. *Be quiet!*, *Don't say anything!*), and also to classify the type of verb form used in an imperative sentence (e.g. *be* is an imperative verb form in *Be quiet!*).

Imperfective See **aspect**.

Impersonal The pronoun *it* is said to be *impersonal* when used as a pronoun which has no **thematic role** (and doesn't refer to any external entity outside the sentence), e.g. in sentences such as *It is rumoured that he is unhappy*, or *It is unlikely that he'll come back*.

Indicative Indicative (auxiliary and nonauxiliary) verb forms are finite forms which are used (*inter alia*) in declarative and interrogative clauses (i.e. statements and questions). Thus, the bold-printed items are indicative forms in the following sentences: *He **is** teasing you, **Can** he speak French?, He **had** been smoking, He **loves** chocolate, He **hated** syntax.* An indicative clause is a clause which contains an indicative (auxiliary or nonauxiliary) verb. See **mood**.

Indices Subscript letters attached to sets of constituents to indicate whether or not there is a **binding** relation between them. For example, in a structure such as *John$_i$ thinks that Harry$_j$ is* *deceiving himself*, the indices indicate that *himself* is bound by (i.e. interpreted as referring to) *Harry*, not by *John*.

Indirect object See **object**.

Indirect theta-marking See **theta-marking**.

Infinitive The *infinitive* form of a verb is the (uninflected) form which is used when the verb is the complement of a modal auxiliary like *can*, or of the infinitive particle *to*. Accordingly, the bold-printed verbs are infinitive forms in the following sentences: *He can **speak** French, He's trying to **learn** French*. An *infinitive clause* is a clause which contains a verb in the infinitive form. Hence, the bracketed clauses are infinitive clauses in the following examples: *He is trying [to help her], Why not let [him help her]*? (In both examples, *help* is an infinitive verb form.) Since clauses are analysed as phrases within the framework used here, the term *infinitive phrase* is used interchangeably with *infinitive clause*, to denote an IP projection headed by the infinitive particle *to* (or by the null counterpart of the infinitive particle *to* discussed in ch. 3).

INFL A category devised by Chomsky whose members include finite auxiliaries (which are *INFL*ected for tense/agreement), and the *INF*initiva*L* particle *to*. See ch. 2.

Inflection(al morphology) An *inflection* is an **affix** which marks grammatical properties such as number, person, tense, case. For example, English has four verb inflections – namely past-tense +*d*, third person singular present-tense +*s*, perfective/passive +*n* and imperfective/progressive +*ing*. By contrast, English has only one noun inflection, namely plural +*s*. The term *inflectional morphology* denotes the study of the grammar of inflections. The term *inflection* is also used (in a different sense) as the full label for the category **INFL**.

+***ing*** An inflectional suffix which has two main roles. On the one hand, it can serve as a *progressive/imperfective suffix* which (when attached to a verb stem) produces a *progressive/imperfective participle* (e.g. in a sentence such as *He was **smoking*** (see **aspect**)). On the other hand, it can serve as a suffix used to derive the **gerund** form of a verb.

In situ A constituent is said to remain *in situ* if it remains in place, and doesn't undergo movement.

Intermediate projection A constituent which is

larger than a word, but smaller than a phrase. See ch. 3 and **projection**.

Internal argument Complement. See **argument**.

Interpretable A feature is interpretable at the level of LF/logical form if it has semantic content: so, for example, a feature such as [Plural] is interpretable at LF, but a phonetic feature like [nasal] is uninterpretable at LF, and so too are purely grammatical/formal features (e.g. case-features). See ch. 3.

Interpretation To say that an expression has a particular *interpretation* is to say that it expresses a particular set of semantic relations. So, for example, we might say that a sentence such as *He loves you more than Sam* has two different interpretations – one on which *Sam* has a subject interpretation and is implicitly understood as the **subject** of *loves you*, and a second on which *Sam* has an object interpretation and is implicitly understood as the **object** of *he loves*. The first interpretation can be paraphrased as 'He loves you more than Sam loves you', and the second as 'He loves you more than he loves Sam.'

Interrogative An *interrogative* clause or sentence is one which is used to ask a question. For example, the overall sentence is interrogative in *Is it raining?*, and the bracketed **complement** clause is interrogative in *I wonder [if it is raining]*.

Intransitive See **transitive**.

Inversion A term used to denote a movement process by which the relative order of two expressions is reversed. It is most frequently used in relation to the more specific operation by which an auxiliary (and, in earlier stages of English, nonauxiliary) verb comes to be positioned before its subject, e.g. in questions such as *Can you speak Swahili?*, where *can* is positioned in front of its subject *you*. See ch. 5.

Inverted auxiliary/verb An auxiliary/verb which is positioned in front of its subject (e.g. *will* in *Will I pass the syntax exam?*).

IP Inflection phrase – i.e. a phrase/clause which is a projection of **INFL**. Thus, a sentence such as *It might rain* is an IP – more specifically, a projection of the INFL constituent *might*.

IP adverb An adverb (like *certainly*) which is positioned internally within IP (i.e. which is adjoined to some projection of **INFL**).

K Case particle. See **case**.

Labelled bracketing See **bracketing**.

Landing site The landing-site for a moved constituent is the position it ends up in after it has been
moved (e.g. the specifier position within CP is the
landing-site for a moved operator expression).

Last resort principle The principle that grammatical
operations do not apply unless they have to as the
only way of satisfying some grammatical requirement: for example, **do-support** is used in questions
only as a last resort, i.e. if there is no other auxiliary
in the structure which can undergo inversion. See
ch. 5.

Learnability A criterion of adequacy for linguistic
theory. An adequate theory must explain how children come to learn the grammar of their native languages in such a short period of time, and hence
must provide for grammars of languages which
are easily learnable by children. See ch.1.

Least effort principle See **economy principle**.

Level (of representation) A level of representation
(of the structure of a sentence) is a stage (in a
derivation) at which representations comprise only
features of a single type. There are two different levels of representation in a grammar, **LF** and **PF**.
LF/logical form is the level at which representations
include only semantic features; **PF/phonetic form** is
the level at which representations include only phonetic features. By contrast, the grammatical structures produced by merger and movement operations
do not constitute a separate level of representation,
since they contain three different sets of features
(phonetic, grammatical and semantic).

Lexical/Lexicon The word *lexical* is used in a number of different ways. Since a *lexicon* is a dictionary
(i.e. a list of all the words in a language and their
idiosyncratic linguistic properties), the expression
lexical item means 'word', the expression *lexical
entry* means 'the entry in the dictionary for a particular word', the term *lexical property* means 'property
associated with some individual word', and the term
lexical learning means 'learning words and their
idiosyncratic properties'. However, the word *lexical*
is also used in a second sense, in which it is contrasted with **functional** (and hence means 'nonfunction-
al'). In this second sense, a *lexical category* is a
category whose members are **contentives** (i.e. items
with idiosyncratic descriptive content): hence, categories such as noun, verb, adjective or preposition

are lexical categories in this sense. So, for example,
the term *lexical verb* means 'nonauxiliary verb' (i.e.
a verb like *go, find, hate, want*, etc.).

LF(-representation) (A representation of the) logical
form (of an expression) (see **representation**). The
LF-component of a grammar is the component
which converts the syntactic structures produced by
merger and movement operations into LF-representations.

License To say that a head *licenses* a certain type of
specifier/complement is to say that it can have such
a specifier/complement. For example, a finite auxiliary licenses a nominative subject (but since this is
the only type of subject licensed by a finite auxiliary,
this in effect means that a finite auxiliary *must* have
a nominative subject).

Light verb An affixal verb (often with a causative
sense like that of *make*) to which a noun, adjective
or verb adjoins. For example, it might be claimed
that the suffix *+en* in a verb like *sadden* is an affixal
light verb which can combine with an adjective like
sad to form the causative verb *sadden* (meaning
'make sad', 'cause to become sad'). This type of
analysis could be extended to verbs like *roll* as they
are used in sentences like *He rolled the ball down
the hill*, where we could suggest that *roll* is used
causatively (in the sense of 'make roll', or 'cause to
roll'), and hence involves adjunction of the verb *roll*
to an abstract light verb (i.e. to a null verbal counterpart of *+en*). See ch. 9.

Link A constituent (or position) which is part of a
movement **chain**.

Local An operation is *local* only if it operates within
a highly restricted domain (e.g. internally within a
phrase, or across no more than one intervening
phrasal boundary). For example, **agreement** typically involves a local relation between the head and
specifier of a given type of phrase (e.g. in a sentence
like *He has gone*, between the INFL constituent *has*
and its specifier/subject *he*). Similarly, anaphors like
himself typically require a local antecedent (i.e. an
antecedent within the phrase containing them). A
movement operation like **head movement** is local
in the sense that a head can only move into the next-
highest head position within the structure (and so
can cross only one intervening phrase boundary
containing it).

Main clause A free-standing clause, i.e. a clause

which is not contained within any other expression (also referred to as a *principal clause* or *independent clause* in traditional grammar, and termed a *root clause* in more recent work). By contrast, a **complement** clause is a clause which is used as the **complement** of some item. So, in a sentence such as *I think he loves you*, the *think*-clause (i.e. the expression *I think he loves you*) is a main clause, whereas the *loves* clause (i.e. the expression *he loves you*) is a complement clause (more specifically, it is the complement of the verb *think*).

Masculine A term used in discussions of grammatical **gender** to denote pronouns like *he/him/his* which refer to male entities.

Mass noun See **count noun**.

Matrix In a sentence like *I think [you are right]*, to say that the *think*-clause is the matrix clause for the bracketed **complement** clause is to say that it is the clause which immediately contains the bracketed clause (hence that the bracketed clause is **embedded** within the *think*-clause).

Maximal projection See **projection**.

Merger An operation by which two categories are combined to form another category. See ch. 3.

Minimalism/Minimalist program A theory of grammar (outlined in Chomsky 1995) whose core assumption is that grammars should be described in terms of the minimal set of theoretical and descriptive apparatus necessary.

Minimal link condition/Minimality condition A principle of grammar requiring that the links in movement chains should be as short as possible (hence that constituents should move from one position to another in the shortest possible steps). See also **shortest movement principle**.

Minimal projection See **projection**.

MIT The Massachusetts Institute of Technology (located in Cambridge, Massachusetts), where Chomsky has worked for the past four decades.

Modal/Modality A modal auxiliary is an auxiliary which expresses modality (i.e. notions such as possibility, futurity or necessity). The set of modal auxiliaries in English is usually assumed to include *will/would/can/could/shall/should/may/might/ must*, and perhaps *ought*, and *need/dare* when followed by a **bare** (*to*-less) infinitive complement.

Modifier/Modify In an expression such as *tall men*, it is traditionally said that the adjective *tall* modifies (i.e. attributes some property to) or is a modifier of the noun *men*. Likewise, in a sentence such as *Eat slowly!*, the adverb *slowly* is said to modify the verb *eat* (in the sense that it describes the manner of eating).

Module An individual autonomous component of a larger system. For example, a grammar might be said to contain a *case module* – i.e. a component which accounts for the case properties of relevant constituents.

Mood This is a term describing inflectional properties of finite verbs. (Auxiliary and nonauxiliary) verbs in English can be in the **indicative** mood, **subjunctive** mood, or **imperative** mood. Examples of each type of mood are given by the bold-printed verb forms in the the following: *He hates* (= indicative) *spaghetti, The court ordered that he be* (= subjunctive) *detained indefinitely, Keep* (= imperative) *quiet!* Occasionally, this term is extended to nonfinite forms of the verb (so that one can talk about a verb in the *infinitive mood* (i.e. in its infinitive form).

Morpheme The smallest unit of grammatical structure. Thus, a plural noun such as *cats* comprises two morphemes, namely the **stem** *cat* and the plural suffix *+s*.

Morphology The study of how **morphemes** are combined together to form words.

Morphosyntactic A morphosyntactic property is a grammatical property, i.e. a property which is morphologically and syntactically conditioned. For instance, **case** is a morphosyntactic property, in that (for example) **personal pronouns** have different morphological forms and occupy different syntactic positions according to their case: e.g. the nominative form of the first person plural pronoun is *we* and its objective form is *us*; the two occupy different syntactic positions in that the nominative form occurs as the subject of a **finite** verb or auxiliary (cf. *we* in *We disagree*), whereas the objective form occurs as the complement of a **transitive** verb or preposition (cf. *us* in *He disagrees with us*).

Movement An operation by which a word or phrase is moved from one position in a structure to another.

Multiple wh-questions Questions containing more than one wh-word. See ch. 6.

N/N̄/N-bar/NP N represents the category of *noun*; N̄ /N-bar is an intermediate projection headed by N; and NP (noun phrase) is a maximal projection headed by N. See **noun**, **noun phrase** and **projection**; see also ch. 4.

+*n* The inflection used to form the perfective/passive participle form of a verb (see **aspect**, **active**). For example, *shown* is a perfective participle in *The referee has already shown him the yellow card once*, but is a passive participle in *He has already been shown the yellow card once*. The term *n-participle* refers to the perfective/passive participle form of a verb (for some verbs, this may end in +*d*/+*t*: cf. *He has **tried**, She has **bought** one*).

Natural language Human language. More specifically, a language acquired in a natural setting by human beings (hence, excluding e.g. computer languages, animal communication systems, etc.).

Negation A process or construction in which some proposition is said to be false. Negation involves the use of some negative item such as *not, n't, nobody, nothing, never*, etc. – though most discussions of negation tend to be about *not/n't*.

Negative particle This informal term typically denotes *not/n't*.

Neuter See **gender**.

Node A term used to denote a point in a tree diagram which carries a category label.

Nominal This is the adjective associated with **noun**, so that in principle a *nominal* or a *nominal constituent* is an expression headed by a noun. However, the term is often extended to mean 'expression which is a projection or **extended projection** of a noun or pronoun'. In current work, a phrase like *a supporter of monetarism* would be analysed as a **determiner phrase**, and hence is not a nominal, if by *nominal* we mean 'expression headed by a noun'. However, if we say that the **DP** (= determiner phrase) here is an extended projection of the noun *supporter*, we can none-the-less continue to say that it is a *nominal*. Further confusion is caused by the fact that in earlier work, what are now analysed as determiner phrases would then have been analysed as noun phrases.

Nominative See **case**.

Nonargument See **argument**.

Nonauxiliary verb A **lexical** verb (like *want, try,*

hate, smell, buy, etc.) which requires *do*-support to form questions, negatives and tags.

Noncount noun See **count noun**.

Nonfinite See **finite**.

Nonuniform chain See **chain uniformity principle**.

Noun A category of word (whose members include items such as *boy/friend/thought/sadness/computer*) which typically denotes an entity of some kind. See ch. 2.

Noun phrase A phrase whose **head** is a noun. Thus, the expression *lovers of opera* is a noun phrase, since its head is the noun *lovers*. In earlier work, determiners were thought to be the specifiers of noun phrases, so that an expression such as *a fan of Juventus* would have been analysed as a noun phrase (though in more recent work it would be analysed as an expression headed by the determiner *a*, and hence as a **determiner phrase**, DP). See chs. 3–4.

NP See **noun phrase**.

Null See **covert**.

Null case The case carried by **PRO** (see **case**).

Null subject A subject which has grammatical/semantic properties but no overt phonetic form. More specifically, this term usually denotes the null **pro** subject found in finite declarative or interrogative clauses in languages like Italian or Early Modern English, and not the covert subject found in imperative clauses like *Shut the door!* or the covert **PRO** subject found in **control** structures like *The prisoners tried to PRO escape from jail*. Accordingly, a *null subject language* is a language which allows finite **declarative** or **interrogative** clauses to have a null *pro* subject. For example, Italian is a null subject language and so allows us to say *Sei simpatica* (literally 'Are nice', meaning '*You* are nice'); by contrast, English is not a null subject language, and so doesn't allow the subject to be omitted in this type of structure (hence **Are nice* is ungrammatical in English). The *null subject parameter* is a dimension of variation between languages according to whether finite (declarative and interrogative) verbs allow null *pro* subjects or not.

Number A term used to denote the contrast between **singular** and **plural** forms. In English, we find number contrasts in nouns (cf. *one **dog**, two **dogs***), in some determiners (cf. *this book, these books*), in pronouns (cf. *he/they*), and in finite verbs (cf. *He smells, They smell*).

Object The **complement** of a **transitive** item (e.g. in *Help me!*, *me* is the object of the transitive verb *help*; and in *for me*, *me* is the object of the transitive preposition *for*). The term *object* is generally restricted to complements which carry objective case – i.e. to nominal or pronominal complements: hence, *nothing* would be the object (and complement) of *said* in *He said nothing*, but the *that*-clause would be the complement (but not the object) of *said* in *He said [that he was tired]* – though some traditional grammars extend the term object to cover clausal complements as well as (pro)nominal complements. In sentences such as *She gave him them*, the verb *give* is traditionally said to have two objects, namely *him* and *them*: the first object *him* (representing the recipient) is termed the *indirect object*, and the second object *them* (representing the gift) is termed the *direct object*; the relevant construction is known as the *double-object construction*. Where a verb has a single object (e.g. *nothing* in *He said nothing*), this is the *direct object* of the relevant verb.

Object-control predicate See **control**.

Objective See **case**.

One-place predicate A **predicate** which has only one **argument** (e.g. *yawn* in *John yawned*, where *John* is the sole argument of the predicate *yawn*).

Op A symbol used to denote the empty question operator found in yes–no questions like *Do you enjoy syntax?* It can be thought of as a counterpart of the question-mark used in the spelling system to indicate that a sentence is a question, or as the counterpart of *whether* in *I wonder whether you enjoy syntax*.

Operator This term is used in syntax to denote (for example) interrogative and negative expressions which have the syntactic property that they trigger auxiliary inversion (cf. *What have you done?*, *Nothing would I ever do to upset anyone*). See ch. 6.

Operator movement Movement of an operator expression into **spec-CP** (i.e. into the specifier position within **CP**). See ch. 6.

Orphaned See **stranded**.

Overt An expression is *overt* if it has phonetic content, but **covert** if it lacks phonetic content. Thus, *him* is an overt pronoun, but **PRO** is a covert (or *null*, or *empty* or *silent*) pronoun.

P See **preposition**.

Parameter A dimension of grammatical variation between different languages or different varieties of the same language (e.g. the **null subject** parameter, **head parameter, wh-parameter**). See ch. 1.

Parameter-setting The process by which children determine which setting of a parameter is appropriate for the native language they are acquiring. See ch. 1.

Parametric variation Variation from one language (variety) to another in respect of some particular **parameter(s)**. For example, there is parametric variation between English and Italian in respect of the **null subject** parameter, in that Italian is a *null subject language* whereas English is a *non-null subject language*. See ch. 1.

Parsing The grammatical analysis of phrases and sentences – most frequently used in connection with analysing their categorial status and their syntactic structure in terms of a **labelled bracketing** or **tree diagram**.

Participle The *+ing* and *+n* forms of a verb (in certain uses) are traditionally said to be *participles*. More specifically, the *+ing* form (when not used as a **gerund**) is said to be an *imperfective/progressive/present participle* (e.g. in *He is **leaving***), whereas the *+n* form is said to function as a *perfective/past participle* in some uses (e.g. in *He has **stolen** them*) and as a *passive participle* in others (e.g. *They have been **stolen***). See **aspect, active**.

Particle This is a pre-theoretical term used to describe a range of items which are invariable in form, and which don't fit easily into traditional systems of grammatical categories. For example, infinitival *to* (cf. *Try **to** be nice*) is said to be an *infinitive particle*, and *not/n't* are said to be *negative particles*. The term is sometimes extended to include prepositions used without a complement (e.g. *up* in *Give up!*).

Partitive A partitive quantifier is a word like *some/any* which quantifies over part of the members of a given set (as in *Some people are lazy*). For a different use of the word in the expression *partitive case*, see **case**.

Passive See **active, passivization**.

Passivization A movement operation whereby the complement of a verb becomes its subject (cf. *The jewels were stolen*), or the subject of an infinitive complement of a passive participle becomes the subject of the clause containing the passive participle (cf. *The ministers were thought to have lied to Parliament*). See ch. 8.

Past tense See **tense**.

PATIENT A particular **thematic role**, associated with an entity which suffers the consequences of some action. For example, in a sentence such as *John killed Harry, Harry* is the PATIENT **argument** of the verb *kill*.

Percolation An operation (also known as **attraction**) by which a feature which is attached to one category comes to be attached to another category higher up in the structure.

Perfective See **aspect, participle**.

Performance A term which denotes observed language behaviour, e.g. the kind of things people actually say when they speak a language, and what meanings they assign to sentences produced by themselves or other people. Performance can be impaired by factors such as tiredness, drunkenness, etc. *Performance* is contrasted with **competence** (which denotes the fluent native speakers' knowledge of the grammar of their native language). See ch. 1.

Person In traditional grammar, English is said to have three grammatical *persons*: A *first person* expression (e.g. *I/we*) is one whose reference includes the speaker(s); a *second person* expression (e.g. *you*) is one which excludes the speaker(s) but includes the addressee(s) (i.e. the person or people being spoken to); a *third person* expression (e.g. *he/she/it/they*) is one whose reference excludes both the speaker(s) and the addressee(s) – i.e. an expression which refers to someone or something other than the speaker(s) or addressee(s).

Personal pronouns These are pronouns which carry inherent **person** properties – i.e. first person pronouns such as *I/we*, second person pronouns such as *you*, and third person pronouns such as *he/she/it/they*.

PF(-representation) (A representation of the) phonetic form (of an expression). See **representation**.

The **PF-component** of a grammar is the component which converts the syntactic structures produced by merger and movement operations into PF-representations.

Phrase The term *phrase* is used to denote an expression larger than a word which is a *maximal projection*: see **projection**. In traditional grammar, the term refers strictly to nonclausal expressions (hence, *reading a book* is a phrase, but *He is reading a book* is a clause, not a phrase). However, in more recent work, clauses are analysed as types of phrases: e.g. *He will resign* is an auxiliary phrase (IP), and *That he will resign* is a complementizer phrase (CP).

Phrase structure See **constituent structure**.

Pied-piping A process by which a moved constituent (or set of features) drags one or more other constituents (or sets of features) along with it when it moves. For example, if we compare a sentence like *Who were you talking to?* with *To whom were you talking?*, we might say that in both cases the pronoun *who(m)* is moved to the front of the sentence, but that in the second sentence the preposition *to* is pied-piped along with *whom*. See ch. 6.

Plural A plural expression is one which denotes more than one entity (e.g. *these cars* is a plural expression, whereas *this car* is a singular expression).

Postmodify To say that *nice* in an expression such as *someone nice* postmodifies *someone* is to say that *nice* **modifies** and follows *someone*.

Postulate A postulate is a theoretical assumption or hypothesis; to postulate is to assume or hypothesize.

PP See **prepositional phrase**.

PPT See **principles-and-parameters theory**.

Preclausal A preclausal expression is one which is positioned in front of a clause.

Predicate On *predicate*, see **argument**. A *predicate nominal* is a nominal expression used as a predicate – e.g. the bold-printed expressions in *John is a fool*, *I consider them fools* (where the expressions *a fool/fools* are said to be predicated of *John/them*).

Predication The process by which a predicate is combined with a subject in order to form a proposition (see **argument**). For example, in a sentence such as *Boris likes vodka*, the property of liking vodka is said to be predicated of Boris.

Predication principle A principle suggested by Rothstein (1995) to the effect that a syntactic predicate (e.g. an I-bar or V-bar constituent) requires a subject.

Predicative An adjective which is used as a **predicate** is said to be predicative in the relevant use – e.g. the bold-printed adjectives in *John is **drunk**, I consider your behaviour **unforgiveable***. Likewise, the nominal *fools* is said to be used predicatively in sentences such as *They are **fools**, I consider them **fools***.

Prefix See **affix**.

Premodify To say that the adjective *tall* premodifies the noun *men* in the expression *tall men* is to say that *tall* precedes and **modifies** *men*.

Prenominal A *prenominal* expression is one which is positioned in front of a nominal (i.e. a noun expression). For example, both *a* and *red* are prenominal in an expression such as *a red car*, because they precede the noun *car*.

Preposing an informal term to indicate a movement operation by which a constituent is moved further to the left within a phrase or sentence.

Preposition A preposition is an invariable word generally used to express location, manner, etc. – e.g. *at/in/on/under/by/with/from/against* etc. It is a characteristic property of most prepositions that they can be premodified by *straight/right*. Where a preposition has a nominal or pronominal complement, it is said to be **transitive**; where it has no complement, it is said to be **intransitive**. So, for example, the preposition *inside* is transitive in *There was nobody inside the house*, but intransitive in *There was nobody inside*. See ch. 2.

Prepositional phrase A phrase whose head is a preposition – e.g. *in town, on Sunday, to the market, for someone else*, etc.

Preposition stranding See **stranded**.

Prescriptive grammar An approach to grammar (often found in traditional textbooks used to teach grammar in secondary schools) which seeks to prescribe (i.e. lay down) norms of linguistic behaviour (taken from the so-called standard language) for all speakers of a language. In such an approach, certain types of colloquial construction found in the spoken language (e.g. **split infinitives**) are stigmatized as alleged instances of 'bad grammar'.

Present See **tense**.

Principles Principles describe potentially universal properties of grammatical operations or structures: the terms *condition* and **constraint** are also used with much the same meaning. Potential principles of Universal Grammar include the **structure dependence principle**, the **head movement constraint**, the **shortest movement principle**, the **economy principle**, the principle of **greed**, the **principle of full interpretation**, etc.

Principles-and-parameters theory A theory devised by Chomsky in work over the past two decades which maintains that universal properties of natural language grammars reflect the operation of a set of universal grammatical **principles**, and that grammatical differences between languages can be characterized in terms of a restricted set of **parameters**. See ch. 1.

PRO/pro *PRO* designates a covert null-case pronoun (known informally as *big PRO*, because it is written in capital letters) which represents the understood subject of an infinitive complement of a **control** predicate, e.g. in a structure such as *John decided to PRO leave* (see chs. 4 and 7). By contrast, *pro* is a covert nominative-case pronoun (known informally as *little pro*, because it is written in lower-case letters) which represents the understood subject of a finite clause in (for example) a Shakespearean sentence such as *Wilt pro come?* (= 'Will [you] come?', Stephano, *The Tempest*, III.ii).

Progressive See **aspect**.

Project(ion) A projection is a constituent which is an expansion of a head word. For example, a noun phrase such as *students of linguistics* is a projection of its head noun *students* (equivalently, we can say that the noun *students* here projects into the noun phrase *students of linguistics*). A *minimal projection* is a constituent which is not a projection of some other constituent: hence, heads (i.e. words) are minimal projections. An *intermediate projection* is a constituent which is larger than a word, but smaller than a phrase. A *maximal projection* is a constituent which is not contained within any larger constituent with the same head. So, for example, in a sentence like *He is proud of you*, the adjectival phrase *proud of you* is a maximal projection, since it is a projection of the adjective *proud* but is not contained within any larger projection of the same adjective *proud*. By contrast, in a sentence such as *He is proud*, the adjective *proud* is both a minimal projection (by virtue of the fact that it is not a projection of some other head) and a maximal projection (by virtue of the fact that it is not contained within any larger structure which has the same head adjective).

Pronominal See **pronoun**.

Pronoun The word *pronoun* is traditionally defined as a word used in place of a noun expression. For example, in a sentence such as *John thinks people dislike him*, the pronoun *him* can be used to replace *John* at the end of the sentence, in order to avoid repeating the noun *John*. (Of course, *him* could also refer to someone other than *John*.) Pronouns differ from nouns in that they have no intrinsic descriptive content, and so are **functors**. In much recent work, most types of pronoun are analysed as **determiners**: for example, *this* is said to be a prenominal determiner in a sentence such as *I don't like **this idea*** (since it modifies the following noun *idea*), but a pronominal determiner (i.e. a determiner used without any following noun expression) in a sentence such as *I don't like **this***. See ch. 2.

Proposition A term used to describe the semantic content (i.e. meaning) of a sentence. For example, we might say that the sentence *Does John smoke?* questions the truth of the proposition that 'John smokes.'

Q In one use, an abbreviation for **quantifier**; in another use, an abbreviation for *question affix*. (On the possibility that COMP in questions may contain an abstract question affix **Q**, see the discussion of structure (6) in ch. 5).

QP/Quantifier phrase A phrase whose head is a quantifier – e.g. an expression such as *many people, few of the students*, etc.

Quantifier A quantifier is a special type of **determiner** used to denote quantity. Typical quantifiers include the universal quantifiers *all/both*, the distributive quantifiers *each/every*, the partitive quantifiers *some/any*, etc.

Quantifier floating See **floating quantifier**.

Question operator See **Op**.

Raising (predicate) The term *raising* is used in two senses. On the one hand, it is used in a general sense to denote any movement operation which involves moving some word or phrase from a lower to a higher position in a structure. On the other hand, it can also be used with the more specific sense of a *subject-to-subject raising* operation by which an

expression is moved from one subject position to another (e.g. from being the subject of VP to being the subject of IP). The term *raising predicate* denotes a word like *seem* whose subject is raised out of subject position in a complement clause to become subject of the *seem* clause. See chs. 7 and 8.

RECIPIENT The name of the thematic role borne by the entity which receives (or comes to possess) something – e.g. *Mary* in *John bought Mary a present*.

Recursive A recursive operation is one which can be repeated any number of times. For example, the process by which an adjective comes to modify a noun might be said to be recursive in that we can position any number of adjectives in front of a noun (e.g. *a **tall, dark, handsome** stranger*).

Reference/Referential The reference of an expression is the entity (e.g. object, concept, state of affairs) in the external world to which it refers. A *referential expression* is one which refers to such an entity; conversely, a *nonreferential expression* is one which does not refer to any such entity. For example the second *there* in a sentence such as *There was nobody there* is referential (it can be paraphrased as 'in that place'), whereas the first *there* is nonreferential and so cannot have its reference questioned by *where?* (cf. **Where was nobody there?*).

Reflexive A reflexive is a +*self*/+*selves* form such as *myself, himself, ourselves, themselves*, etc. See also **anaphor**.

Representation An *LF-representation* is a representation of the logical form of an expression; a *PF-representation* is a representation of the phonetic form of an expression. See also **level of representation**.

Restrictive A restrictive theory is one which imposes strong constraints on the types of structures and operations found in natural language grammars. See ch. 1.

Resultative A verb such as *paint* in a sentence such as *John painted his house pink* is said to be a resultative verb in that the result of the action of painting is that the house becomes pink.

+s In one use, this denotes the plural suffix found in plural nouns such as *dog+s*; in another use, it denotes the third person singular present-tense suffix found in verbs such as *adore+s*.

Schwa The neutral vowel /ə/ – e.g. the vowel corresponding to the bold-printed letters in words like *about*, *affair*, *potato*, etc.

Scrambling A process which reorders maximal **projections** internally within clauses, moving them further to the front of the clause. For example, in an Early Modern English sentence like *The king your mote did see*, we might say that *your mote* has been *scrambled* out of its normal postverbal position (after *see*) into a position in front of *did* (see the discussion of (11) in ch. 10).

Second person See **person**.

Select(ion) When a word can have a particular type of **complement**, we say that it *selects* (i.e. 'takes') the relevant type of complement (and the relevant property is referred to as *complement selection*). So, for example, we can say that it is a complement-selection property of the verb *want* that it selects (i.e. 'can take') a *to*-infinitive complement (as in *I want to help you*).

Semantics The study of linguistic aspects of meaning.

Sentence This term denotes a free-standing **clause** which is not contained within some larger expression. In terms of the conventions of the English spelling system, a sentence might be defined (rather inaccurately) as a string of words which starts with a word beginning with a capital letter and which ends with a word immediately followed by a full-stop, so that this entry for **sentence** contains two sentences.

Shell This term is used in connection with the idea (discussed in ch. 9) that verb phrases comprise two different projections, an outer **vp** shell headed by a **light verb**, and an inner **VP** core headed by a lexical verb.

Shortest movement principle A principle of grammar requiring that a constituent should move the shortest distance possible in any single movement operation.

Silent See **covert**.

Singular A singular expression is one which denotes a single entity (e.g. *this car* is a singular expression, whereas *these cars* is a plural expression).

Spec See **specifier**.

Spec-CP/Spec-IP/Spec-VP (etc.) The **specifier** position within CP/IP/VP.

Spec–head A *spec–head* relation is a relation between a head and its **specifier**. For example, we might say that subject–auxiliary **agreement** involves a spec–head relation in sentences like *He has gone*, since *has* is the head of the clause and agrees with its specifier *he*.

Specifier The grammatical function fulfilled by certain types of constituent which (in English) precede the head of their containing phrase. For example, in a sentence such as *John is working*, *John* is the specifier (and **subject**) of *is working* (see ch. 3). In a sentence such as *What did John do?*, *what* is the specifier of the CP headed by the inverted auxiliary *did* (See ch. 6).

Specifier-features Features which determine the kind of specifier which a given type of head can have. For example, the specifier-features of the auxiliary *has* are [3SNom], and these tell us that it requires a third person singular nominative subject like *he/she/it*. See ch. 3.

Spellout The point in a derivation at which phonetic and semantic features are processed by separate components of the grammar (the **PF** component and the **LF** component respectively).

Split infinitive A structure in which the infinitive particle *to* is separated from the verb with which it is associated: a sentence such as *It's important to really try hard* contains an example of a split infinitive, since the particle *to* has been separated from the verb *try* by the intervening adverb *really*.

Split INFL hypothesis The hypothesis that there is not just one auxiliary position in clauses (= **INFL**), but rather two (**T** and **AgrS**). See ch. 10.

Split VP hypothesis The hypothesis that verb phrases have a complex internal structure comprising an outer **vp** shell headed by a light verb, **AgrOP/AgrIOP** projections, and an inner **VP** core headed by a lexical verb. See ch. 10.

Stem A **morpheme** which contains no inflectional or derivational **affixes**. For example, the stem form of the verb *going* is *go*.

Stranded A stranded (or orphaned) preposition is one which has been separated from its complement (by movement of the complement). For example, in a sentence such as *Who were you talking to?*, *to* is a stranded/orphaned preposition by virtue of the fact that it is separated from its complement *who* (which has been moved to the front of the sentence). By extension, in a sentence such as *They have all left*, the quantifier *all* could be said to have been stranded, since it is separated from the pronoun *they* which it quantifies.

String A continuous sequence of words contained within the same phrase or sentence. For example, in the phrase *a couple of drinks*, the sequences *a couple, couple of, of drinks, a couple of* and *couple of drinks* are all strings, whereas the sequences *a of, a drinks, a couple drinks, a of drinks* and *couple drinks* are not. Note that a *string* need not be a **constituent**.

Strong feature A strong feature is one which can trigger movement; a weak feature is one which cannot trigger movement. For example, finite verbs carry strong agreement-features in Early Modern English, and so raise to INFL; but finite verbs carry weak agreement-features in Modern Standard English, and so cannot move to INFL but rather remain *in situ*. See ch. 5.

Structural representation See **representation**.

Structure See **constituent structure**.

Structure dependence principle A principle which states that grammatical operations are sensitive to grammatical structure, so that whether or not a particular grammatical operation can apply to a particular expression depends on the syntactic structure of the expression. See ch. 1.

Subject The subject is one of the major constituents of a **clause**, since the smallest type of clause which we can construct is one which comprises a **subject** and a **predicate** (the predicate in most cases being a verb). Thus, in a clause such as *John smokes*, the subject is *John* and the predicate is the verb *smokes*. In semantic terms, the **subject** of a clause is typically the entity performing the action described by the verb. In grammatical terms, the subject of a clause is typically the expression which (for example) **agrees** with the verb, which precedes the verb, and which carries nominative **case** if the verb is **finite**: e.g. in *He smokes cigars, he* is the subject of the verb *smokes* by virtue of the fact that *he* is nominative, *he* precedes the verb *smokes* and *he* agrees with *smokes* (in that both are third person singular).

Subject control predicate See **control**.

Subjunctive In a (**formal** style) sentence such as *The judge ordered that he be detained indefinitely*, the verb *be* is said to be a (present-tense) subjunctive

form, since, although it has exactly the same form as the infinitive *to be*, it has a nominative subject *he*, and hence is a finite form. In a sentence such as *If he were here, he'd tell you what to do*, the verb *were* is said to be a past-tense subjunctive form. (For all verbs other than *be*, there is no morphological distinction between past-tense **indicative** and past-tense subjunctive verb forms.) In present-day spoken English, constructions containing subjunctive verbs are generally avoided, as they are felt to be archaic or excessively formal in style by many speakers.

Substitution A technique used to determine the category which a given expression belongs to. An expression belongs to a given type of category if it can be substituted (i.e. replaced) in the phrase or sentence in which it occurs by another expression which clearly belongs to the category in question. For example, we might say that *clearer* is an adverb in *John speaks clearer than you* because it can be replaced by the adverbial expression *more clearly*. See ch. 2.

Successive cyclic movement Movement in a succession of short steps. See ch. 5.

Suffix See **affix**.

Superlative The superlative is a form of an adjective/adverb which carries the suffix +*est* (e.g. *John is the **hardest** worker because he works **hardest***) to mark the highest value for a particular property in comparison with others.

Synonym/synonymous Two expressions are said to be synonyms/synonymous if they have much the same **interpretation**: for example, *dad* and *father* are synonyms.

Syntactic representation See **representation**.

Syntax The study of how words are combined together to form phrases and sentences.

T/T̄/T-bar/TP T is an abstract **tense** morpheme (considered as one of the head constituents in clauses – see ch. 10); T̄/T-bar is an intermediate projection of T; TP (tense phrase) is a maximal projection headed by T. See ch. 10.

Tag (question) A *tag* is a **string** usually consisting of an auxiliary and a pronoun which is added onto the end of a sentence. Thus, the bold-printed string is the tag in the following: *The president isn't underestimating his opponents, is he?'*, and the overall sentence is known as a *tag question*.

Tense Finite auxiliary and nonauxiliary verbs in English show a binary (two-way) tense contrast, traditionally said to be between *present-tense* forms and *past-tense* forms. Thus, in *John hates syntax, hates* is a present-tense verb form, whereas in *John hated syntax, hated* is a past-tense verb form. (An alternative classification which many linguists prefer is to say that *hated* carries *past* tense, and *hates* carries *non-past* tense.) The present/past tense distinction correlates (to some extent) with time-reference, so that (for example) past-tense verbs typically describe an event taking place in the past, whereas present-tense verbs typically describe an event taking place in the present (or future). However, the correlation is an imperfect one, since e.g. in a sentence such as *If I went there tomorrow, would you come with me?*, the verb *went* is a past-tense (**subjunctive**) form, but has future rather than past time-reference.

Ternary Three-way. For example, we might say that English has a ternary **person** system in personal pronouns, in that we find first person pronouns like *I/we*, second person pronouns like *you* and third person pronouns like *he/she/it/they*.

Thematic role/θ-role The semantic role played by an argument in relation to its predicate (e.g. AGENT, THEME, RECIPIENT, etc.). See the list of thematic roles given in (30), ch. 7.

THEME The name of a specific theta-role (sometimes also termed PATIENT) associated with the entity undergoing the effect of some action. For example, *Harry* is the THEME **argument** of the verb *kill* in a sentence like *John killed Harry*.

Theta-criterion/θ-criterion A principle of UG which specifies that each argument bears one and only one theta-role, and each theta-role is assigned to one and only one argument. See ch. 8.

Theta-marking/θ-marking The assignment of **thematic roles** by predicates to **arguments**. For example, the verb *arrest* assigns the θ-role of PATIENT to its complement and assigns the θ-role AGENT to its subject, and is said to (directly) θ-mark its complement and (indirectly) θ-mark its subject. See ch. 7.

Theta-role/θ-role See **thematic role**.

Third person See **person**.

Three-place predicate A **predicate** which has three arguments – e.g. the verb *give* in *John gave Mary something* (where the three arguments of *give* are *John*, *Mary* and *something*).

Topicalization A process by which a constituent is made into the *topic* of a sentence by being moved into a more prominent position at the front of the sentence (e.g. *such behaviour* might be said to be topicalized in a sentence such as *Such behaviour, we cannot tolerate in a civilized society*).

TP Tense phrase – i.e. phrase headed by an abstract tense morpheme **T**. See ch. 10.

TP adverb An adverb which adjoins to some projection of **T**. See ch. 10.

Trace (theory) A *trace* is an empty category left behind (as a result of movement) in each position out of which a constituent moves. *Trace theory* is a theory which posits that moved constituents leave behind a trace in each position out of which they move. See ch. 5.

Transitive A word is said to be transitive (in a given use) if it checks objective case. So, for example, *hate* is a transitive verb in sentences like *I hate him* because it checks the objective case of *him*. In much the same way, the preposition *for* is transitive in *He bought it for us*, since it checks the objective case of *us*. By contrast, words which (in a given use) don't check objective case are intransitive (in the relevant use): for example, adjectives (e.g. *fond*) are generally intransitive and so can't have an objective complement (cf. **fond him*), and likewise all nouns (e.g. *loss*) are similarly intransitive (cf. **loss earnings*). Simplifying somewhat, we can say that a word is intransitive if it has no complement (e.g. *leave* in *He may leave*), or if it has a complement which is not a D or DP (e.g. *got* in *She got angry*, or *spoke* in *He spoke to her*). However, this is oversimplistic in that it overlooks the fact that a word with a clausal complement is transitive if its clausal complement has an objective subject (e.g. *expect* is transitive in a sentence like *We expect him to win* since *expect* checks the case of *him*), but words are generally taken to be intransitive when they have other types of clausal complement (e.g. *expect* is generally considered intransitive when it has a *that*-clause complement, as in *Nobody expected that he would win*). See also **object**.

Tree (diagram) A way of representing the syntactic structure of a phrase or sentence. See ch. 3.

Two-place predicate A **predicate** which has two arguments. For example, *kill* is a two-place predicate in a sentence such as *John killed Harry*, because it has two arguments (*John* and *Harry*). See ch. 7.

UG See **Universal Grammar**.

Unaccusative An unaccusative predicate is a verb like *come* whose apparent subject originates in **VP** rather than **vp**. See ch. 9.

Unbound A constituent is unbound if it has no appropriate **antecedent** in an appropriate position within the relevant structure. For example, the **anaphor** *himself* is unbound in a sentence such as **She helped himself*, since *she* is not an appropriate antecedent for *himself*, and there is no other appropriate antecedent for *himself* anywhere within the sentence.

Underlying structure A structure as it was before the application of some movement operation(s).

Unergative An unergative verb is a verb like *groan* in a sentence such as *He was groaning* which has an agent subject but seems to have no object. See ch. 9.

Ungradable See **gradable**.

Ungrammatical An expression is ungrammatical if it contains a morphological error (e.g. if some word is in the wrong form) or syntactic error (e.g. if some word occupies the wrong position). Hence, a sentence like *He seed me is ungrammatical because *seed* is in the wrong form (*saw* is required), and a sentence like *He me saw is ungrammatical because *me* is in the wrong position (cf. *He saw me*).

Uniform(ity) See **chain uniformity principle**, or **uniform theta-assignment hypothesis**.

Uniform theta-assignment hypothesis/UTAH This hypothesis (put forward in Baker 1988) maintains that each theta-role assigned by a particular type of predicate is canonically associated with a specific syntactic position: e.g. **spec-vp** is the canonical position associated with an AGENT argument. See ch. 9.

Uninterpretable See **interpretable**.

Universal Grammar/UG The study of the common grammatical properties shared by all natural languages (and of the **parameters** of variation between languages).

Universality A criterion of adequacy for a theory of grammar, requiring that the theory be applicable to all natural languages. See ch. 1.

UTAH See **uniform theta-assignment hypothesis**.

V/V̄/V-bar/VP V is a lexical verb; V̄/V-bar is an intermediate projection headed by a lexical verb;

VP is a maximal projection headed by a lexical verb. See **lexical** and **projection**.

v/v̄/v-bar/vp v is a light verb; v̄/v-bar is an intermediate projection headed by a light verb; vp is is a maximal projection headed by a light verb. See **light verb** and **projection**.

Verb A category of word which has the morphological property that it can carry a range of inflections including past tense +*d*, third person singular present-tense +*s*, perfective +*n* and progressive +*ing* (cf. *show/shows/showed/shown/showing*), and the syntactic property that it can head the complement of infinitival *to* (cf. *Do you want to show me?*). See ch. 2.

Verb movement See **V movement**.

Verb phrase A phrase/maximal projection which is headed by a verb – e.g. the bracketed phrase in *They will* [*help you*] (see ch. 3). In terms of the **shell** analysis presented in ch. 9, there are two different types of *verb phrase* – a **VP** headed by a **lexical verb**, and a **vp** headed by a **light verb**.

V(-to-I) movement An operation by which a finite verb moves from V to INFL (e.g. in Early Modern English). See ch. 5.

Voice See **active**.

VP See **V**.

vp See **v**.

vp adverb An adverb which adjoins to a projection of **v**.

VP adverb An adverb (like *perfectly*) which adjoins to some projection of V.

VP-internal subject hypothesis The hypothesis that subjects originate internally within **VP/vp**: see chs. 7 and 9.

Wanna-contraction The process by which the string *want to* contracts to *wanna*.

Weak features See **strong features**.

Wh A feature marking some word, phrase, clause or sentence as **interrogative**. See ch. 6.

Wh-expression An expression containing a **wh-word**.

Wh-movement A type of **operator movement** whereby an expression containing a wh-word (i.e. a word such as *who/which/what/where/why/when*) is moved to the front of a particular clause. See ch. 6.

Wh-parameter The parameter which determines whether wh-expressions can (or can't) be moved to the front of an appropriate clause (especially in relation to wh-questions). See ch. 1.

Wh-phrase A phrase containing a wh-word.

Wh-question A question which contains a **wh-word**, e.g. *What are you doing?*

Wh-word A word which begins with *wh* (e.g. *who/ what/which/where/when/why*), or which has a similar syntax to wh-words (e.g. *how*).

X/$\overline{\text{X}}$/X-bar/XP The symbol **X** (and sometimes **Y** similarly) is used as a variable denoting 'any word category you care to choose' (so X could be a noun, verb, adjective, determiner, complementizer, etc.). $\overline{\text{X}}$/X-bar is an intermediate projection headed by a word category; XP is a maximal projection headed by a word category. See **projection**.

Y/$\overline{\text{Y}}$/Y-bar/YP See **X**.

Yes–no question A question to which *Yes* or *No* would be an appropriate answer – e.g. *Do you like syntax?*

References

Abney, S.P. (1987) 'The English noun phrase in its sentential aspect', PhD diss., MIT.

Akmajian, A. and F. Heny (1975) *An Introduction to the Principles of Transformational Syntax*, MIT Press, Cambridge, Mass.

Aronoff, M. (1976) *Word Formation in Generative Grammar*, MIT Press, Cambridge, Mass.

Authier, J.-M. (1991) 'V-governed expletives, case theory and the projection principle', *Linguistic Inquiry* 22: 721–40.

Bailey, B.L. (1966) *Jamaican Creole Syntax: a Transformational Approach*, Cambridge University Press.

Baker, M. (1988) *Incorporation*, University of Chicago Press.

Baker, M., K. Johnson and I. Roberts (1989) 'Passive arguments raised', *Linguistic Inquiry* 20: 219–51.

Baltin, M. (1995) 'Floating quantifiers, PRO and predication', *Linguistic Inquiry* 26: 199–248.

Belletti, A. (1988) 'The case of unaccusatives', *Linguistic Inquiry* 19: 1–34.

  (1990) *Generalized Verb Movement*, Rosenberg and Sellier, Turin.

Bobaljik, J.D. (1995) 'Morphosyntax: the syntax of verbal inflection', PhD diss., MIT.

Bošković, Z. (1995) 'Principles of economy in nonfinite complementation', PhD diss., University of Connecticut.

Bowerman, M. (1995) 'Don't giggle me!', talk presented at the University of Essex, 30 November 1995.

Bowers, J. (1993) 'The syntax of predication', *Linguistic Inquiry* 24: 591–656.

Burton, S. and J. Grimshaw (1992) 'Coordination and VP-internal subjects', *Linguistic Inquiry* 23: 305–13.

Burzio, L. (1986) *Italian Syntax*, Reidel, Dordrecht.

Carnie, A. (1995) 'Non-verbal predication and head movement', PhD diss., MIT.

Carrier, J. and J.H. Randall (1992) 'The argument structure and syntactic structure of resultatives', *Linguistic Inquiry* 23: 173–234.

Chomsky, N. (1965) *Aspects of the Theory of Syntax*, MIT Press, Cambridge, Mass.

  (1968) Interview with S. Hamshire in *The Listener*, May 1968.

  (1972) *Language and Mind* (enlarged edition), Harcourt Brace Jovanovich, New York.

  (1981) *Lectures on Government and Binding*, Foris, Dordrecht.

  (1986a) *Knowledge of Language: Its Nature, Origin and Use*, Praeger, New York.

  (1986b) *Barriers*, MIT Press, Cambridge, Mass.

  (1993) 'A minimalist program for linguistic theory', in K. Hale and S.J. Keyser (eds.) *The View from Building 20*, MIT Press, Cambridge, Mass., pp. 41–58 (reprinted as chapter 3 of Chomsky 1995).

  (1995) *The Minimalist Program*, MIT Press, Cambridge Mass.

Chomsky, N. and H. Lasnik (1995) 'The theory of principles and parameters', in Chomsky 1995, pp. 13–127.

Cinque, G. (1995) 'Romance past particle agreement and clause structure', talk presented to the Romance Linguistics Seminar, University of Cambridge.

Contreras, H. (1986) 'Spanish bare NPs and the ECP', in I. Bordelois, H. Contreras and K. Zagona (eds.) *Generative Studies in Spanish Syntax*, Foris, Dordrecht, pp. 25–49.

Contreras, J. (1987) 'Small clauses in Spanish and English', *Natural Language and Linguistic Theory* 5: 225–44.

Ernst, T. (1991) 'On the scope principle', *Linguistic Inquiry* 22: 750–6.

Fabb, N. (1988) 'English suffixation is constrained only by selectional restrictions', *Natural Language and Linguistic Theory* 6: 527–39.

Fillmore, C.J. (1968) 'The case for case', in E. Bach and R.T. Harms (eds.) *Universals in Linguistic Theory*, Holt Rinehart and Winston, New York, pp. 1–88.

Grice, H.P. (1975) 'Logic and conversation', in P. Cole and J. Morgan (eds.) *Syntax and Semantics*, vol. III: *Speech Acts*, Academic Press, New York, pp. 41–58.

Grimshaw, J. (1990) *Argument Structure*, MIT Press, Cambridge, Mass.

  (1991) 'Extended projection', draft manuscript, Brandeis University, July 1991.

  (1993) 'Minimal projection, heads, and optimality', draft manuscript, Rutgers University, June 1993.

Groat, E. (1995) 'English expletives: a minimalist approach', *Linguistic Inquiry* 26: 354–65.

Gruber, J.S. (1965) 'Studies in lexical relations', PhD diss., MIT.

Guilfoyle, E. (1983) 'Habitual aspect in Hiberno-English', *McGill Working Papers in Linguistics* 1: 22–32.

Guilfoyle, E., H. Hung and L. Travis (1992) 'Spec of IP and spec of VP: two subjects in Austronesian languages', *Natural Language and Linguistic Theory* 10: 375–414.

Haegeman, L. (1994) *Introduction to Government and Binding Theory*, 2nd edn, Blackwell, Oxford.

Hale, K. and S. J. Keyser (1991) *On the Syntax of Argument Structure*, Lexicon Project Working Papers, MIT, Center for Cognitive Science, Cambridge, Mass.

(1993) 'On argument structure and the lexical expression of semantic relations', in K. Hale and S.J. Keyser (eds.) *The View from Building 20*, MIT Press, Cambridge, Mass., pp. 53–109.

(1994) 'Constraints on argument structure', in B. Lust, M. Suñer and J. Whitman (eds.) *Heads, Projections and Learnability*, Erlbaum, Hillsdale, N.J. vol. I, pp. 53–71.

Harley, H. (1995) 'Subjects, events and licensing', PhD diss., MIT.

Harris, J. (1986) 'Expanding the superstrate: habitual aspect markers in Atlantic Englishes', *English World-Wide* 7: 171–99.

Henry, A. (1995) *Belfast English and Standard English: Dialect Variation and Parameter-Setting*, Oxford University Press.

Huang, C.-T.J. (1993) 'Reconstruction and the structure of VP: some theoretical consequences', *Linguistic Inquiry* 24: 103–38.

Jackendoff, R.S. (1972) *Semantic Interpretation in Generative Grammar*, MIT Press, Cambridge, Mass.

Johnson, K. (1991) 'Object positions', *Natural Language and Linguistic Theory* 9: 577–636.

Jones, M.A. (1994) *Sardinian Syntax*, Routledge, London.

Kayne, R.S. (1984) 'Principles of particle constructions', in J. Guéron, H.-G. Obenauer and J.-Y. Pollock (eds.) *Grammatical Representation*, Foris, Dordrecht, pp. 101–40.

Keyser, S.J. and T. Roeper (1992) 'Re: the abstract clitic hypothesis', *Linguistic Inquiry* 23: 89–125.

Kitagawa, Y. (1986) 'Subjects in English and Japanese', PhD diss., University of Massachusetts.

Koizumi, M. (1995) 'Phrase structure in minimalist syntax', PhD diss., MIT.

Koopman, H. and D. Sportiche (1991) 'The position of subjects', in J. McCloskey (ed.) *The Syntax of Verb-Initial Languages*, Elsevier, North Holland (published as a special issue of *Lingua*).

Kuroda, Y. (1988) 'Whether we agree or not', *Lingvisticae Investigationes* 12: 1–47.

Lakoff, G. (1971) 'Presupposition and relative well-formedness', in D.D. Steinberg and L.A. Jakobovits (eds.) *Semantics*, Cambridge University Press, pp. 329–40.

Larson, R. (1988) 'On the double object construction', *Linguistic Inquiry* 19: 335–91.

(1990) 'Double objects revisited: reply to Jackendoff', *Linguistic Inquiry* 21: 589–632.

(1991) '*Promise* and the theory of control', *Linguistic Inquiry* 2: 103–39.

Lasnik, H. (1992) 'Case and expletives: notes toward a parametric account', *Linguistic Inquiry* 23: 381–405.

(1995) 'Case and expletives revisited: on greed and other human failings', *Linguistic Inquiry* 26: 615–33.

Longobardi, G. (1994) 'Reference and proper names', *Linguistic Inquiry* 25: 609–66.

McNally, L. (1992) 'VP-coordination and the VP-internal subject hypothesis', *Linguistic Inquiry* 23: 336–41.

Marantz, A. (1984) *On the Nature of Grammatical Relations*, MIT Press, Cambridge, Mass.

Ouhalla, J. (1991) *Functional Categories and Parametric Variation*, Routledge, London.

Pesetsky, D. (1995) *Zero Syntax: Experiencers and Cascades*, MIT Press, Cambridge, Mass.

Pollock, J.-Y. (1989) 'Verb movement, Universal Grammar, and the structure of IP', *Linguistic Inquiry* 20: 365–424.

Postal, P.M. (1966) 'On so-called pronouns in English', in F. Dinneen (ed.) *Nineteenth Monograph on Language and Linguistics*, Georgetown University Press, Washington, D.C.

(1974) *On Raising*, MIT Press, Cambridge, Mass.

Radford, A. (1981) *Transformational Syntax*, Cambridge University Press.

(1988) *Transformational Grammar*, Cambridge University Press.

Rickford, J.R. (1986) 'Social contact and linguistic diffusion: Hiberno-English and New World Black English', *Language* 62: 245–89.

Ritter, E. and S.T. Rosen (1993) 'Deriving causation', *Natural Language and Linguistic Theory* 11: 519–55.

Roberts, I. (1986) *The Representation of Implicit and Dethematized Subjects*, Foris, Dordrecht.

(1991) 'Excorporation and minimality', *Linguistic Inquiry* 22: 209–18.

(1993) *Verbs and Diachronic Syntax*, Kluwer, Dordrecht.

Rohrbacher, B. (1994) *The Germanic VO Languages and the Full Paradigm: a Theory of V to I Raising*, GLSA Publications, Amherst.

Rosen, S.T. (1990) *Argument Structure and Complex Predicates*, Garland, New York.

Ross, J.R. (1967) 'Constraints on variables in syntax', PhD diss., MIT (published as *Infinite Syntax!* by Ablex, Norwood, N.J., 1986).

Rothstein, S.D. (1995) 'Pleonastics and the interpretation of pronouns', *Linguistic Inquiry* 26: 499–529.

Salles, H. M.-L. (1995) 'Preposition pied-piping and preposition stranding: a minimalist approach', *Research Papers in Linguistics*, University of Wales, Bangor, 6: 97–123.

Speas, P. (1986) 'Adjunction and projections in syntax', PhD diss., MIT.

Spencer, A.J. (1991) *Morphological Theory*, Blackwell, Oxford.

Sportiche, D. (1988) 'A theory of floating quantifiers and its corollaries for constituent structure', *Linguistic Inquiry* 19: 425–49.

Stowell, T. (1981) 'Origins of phrase structure', PhD diss., MIT.

Stroik, T. (1990) 'Adverbs as V-sisters', *Linguistic Inquiry* 21: 654–61.

Tieken-Boon van Ostade, I. (1988) 'The origins and development of periphrastic auxiliary *do*: a case of destigmatisation', *Dutch Working Papers in English Language and Linguistics* 3: 1–30.

Travis, L. (1984) 'Parameters and effects of word order variation', PhD diss., MIT.

Trudgill, P. and J.K. Chambers (1991) (eds.) *Dialects of English: Studies in Grammatical Variation*, Longman, London.

Vikner, S. (1995) *Verb Movement and Expletive Subjects in Germanic Languages*, Oxford University Press.

Wakelin, M.F. (1977) *English Dialects: an Introduction*, 2nd edn, Athlone, London.

Woolford, E. (1991) 'VP-internal subjects in VSO and nonconfigurational languages', *Linguistic Inquiry* 22: 503–40.

Zagona, K. (1987) *Verb Phrase Syntax*, Kluwer, Dordrecht.

Index